ARISTOTLE'S POETICS

A Translation and Commentary for Students of Literature

ARISTOTLE'S

POETICS

A Translation and Commentary for Students of Literature

Translation by

LEON GOLDEN

Professor of Classics
Florida State University

Commentary by

O. B. HARDISON, Jr.

Professor of English
University of North Carolina

PRENTICE-HALL, Inc., Englewood Cliffs, N.J.

Library of Congress Catalog Card No.: 68–19424

Current printing (*last number*):
10 9 8 7 6 5 4 3 2 1

Printed in the United States of America

Chapter I of the commentary appeared in slightly different form in Number 16 (1967) of the *Yearbook of Comparative and General Literature* and is reprinted by permission of the editors.

PRENTICE-HALL INTERNATIONAL, INC., *London*
PRENTICE-HALL OF AUSTRALIA, PTY. LTD., *Sydney*
PRENTICE-HALL OF CANADA, LTD., *Toronto*
PRENTICE-HALL OF INDIA PRIVATE LTD., *New Delhi*
PRENTICE-HALL OF JAPAN, INC., *Tokyo*

Preface

The present volume is intended to fill the need for a chapter-by-chapter commentary on the *Poetics* that draws on modern scholarship and that is adopted to the needs of students of literature and criticism who are not proficient in Greek. Most editions intended for the general reader consist of a brief, simplified introduction, a translation offered without explanation of the assumptions on which it is based, and notes that often mislead by giving as fact what is really conjecture. Even the most widely used popular interpretations of the *Poetics* have serious drawbacks. Butcher's *Aristotle's Theory of Poetry and Fine Arts* was first published in 1895, and its last revision was in 1907. In addition to being dated, it takes the form of an essay on selected Aristotelian topics rather than a commentary. This means that it necessarily omits many important and difficult passages, quotes others out of context, and gives disproportionate emphasis to others. Lane Cooper's popular treatments of the *Poetics,* intended primarily for students of English literature, are equally dated. Moreover, his interpretations and inferences are generally far more questionable than Butcher's. Finally, Humphrey House's graceful *Aristotle's Poetics* (1964) is both an intentional simplification that makes little use of recent scholarship and—like Butcher's work—an essay on selected topics rather than a commentary.

The translation of the *Poetics* is based on a review of the important Greek texts from Bywater (1909) to Kassel (1965). Its two guiding principles are accuracy and readability. The first version of the translation was made independently of the commentary. Later, translation and commentary were collated and both were modified. In the process, a fruitful interchange of ideas occurred, which resulted, we believe, in the enrichment of both through enhanced objectivity, clarity, and suggestiveness.

The commentary treats the *Poetics* chapter-by-chapter. It draws heavily on the rich accumulation of scholarship from Butcher to the present. Gerald Else's *Aristotle's Poetics: The Argument* (1957) is especially important in this regard. As the most recent and most exhaustive treatment of the *Poetics* in English, it has opened many exciting new vistas and given rise to much highly stimulating (and occasionally acrimonious) debate. A special effort has been made to represent Professor Else's views in the commentary, even though the positions finally taken on such major topics as the integrity of Aristotle's text, the meaning of catharsis and hamartia, the significance of recognition, and the like differ fundamentally from his. Among other recent interpretations of the *Poetics,* that offered by Professor Richard McKeon and his followers has also been given prominent representation. Debts for specific points of interpretation are too numerous to list here, but special mention may be made of Martin Ostwald's analysis of hamartia and of Rostagni's interpretation of the twelve "answers to critics" in Chapter XXV.

The general aim of the commentary is a consistent, readable analysis, original in outline but eclectic and representative in treatment of specific topics. On key issues, however, an effort has been made to refer to the principal theories, and such references are supplemented by the list of works in the selective bibliography following the commentary. The result, it is hoped, will be valid as a continuous essay and also useful as a reference work so that the reader who is curious about a passage in Aristotle's treatise can turn to the section of the commentary where it is discussed and find at least preliminary guidance.

Line numbers in parentheses in the commentary refer to line numbers as given in the margins of the Golden translation. Works by Aristotle other than the *Poetics* are cited by the page and line numbers of Bekker's Greek text, which are reproduced in most of the standard translations of Aristotle's works. To facilitate comparison of the present translation with the Greek and with other English versions, Bekker's page numbers for the *Poetics* are also given in the margins of the text, along with the line numbers.

It is a pleasure to record a special debt of gratitude to Father Norman McKendrick of the Classics Department of the University of Detroit for unfailingly generous and valuable advice.

Leon Golden
O. B. Hardison, Jr.

Contents

A Translation of Aristotle's POETICS

A Commentary on Aristotle's POETICS

Diagrams

A Translation of

ARISTOTLE'S POETICS

by

Leon Golden

I

Let us discuss the art of poetry, itself, and its species, de- 1447a
scribing the character of each of them, and how it is necessary to construct plots if the poetic composition is to be successful and, furthermore, the number and kind of parts to be found in the poetic work, and as many other matters as are relevant. Let us follow the order of nature, beginning with first principles.

Now epic poetry, tragedy, comedy, dithyrambic poetry, and most forms of flute and lyre playing all happen to be, in general, imitations, but they differ from each other in three ways: either because the imitation is carried on by different means or because it is concerned with different kinds of objects or because it is presented, not in the same, but in a different manner.

For just as some artists imitate many different objects by using color and form to represent them (some through art, others only through habit), other artists imitate through sound, as indeed, in the arts mentioned above; for all these accomplish imitation through rhythm and speech and harmony, making use of these elements separately or in combination. Flute playing and lyre playing, for example, use harmony and rhythm alone; and this would also be true of any other arts (for example, the art of playing the shepherd's pipe) that are similar in character to these. Dancers imitate by using rhythm without harmony, since they imitate characters, emotions, and actions by rhythms that are arranged into dance-figures.

The art that imitates by words alone, in prose and in verse, and in the latter case, either combines various meters or makes use of only one, has been nameless up to the present time. For 1447b
we cannot assign a common name to the mimes of Sophron and Xenarchus and the Socratic dialogues; nor would we have

a name for such an imitation if someone should accomplish it through trimeters or elegiacs or some other such meter, except that the public at large by joining the term "poet" to a meter gives writers such names as "elegiac poets" and "epic poets." Here the public classifies all those who write in meter as poets and completely misses the point that the capacity to produce an imitation is the essential characteristic of the poet. The public is even accustomed to apply the name "poet" to those who publish a medical or scientific treatise in verse, although Homer has nothing at all in common with Empedocles except the meter. It is just to call Homer a poet, but we must consider Empedocles a physicist rather than a poet.

And in the same way, if anyone should create an imitation by combining all the meters as Chairemon did when he wrote *The Centaur,* a rhapsody composed by the use of all the meters, he must also be designated a poet. Concerning these matters let us accept the distinctions we have just made.

There are some arts that use all the means that have been discussed, namely, rhythm and song and meter, as in the writing of dithyrambs and nomic poetry[1] and in tragedy and comedy. A difference is apparent here in that some arts use all the various elements at the same time, whereas others use them separately. These, then, are what I call the differences in the artistic means through which the imitation is accomplished.

II

Artists imitate men involved in action and these must either 1448a
be noble or base since human character regularly conforms to these distinctions, all of us being different in character because

[1] The dithyramb was originally a choral ode sung in honor of Dionysus, whereas nomic poetry was originally concerned with texts taken from the epic and was presented with a flute or lyre accompaniment.

of some quality of goodness or evil. From this it follows that the objects imitated are either better than or worse than or like the norm. We find confirmation of this observation in the practice of our painters. For Polygnotus represents men as better, Pauson as worse, and Dionysius as like the norm.[2] It is clear that each of the above-mentioned forms of imitation will manifest differences of this type and will be different through its choosing, in this way, a different kind of object to imitate. Even in dancing, flute-playing, and lyre-playing it is possible for these differences to exist, and they are seen also in prose, and in verse that does not make use of musical accompaniment, as is shown by the fact that Cleophon represents men like the norm, Homer as better, and both Hegemon the Thasian (who was the first writer of parodies) and Nicochares, the author of the *Deiliad,* as worse.[3] The same situation is found in dithyrambic and nomic poetry,[4] as we see in the way Timotheus and Philoxenus handled the Cyclops theme.[5] It is through the same distinction in objects that we differentiate comedy from tragedy, for the former takes as its goal the representation of men as worse, the latter as better, than the norm.

III

There is, finally, a third factor by which we distinguish imitations, and that is the manner in which the artist represents

[2] Polygnotus was one of the great painters of the fifth century B.C. Neither Pauson nor Dionysius are identified with certainty.

[3] Not much is known about the poets other than Homer mentioned here. Cleophon was a dramatic or epic writer; a small fragment of a parody of Hegemon of Thasos is preserved in Athenaeus; we have no further certain information about Nicochares.

[4] There is a lacuna in the text at this point where the name of another writer of nomic poetry was probably mentioned.

[5] Timotheus was a dithyrambic poet who lived in Miletus from 450-360 B.C.; Philoxenus was a dithyrambic poet who lived in Cythera from 436 to 380 B.C.

the various types of object. For, using the same means and imitating the same kinds of object, it is possible for the poet on different occasions to narrate the story (either speaking in the person of one of his characters as Homer does or in his own person without changing roles) [6] or to have the imitators performing and acting out the entire story.

As we said at the beginning, imitations are to be distinguished under these three headings: means, object, and manner. Thus, in one way, Sophocles is the same kind of imitative artist as Homer, since they both imitate noble men; but in another sense, he resembles Aristophanes, since they both imitate characters as acting and dramatizing the incidents of the story. It is from this, some tell us, that these latter kinds of imitations are called "dramas" because they present characters who "dramatize" the incidents of the plot.

By the way, it is also for this reason that the Dorians claim to be the originators of both tragedy and comedy. The Megarians—both those in Megara itself, who assert that comedy arose when democracy was established among them, and those Megarians in Sicily, who point out that their poet Epicharmus far antedates Chionides and Magnes[7]—claim to have originated comedy; in addition, some of the Dorians in the Peloponnesus claim to be the originators of tragedy. As proof of their contentions, they cite the technical terms they use for these art forms; for they say that they call the towns around their city *komai,* but that the Athenians call their towns *demoi.* By this they argue that the root of the name "comedian" is not derived from *komazein* [the word for "reveling"] but from *komai* [their word for the towns] that the comic artists visited in

[6] The translation given of this phrase is based on the traditional text, which has been accepted by Butcher, Hardy, and Kassel. On philosophical and linguistic grounds, Bywater prefers to emend the text of the passage so that it reads as follows: "Given both the same means and the same kind of object for imitation, one may either (1) speak at one moment in narrative and at another in an assumed character, as Homer does; or (2) one may remain the same throughout, without any such change; or (3) the imitators may represent the whole story dramatically, as though they were actually doing the things described," (p. 7).

[7] Not much is known, in addition to what Aristotle tells us in the *Poetics,* about these three comic writers who lived in the early part of the fifth century B.C.

their wanderings after they had been driven in disgrace from the city. In support of their claim to be the originators of "drama," they point out that the word for "doing" is *dran* in 1448b
their dialect, whereas Athenians use the word *prattein* for this concept.

Concerning the number and kind of distinctions that characterize "imitations," let us accept what has been said above.

IV

Speaking generally, the origin of the art of poetry is to be found in two natural causes. For the process of imitation is natural to mankind from childhood on: Man is differentiated from other animals because he is the most imitative of them, and he learns his first lessons through imitation, and we observe that all men find pleasure in imitations. The proof of this point is what actually happens in life. For there are some things that distress us when we see them in reality, but the most accurate representations of these same things we view with pleasure—as, for example, the forms of the most despised animals and of corpses. The cause of this is that the act of learning is not only most pleasant to philosophers but, in a similar way, to other men as well, only they have an abbreviated share in this pleasure. Thus men find pleasure in viewing representations because it turns out that they learn and infer what each thing is—for example, that this particular object is that kind of object; since if one has not happened to see the object previously, he will not find any pleasure in the imitation *qua* imitation but rather in the workmanship or coloring or something similar.

Since imitation is given to us by nature, as are harmony and rhythm (for it is apparent that meters are parts of the rhythms), men, having been naturally endowed with these gifts from the beginning and then developing them gradually, for the most part, finally created the art of poetry from their early improvisations.

Poetry then diverged in the directions of the natural dispositions of the poets. Writers of greater dignity imitated the noble actions of noble heroes; the less dignified sort of writers imitated the actions of inferior men, at first writing invectives as the former writers wrote hymns and encomia. We know of no "invective" by poets before Homer, although it is probable that there were many who wrote such poems; but it is possible to attribute them to authors who came after Homer—for example, the *Margites* of Homer himself, and other such poems. In these poems, the fitting meter came to light, the one that now bears the name "iambic" [i.e., invective] because it was originally used by men to satirize each other. Thus, of our earliest writers, some were heroic and some iambic poets. And just as Homer was especially the poet of noble actions (for he not only handled these well but he also made his imitations dramatic), so also he first traced out the form of comedy by dramatically presenting not invective but the ridiculous. For his *Margites* has the same relation to comedy as the *Iliad* and *Odyssey* have to tragedy. But when tragedy and com- 1449a
edy began to appear, poets were attracted to each type of poetry according to their individual natures, one group becoming writers of comedies in place of iambics, and the other, writers of tragedies instead of epics because these genres were of greater importance and more admired than the others.

Now then, the consideration of whether or not tragedy is by now sufficiently developed in its formal elements, judged both in regard to its essential nature and in regard to its public performances, belongs to another discussion. What is relevant is that it arose, at first, as an improvisation (both tragedy and comedy are similar in this respect) on the part of those who led the dithyrambs, just as comedy arose from those who led the phallic songs that even now are still customary in many of our cities. Tragedy, undergoing many changes (since our poets were developing aspects of it as they emerged), gradually progressed until it attained the fulfillment of its own nature. Aeschylus was the first to increase the number of actors from one to two; he also reduced the role of the chorus and made the dialogue the major element in the play. Sophocles increased the number of actors to three and introduced scene painting. Then tragedy acquired its magnitude. Thus by developing away from a satyr-play of short plots and absurd diction, tragedy achieved, late in its history, a dignified level. Then the iambic meter took the place of the tetrameter. For the poets first used the trochaic tetrameter because their poetry was satyric and very closely associated with dance; but when dialogue was introduced, nature itself discovered the appropriate meter. For the iambic is the most conversational of the meters—as we see from the fact that we speak many iambs when talking to each other, but few [dactylic] hexameters, and only when departing from conversational tone. Moreover, the number of episodes was increased. As to the other elements by which, we are told, tragedy was embellished, we must consider them as having been mentioned by us. For it would probably be an enormous task to go through each of these elements one by one.

V

As we have said, comedy is an imitation of baser men. These are characterized not by every kind of vice but specifically by "the ridiculous," which is a subdivision of the category of "deformity." What we mean by "the ridiculous" is some error or ugliness that is painless and has no harmful effects. The example that comes immediately to mind is the comic mask, which is ugly and distorted but causes no pain.

Now then, the successive changes in the history of tragedy and the men who brought them about have been recorded; but the analogous information about the history of comedy is lacking because the genre was not treated, at the beginning, as a serious art form. It was only recently that the archons 1449b
began to grant choruses to the comic poets; until then, the performers were all volunteers. And it was only after comedy had attained some recognizable form that we began to have a record of those designated as "comic poets." Who introduced masks or prologues, who established the number of actors, and many other matters of this type, are unknown. The creation of plots came first from Sicily, where it is attributed to Epicharmus and Phormis; and it was first Crates among the Athenian poets who departed from iambic [or invective] poetry and began to write speeches and plots of a more universal nature.

Now epic poetry follows the same pattern as tragedy insofar as it is the imitation of noble subjects presented in an elevated meter. But epic differs from tragedy in that it uses a single meter, and its manner of presentation is narrative. And further, there is a difference in length. For tragedy attempts, as far as possible, to remain within one circuit of the sun or, at least, not depart from this by much. Epic poetry, however, has no limit in regard to time, and differs from tragedy in this respect; although at first the poets proceeded in tragedy in the same way as they did in epic. Some of the parts of a poem are common to both tragedy and epic, and some belong to tragedy alone. Therefore, whoever can judge what is good and bad in tragedy can also do this in regard to epic. For whatever parts epic poetry has, these are also found in tragedy; but, as we have said, not all of the parts of tragedy are found in epic poetry.

VI

We shall speak about the form of imitation that is associated with hexameter verse and about comedy later. Let us now discuss tragedy, bringing together the definition of its essence that has emerged from what we have already said. Tragedy is, then, an imitation of a noble and complete action, having the proper magnitude;[8] it employs language that has been artistically enhanced by each of the kinds of linguistic adornment, applied separately in the various parts of the play; it is presented in dramatic, not narrative form, and achieves, through the representation of pitiable and fearful incidents, the catharsis of such pitiable and fearful incidents. I mean by "language that has been artistically enhanced," that which is accompanied by rhythm and harmony and song; and by the phrase "each of the kinds of linguistic adornment applied separately in the various parts of the play," I mean that some parts are accomplished by meter alone and others, in turn, through song.

And since [in drama] agents accomplish the imitation by acting the story out, it follows, first of all, that the arrangement of the spectacle should be, of necessity, some part of the tragedy as would be melody and diction, also; for these are the means through which the agents accomplish the imitation. I mean by diction the act, itself, of making metrical compositions, and by melody, what is completely obvious. Since the imitation is of an action and is accomplished by certain agents, the sort of men these agents are is necessarily dependent upon their "character" and "thought." It is, indeed, on the basis of these two considerations that we designate the quality of actions, because the two natural causes of human action are 1450a thought and character. It is also in regard to these that the

[8] There is no word in the Greek text for "proper" but I have followed the practice of several other translators who add a modifier to the term "magnitude" where it is logically warranted. The term "representation" has also been added to the final clause of this sentence because of Aristotle's insistence that the pleasure of tragedy is achieved *through imitation* (Ch. XIV, ll. 15-6). See L. Golden, "Catharsis," *TAPA*, XCIII (1962), 58.

lives of all turn out well or poorly. For this reason we say that tragic plot is an imitation of action.

Now I mean by the plot the arrangement of the incidents, and by character that element in accordance with which we say that agents are of a certain type; and by thought I mean that which is found in whatever things men say when they prove a point or, it may be, express a general truth. It is necessary, therefore, that tragedy as a whole have six parts in accordance with which, as a genre, it achieves its particular quality. These parts are plot, character, diction, thought, spectacle, and melody. Two of these parts come from the means by which the imitation is carried out; one from the manner of its presentation, and three from the objects of the imitation. Beyond these parts there is nothing left to mention. Not a few poets, so to speak, employ these parts; for indeed, every drama [theoretically] has spectacle, character, plot, diction, song, and thought.

The most important of these parts is the arrangement of the incidents; for tragedy is not an imitation of men, *per se,* but of human action and life and happiness and misery. Both happiness and misery consist in a kind of action; and the end of life is some action, not some quality.[9] Now according to their characters men have certain qualities; but according to their actions they are happy or the opposite. Poets do not, therefore, create action in order to imitate character; but character is included on account of the action. Thus the end of tragedy is the presentation of the individual incidents and of the plot; and the end is, of course, the most significant thing of all. Furthermore, without action tragedy would be impossible, but without character it would still be possible. This point is illustrated both by the fact that the tragedies of many of our modern poets are characterless, and by the fact that many poets, in general, experience this difficulty. Also, to take an example from our painters, Zeuxis illustrates the point when compared to Polygnotus; for Polygnotus is good at incorporating character into his painting, but the work of Zeuxis shows no real characterization at all. Furthermore, if someone

[9] The text is corrupt here. The translation follows an emendation suggested by Vahlen and accepted by Bywater and Hardy.

arranges a series of speeches that show character and are well-constructed in diction and thought, he will not, by this alone, achieve the end of tragedy; but far more will this be accomplished by the tragedy that employs these elements rather inadequately but, nevertheless, has a satisfactory plot and arrangement of incidents. In addition to the arguments already given, the most important factors by means of which tragedy exerts an influence on the soul are parts of the plot, the reversal, and the recognition. We have further proof of our view of the importance of plot in the fact that those who attempt to write tragedies are able to perfect diction and character before the construction of the incidents, as we see, for example, in nearly all of our early poets.

The first principle, then, and to speak figuratively, the soul of tragedy, is the plot; and second in importance is character. A closely corresponding situation exists in painting. For if someone should paint by applying the most beautiful colors, 1450b
but without reference to an over-all plan, he would not please us as much as if he had outlined the figure in black and white. Tragedy, then, is an imitation of an action; and it is, on account of this, an imitation of men acting.

Thought is the third part of tragedy and is the ability to say whatever is pertinent and fitting to the occasion, which, in reference to the composition of speeches, is the essential function of the arts of politics and rhetoric. As proof of this we point out that our earlier poets made their characters speak like statesmen, and our contemporary poets make them speak like rhetoricians. Now character is that part of tragedy which shows an individual's purpose by indicating, in circumstances where it is not clear, what sort of things he chooses or rejects. Therefore those speeches do not manifest character in which there is absolutely nothing that the speaker chooses or rejects. Thought we find in those speeches in which men show that something is or is not, or utter some universal proposition.

The fourth literary part is diction, and I mean by diction, as has already been said, the expression of thoughts through language which, indeed, is the same whether in verse or prose.

Of the remaining parts, melody is the greatest of the linguistic adornments; and spectacle, to be sure, attracts our attention but is the least artistic and least essential part of the art of poetry. For the power of tragedy is felt even without a dramatic performance and actors. Furthermore, for the realization of spectacle, the art of the costume designer is more effective than that of the poet.

VII

Now that we have defined these terms, let us discuss what kind of process the arrangement of incidents must be, since this is the first and most important element of tragedy. We have posited that tragedy is the imitation of a complete and whole action having a proper magnitude.[10] For it is possible for something to be a whole and yet not have any considerable magnitude. To be a whole is to have a beginning and a middle and an end. By a "beginning" I mean that which is itself not, by necessity, after anything else but after which something naturally is or develops. By an "end" I mean exactly the opposite: that which is naturally after something else, either necessarily or customarily, but after which there is nothing else. By a "middle" I mean that which is itself after something else and which has something else after it. It is necessary, therefore, that well-constructed plots not begin by chance, anywhere, nor end anywhere, but that they conform to the distinctions that have been made above.

Furthermore, for beauty to exist, both in regard to a living being and in regard to any object that is composed of separate parts, not only must there be a proper arrangement of the component elements, but the object must also be of a magni-

[10] For the phrase "proper magnitude" see Ch. VI, f.n. 8.

tude that is not fortuitous. For beauty is determined by magnitude and order; therefore, neither would a very small animal be beautiful (for one's view of the animal is not clear, taking place, as it does, in an almost unperceived length of time), nor is a very large animal beautiful (for then one's view does not occur all at once, but, rather, the unity and wholeness of the 1451a
animal are lost to the viewer's sight as would happen, for example, if we should come across an animal a thousand miles in length). So that just as it is necessary in regard to bodies and animals for there to be a proper magnitude—and this is the length that can easily be perceived at a glance—thus, also, there must be a proper length in regard to plots, and this is one that can be easily taken in by the memory. The limit of length in regard to the dramatic contests and in terms of the physical viewing of the performance is not a matter related to the art of poetry. For if it were necessary for a hundred tragedies to be played, they would be presented by timing them with water clocks as we are told happened on some occasions in the past. The limit, however, that is set in regard to magnitude by the very nature of the subject itself is that whatever is longer (provided it remains quite clear) is always more beautiful. To give a general rule, we say that whatever length is required for a change to occur from bad fortune to good or from good fortune to bad through a series of incidents that are in accordance with probability or necessity, is a sufficient limit of magnitude.

VIII

A plot is a unity not, as some think, merely if it is concerned with one individual, for in some of the many and infinitely varied things that happen to any one person, there is no unity. Thus, we must assert, there are many actions in the life of a single person from which no over-all unity of action emerges. For this reason all those poets seem to have erred who have written a *Heracleid* and a *Theseid* and other poems of this type; for they think that since Heracles was one person it is appropriate for his story to be one story. But Homer, just as he was superior in other respects, also seems to have seen this point well, whether through his technical skill or his native talent, since in making the *Odyssey* he did not include all the things that ever happened to Odysseus. (For example, it happened that Odysseus was wounded on Parnassus and that he feigned madness at the time of the call to arms; but between these two events there is no necessary or probable relation.) Homer, rather, organized the *Odyssey* around one action of the type we have been speaking about and did the same with the *Iliad*. Necessarily, then, just as in other forms of imitation, one imitation is of one thing, so also, a plot, since it is an imitation of an action, must be an imitation of an action that is one and whole. Moreover, it is necessary that the parts of the action be put together in such a way that if any one part is transposed or removed, the whole will be disordered and disunified. For that whose presence or absence has no evident effect is no part of the whole.

IX

It is apparent from what we have said that it is not the function of the poet to narrate events that have actually happened, but rather, events such as might occur and have the capability of occurring in accordance with the laws of probability or necessity. For the historian and the poet do not differ 1451b
by their writing in prose or verse (the works of Herodotus

might be put into verse but they would, nonetheless, remain a form of history both in their metrical and prose versions). The difference, rather, lies in the fact that the historian narrates events that have actually happened, whereas the poet writes about things as they might possibly occur. Poetry, therefore, is more philosophical and more significant than history, for poetry is more concerned with the universal, and history more with the individual. By the universal I mean what sort of man turns out to say or do what sort of thing according to probability or necessity—this being the goal poetry aims at, although it gives individual names to the characters whose actions are imitated. By the individual I mean a statement telling, for example, "what Alcibiades did or experienced."

Now then, this point has already been made clear in regard to comedy; for the comic poets, once they have constructed the plot through probable incidents, assign any names that happen to occur to them, and they do not follow the procedure of the iambic poets who write about specific individuals. In regard to tragedy, however, our poets cling to the names of the heroes of the past on the principle that whatever is clearly capable of happening is readily believable. We cannot be sure that whatever has not yet happened is possible; but it is apparent that whatever has happened is also capable of happening for, if it were not, it could not have occurred. Nevertheless in some tragedies one or two of the names are well known and the rest have been invented for the occasion; in others not even one is well-known, for example, Agathon's *Antheus,*[11] since in this play both the incidents and the names have been invented, and nonetheless they please us. Thus we must not seek to cling exclusively to the stories that have been handed down and about which our tragedies are usually written. It would be absurd, indeed, to do this since the well-known plots are known only to a few, but nevertheless please everyone. It is clear then from these considerations that it is necessary for the poet to be more the poet of his plots than of his meters, insofar as he is a poet because he is an imitator and imitates human actions. If the poet happens to write about things that have actually

[11] Agathon was a late fifth-century B.C. tragic poet whose work has not survived except in fragments. He appears, prominently, in Plato's *Symposium.*

occurred, he is no less the poet for that. For nothing prevents some of the things that have actually occurred from belonging to the class of the probable or possible, and it is in regard to this aspect that he is the poet of them.

Of the simple plots and actions the episodic are the worst; and I mean by episodic a plot in which the episodes follow each other without regard for the laws of probability or necessity. Such plots are constructed by the inferior poets because of their own inadequacies, and by the good poets because of the actors. For since they are writing plays that are to be entered in contests (and so stretch the plot beyond its capacity) they are frequently forced to distort the sequence of action. 1452a

Since the imitation is not only a complete action but is also of fearful and pitiable incidents, we must note that these are intensified when they occur unexpectedly, yet because of one another. For there is more of the marvelous in them if they occur this way than if they occurred spontaneously and by chance. Even in regard to coincidences, those seem to be most astonishing that appear to have some design associated with them. We have an example of this in the story of the statue of Mitys in Argos killing the man who caused Mitys' death by falling upon him as he was a spectator at a festival.[12] The occurrence of such an event, we feel, is not without meaning and thus we must consider plots that incorporate incidents of this type to be superior ones.

X

Plots are divided into the simple and the complex, for the actions of which the plots are imitations are naturally of this

[12] I have followed Butcher's, Hardy's, and Bywater's interpretation of this passage. Others, however, understand the phrase to mean "when he was looking at the statue."

character. An action that is, as has been defined, continuous and unified I call simple when its change of fortune arises without reversal and recognition, and complex when its change of fortune arises through recognition or reversal or both. Now these aspects of the plot must develop directly from the construction of the plot, itself, so that they occur from prior events either out of necessity or according to the laws of probability. For it makes quite a difference whether they occur *because* of those events or merely *after* them.

XI

Reversal is the change of fortune in the action of the play to the opposite state of affairs, just as has been said; and this change, we argue, should be in accordance with probability and necessity. Thus, in the *Oedipus* the messenger comes to cheer Oedipus and to remove his fears in regard to his mother; but by showing him who he actually is he accomplishes the very opposite effect. And in *Lynceus,* Lynceus is being led away to die and Danaus is following to kill him; but it turns out, because of the action that has taken place, that Danaus dies and Lynceus is saved. Recognition, as the name indicates, is a change from ignorance to knowledge, bringing about either a state of friendship or one of hostility on the part of those who have been marked out for good fortune or bad. The most effective recognition is one that occurs together with reversal, for example, as in the *Oedipus.* There are also other kinds of recognition for, indeed, what we have said happens, in a way, in regard to inanimate things, even things of a very casual kind; and it is possible, further, to "recognize" whether someone has or has not done something. But the type of recognition that is especially a part of the plot and the action is the one that has been mentioned. For such a recognition and reversal will evoke pity or fear, and we have defined tragedy as an imitation 1452b of actions of this type; and furthermore, happiness and misery will appear in circumstances of this type. Since this kind of recognition is of persons, some recognitions that belong to this class will merely involve the identification of one person by another when the identity of the second person is clear; on other occasions it will be necessary for there to be a recognition on the part of both parties: for example, Iphigenia is recognized by Orestes from her sending of the letter; but it is necessary that there be another recognition of him on her part.

Now then, these are two parts of the plot, reversal and recognition, and there is also a third part, suffering. Of these, reversal and recognition have been discussed; the incident of suffering results from destructive or painful action such as death on the stage, scenes of very great pain, the infliction of wounds, and the like.

XII

The parts of tragedy that we must view as formal elements we have discussed previously; looking at the quantitative aspect of tragedy and the parts into which it is divided in this regard, the following are the distinctions to be made: prologue, episode, exode, and the choral part, which is divided into parode and stasimon. These are commonly found in all plays, but only in a few are found songs from the stage and *kommoi*. The prologue is the complete section of a tragedy before the parode of the chorus; an episode is the complete section of a tragedy between complete choric songs; the exode is the complete section of a tragedy after which there is no song of the chorus. Of the choral part, the parode is the entire first speech of the chorus, the stasimon is a song of the chorus without anapests and trochees, and a *kommos* is a lament sung in common by the chorus and the actors. The parts of tragedy that we must view as formal elements we have discussed previously; the above distinctions have been made concerning the quantitative aspect of tragedy, and the parts into which it is divided in this regard.

XIII

What goals poets must aim at, what difficulties they must be wary of when constructing their plots, and how the proper function of tragedy is accomplished are matters we should discuss after the remarks that have just been made.

Since the plots of the best tragedies must be complex, not simple, and the plot of a tragedy must be an imitation of pitiable and fearful incidents (for this is the specific nature of the imitation under discussion), it is clear, first of all, that unqualifiedly good human beings must not appear to fall from good fortune to bad; for that is neither pitiable nor fearful; it is, rather, repellent. Nor must an extremely evil man appear to move from bad fortune to good fortune for that is the most untragic situation of all because it has none of the necessary requirements of tragedy; it both violates our human sympathy and contains nothing of the pitiable or fearful in it. 1453a
Furthermore, a villainous man should not appear to fall from good fortune to bad. For, although such a plot would be in accordance with our human sympathy, it would not contain the necessary elements of pity and fear; for pity is aroused

by someone who undeservedly falls into misfortune, and fear is evoked by our recognizing that it is someone like ourselves who encounters this misfortune (pity, as I say, arising for the former reason, fear for the latter). Therefore the emotional effect of the situation just mentioned will be neither pitiable nor fearful. What is left, after our considerations, is someone in between these extremes. This would be a person who is neither perfect in virtue and justice, nor one who falls into misfortune through vice and depravity; but rather, one who succumbs through some miscalculation. He must also be a person who enjoys great reputation and good fortune, such as Oedipus, Thyestes, and other illustrious men from similar families. It is necessary, furthermore, for the well-constructed plot to have a single rather than a double construction, as some urge, and to illustrate a change of fortune not from bad fortune to good but, rather, the very opposite, from good fortune to bad, and for this to take place not because of depravity but through some great miscalculation on the part of the type of person we have described (or a better rather than a worse one).

A sign of our point is found in what actually happens in the theater. For initially, our poets accepted any chance plots; but now the best tragedies are constructed about a few families, for example, about Alcmaeon, Oedipus, Orestes, Meleager, Thyestes, Telephon, and any others who were destined to experience, or to commit, terrifying acts. For as we have indicated, artistically considered, the best tragedy arises from this kind of plot. Therefore, those critics make the very mistake that we have been discussing who blame Euripides because he handles the material in his tragedies in this way, and because many of his plots end in misfortune. For this is, indeed, the correct procedure, as we have said. The very great proof of this is that on the stage and in the dramatic contests such plays appear to be the most tragic, if they are properly worked out; and Euripides, even if, in other matters he does not manage things well, nevertheless appears to be the most tragic of the poets. The second ranking plot, one that is called first by some, has a double structure of events, as in the *Odyssey*, ending in opposite ways for the better and worse characters. It seems to be first on account of the inadequacy of the audience. For our poets trail along writing to please the tastes of the audience. But this double structure of events involves a pleasure that is not an appropriate pleasure of tragedy but rather of comedy. For in comedy, whoever are the greatest enemies in the story—for example, Orestes and Aegisthus—becoming friends at the end, go off together, and no one is killed by anyone.

XIV

Pity and fear can arise from the spectacle and also from 1453b
the very structure of the plot, which is the superior way and shows the better poet. The poet should construct the plot so that even if the action is not performed before spectators, one who merely hears the incidents that have occurred both shudders and feels pity from the way they turn out. That is what anyone who hears the plot of the *Oedipus* would experience. The achievement of this effect through the spectacle does not have much to do with poetic art and really belongs to the business of producing the play. Those who use the spectacle to create not the fearful but only the monstrous have no share in the creation of tragedy; for we should not seek every pleasure from tragedy but only the one proper to it.

Since the poet should provide pleasure from pity and fear through imitation, it is apparent that this function must be worked into the incidents. Let us try to understand what type of occurrences appear to be terrifying and pitiable. It is, indeed, necessary that any such action occur either between those who are friends or enemies to each other, or between those who have no relationship, whatsoever, to each other. If an enemy takes such an action against an enemy, there is nothing pitiable in the performance of the act or in the intention to perform it, except the suffering itself. Nor would there be anything pitiable if neither party had any relationship with the other. But whenever the tragic incidents occur in situations involving strong ties of affection—for example, if a brother kills or intends to kill a brother or a son a father or a mother a son or a son a mother or commits some equally terrible act—there will be something pitiable. These situations, then, are the ones to be sought. Now, it is not possible for a poet to alter completely the traditional stories. I mean, for example, the given fact that Clytemnestra dies at the hands of Orestes, and Eriphyle at the hands of Alcmaeon; but it is necessary for the poet to be inventive and skillful in adapting the stories that have been handed down. Let us define more clearly what we mean by the skillful adaptation of a story. It is possible for the action to occur, as our early poets handled it, with the characters knowing and understanding what they are doing, as indeed Euripides makes Medea kill her children. It is also possible to have the deed done with those who accomplish the terrible deed in ignorance of the identity of their victim, only later recognizing the relationship as in Sophocles' *Oedipus*. The incident, here, is outside the plot, but we find an example of such an incident in the play itself, in the action of Astydamas' *Alcmaeon* or of Telegonus in the *Wounded Odysseus*;[13] and there is further a third type in addition to these that involves someone who intends to commit some fatal act through ignorance of his relationship to another person but recognizes this relationship before doing it. Beyond these possibilities, there is no other way to have an action take place. For it is necessary either to do the deed or not and either knowingly or in ignorance.

Of these possibilities, the case in which one knowingly is about to do the deed and does not is the worst; for it is repel-

[13] Astydamas was a fourth-century B.C. poet; the *Wounded Odysseus* may have been a play by Sophocles.

lent and not tragic because it lacks the element of suffering. Therefore, no one handles a situation this way, except rarely; 1454a
for example, in the *Antigone,* Haemon is made to act in this way toward Creon. To do the deed knowingly is the next best way. Better than this is the case where one does the deed in ignorance and after he has done it recognizes his relationship to the other person. For the repellent aspect is not present, and the recognition is startling. But the most effective is the final type, for example, in the *Cresphontes,* where Merope is going to kill her son and does not, but, on the contrary, recognizes him, and in the *Iphigenia,* where a sister is involved in a similar situation with a brother, and in the *Helle,* where a son who is about to surrender his mother recognizes her.[14]

It is for this reason that, as we have said previously, tragedies are concerned with a few families. For proceeding not by art, but by trial and error, poets learned how to produce the appropriate effect in their plots. They are compelled, therefore, to return time and again to that number of families in which these terrifying events have occurred. We have now spoken sufficiently about the construction of the incidents and of what type the plot must be.

XV

In regard to character, there are four points to be aimed at. First and foremost, character should be good. If a speech or action has some choice connected with it, it will manifest character, as has been said, and the character will be good if the choice is good. Goodness is possible for each

[14] The *Cresphontes* and the *Iphigenia,* the former no longer extant, are plays by Euripides. We have no further information concerning the *Helle.*

class of individuals. For, both a woman and a slave have their particular virtues even though the former of these is inferior to a man, and the latter is completely ignoble. Second, character must be appropriate. For it is possible for a person to be manly in terms of character, but it is not appropriate for a woman to exhibit either this quality or the intellectual cleverness that is associated with men. The third point about character is that it should be like reality, for this is different from making character virtuous and making it appropriate, as we have defined these terms. The fourth aspect of character is consistency. For even if it is an inconsistent character who is the subject of the imitation (I refer to the model that suggested the kind of character being imitated), it is nevertheless necessary for him to be consistently inconsistent. We have an example of unnecessarily debased character in the figure of Menelaus in the *Orestes,* of unsuitable and inappropriate character in the lament of Odysseus in the *Scylla* and the speech of Melanippe, and of inconsistency of character in *Iphigenia at Aulis* where the heroine's role as a suppliant does not fit in with her character as it develops later in the play.

In character, as in the construction of the incidents, we must always seek for either the necessary or the probable, so that a given type of person says or does certain kinds of things, and one event follows another according to necessity or probability. Thus, it is apparent that the resolutions of
the plots should also occur through the plot itself and not 1454b
by means of the *deus ex machina,* as in the *Medea,* and also in regard to the events surrounding the departure of the fleet in the *Iliad.* The *deus ex machina* must be reserved for the events that lie outside the plot, either those that happened before it that are not capable of being known by men, or those that occur after that need to be announced and spoken of beforehand. For we grant to the gods the power of seeing all things. There should, then, be nothing improbable in the action; but if this is impossible, it should be outside the plot as, for example, in Sophocles' *Oedipus.*

Because tragedy is an imitation of the nobler sort of men it is necessary for poets to imitate the good portrait painters.

For even though they reproduce the specific characteristics of their subjects and represent them faithfully, they also paint them better than they are. Thus, also, the poet imitating men who are prone to anger or who are indifferent or who are disposed in other such ways in regard to character makes them good as well, even though they have such characteristics, just as Agathon[15] and Homer portray Achilles.

It is necessary to pay close attention to these matters and, in addition, to those that pertain to the effects upon an audience that follow necessarily from the nature of the art of poetry. For, indeed, it is possible frequently to make mistakes in regard to these. We have spoken sufficiently about these matters in our published works.

XVI

What we mean by "recognition" we have indicated previously. Of the kinds of recognition that occur, there is one, first of all, that is least artistic, which poets mainly use through the poverty of their inspiration. This is the form of recognition that is achieved through external signs; some of these are birthmarks, for example, "the spearhead which the Earth-born are accustomed to bear," or the "stars" such as Carcinus wrote about in his *Thyestes*. Then there are characteristics that we acquire after birth. Of these some are found on the body, for example, scars; and others are external to the body, such as necklaces, and as another example, the ark through which the recognition is accomplished in the *Tyro*. It is also possible to employ these recognitions in better and

[15] I have followed Butcher, Hardy, and Bywater in reading the name of the tragic poet here. Other scholars accept a manuscript reading of the word meaning "good."

worse ways; for example, Odysseus was recognized through his scar in one way by the nurse and in another way by the swineherds. Now those recognitions are less artistic that depend on signs as proof, as well as all that are similar to these; but those that derive from the reversal of action, as in the Bath Scene of the *Odyssey,* are better.

In second place come those recognitions that have been contrived for the occasion by the poet and are therefore inartistic. For example, the way Orestes in the *Iphigenia* makes known that he is Orestes; for Iphigenia made herself known through the letter, but he himself says what the poet wishes him to say but not what the plot requires. Therefore this type of recognition is rather close to the error that has already been mentioned; for it would have been just as possible for him to carry tokens with him. Another example of this type of recognition is the use of the "voice of the shuttle" in the *Tereus* of Sophocles.

The third type arises from our being stimulated by something that we see to remember an event that has an emotional significance for us. This type of recognition occurs in the
Cyprioe of Dicaeogenes where the sight of the painting brings 1455a
forth tears, and also in the story of Alcinous where Odysseus hears the lyre player and, reminded of his past fortunes, weeps; in both instances, it was by their emotional reactions that the characters were recognized.

The fourth type of recognition occurs through reasoning, for example, in the *Choëphoroe* it is achieved by the deduction: Someone like me has come; there is no one resembling me except Orestes; he, therefore, has come. Another recognition of this type was suggested by Polyidus the Sophist in regard to Iphigenia; for it was reasonable for Orestes to infer that, since his sister was sacrificed, he was also going to be sacrificed. Again, in the *Tydeus* of Theodectes, the deduction is made that he who had come to find a son was, himself, to perish. Another example is in the *Phinidae* where the women, when they had seen the place, inferred their destiny: that since they had been exposed there, they were fated to die there.

There is also a type of composite recognition from false

reasoning on the part of another character,[16] for example, in the story of Odysseus, the False Messenger; for he said that he would know the bow that he had not seen, but it is false reasoning to suppose through this that he *would* recognize it again (as if he had seen it before).[17]

The best recognition is the one that arises from the incidents themselves, striking us, as they do, with astonishment through the very probability of their occurrence as, for example, in the action of the *Oedipus* of Sophocles and in the *Iphigenia,* where it is reasonable for the heroine to wish to dispatch a letter. Such recognitions, alone, are accomplished without contrived signs and necklaces. The second best type of recognition is the one that is achieved by reasoning.

XVII

In constructing plots and working them out with diction, the poet must keep the action as much as possible before his eyes. For by visualizing the events as distinctly as he can, just as if he were present at their actual occurrence, he will discover what is fitting for his purpose, and there will be the least chance of incongruities escaping his notice. A sign of this is found in the criticism that is made of Carcinus. For Amphiarus is coming back from the temple, a point that would have escaped the audience's notice if it had not actually seen it; and on the stage, the play failed because the audience was annoyed at this incongruity.[18]

[16] I have followed Bywater in accepting an emendation meaning "another" in place of the manuscript reading "audience" followed by Kassel and Hardy.

[17] In this passage, Bywater notes that, "both text and interpretation here are in the highest degree doubtful." I have followed his interpretation of this difficult passage. Except for the *Choëphoroe,* we do not have any information about the plays mentioned in the previous paragraph.

[18] Carcinus was a fifth-century B.C. tragic poet; nothing further is known of the play mentioned here.

As much as is possible the poet should also work out the action with gestures. For, given poets of the same natural abilities, those are most persuasive who are involved in the emotions they imitate; for example, one who is distressed conveys distress, and one who is enraged conveys anger most truly. Therefore, the art of poetry is more a matter for the well-endowed poet than for the frenzied one.[19] For poets marked by the former characteristic can easily change character, whereas those of the latter type are possessed.

In regard to arguments, both those that already are in existence and those he himself invents, the poet should first put them down in universal form and then extend them by adding 1455b
episodes. I mean that the poet should take a general view of the action of the play, like, for example, the following general view of the *Iphigenia*: A young girl had been sacrificed and had disappeared in a way that was obscure to the sacrificers. She settled in another country in which it was the custom to sacrifice strangers to the goddess, and she came to hold the priesthood for this sacrifice. Later, it turned out that the brother of the priestess came to this country (the fact that the god, for some reason, commanded him to come is outside the argument; the purpose of his coming is outside of the plot). When he came he was seized, and on the point of being sacrificed he made himself known, either as Euripides handled the situation or as Polyidus arranged it, by his saying, in a very reasonable way, that not only had it been necessary for his sister to be sacrificed but also for him; and from this came his deliverance. After this, when the names have already been assigned, it is necessary to complete the episodes. The episodes must be appropriate, as, for example, the madness of Orestes through which he was captured and his deliverance through purification.

In drama, the episodes are short, but epic achieves its length by means of them. For the argument of the *Odyssey* is not long: A certain man is away from home for many years, closely watched by Poseidon but otherwise completely alone. His family at home continually faces a situation where his

[19] See the commentary for a discussion of the textual basis of this translation.

possessions are being squandered by the suitors who plot against his son. Storm-driven, he arrives home and, having made certain people acquainted with him, he attacks the suitors and, while destroying his enemies, is himself saved. This is the essence of the story; everything else is episode.

XVIII

In every tragedy, we find both the complication and the resolution of the action. Frequently some matters outside the action together with some within it comprise the complication, and the rest of the play consists of the resolution. By complication I mean that part of the play from the beginning up to the first point at which the change occurs to good or to bad fortune. By resolution I mean the part of the play from the beginning of the change in fortune to the end of the play. For example, in the *Lynceus* of Theodectes, the complication comprises everything done before the action of the play begins and the seizing of the child, and, in turn, of the parents; the resolution comprises all that happens from the accusation of murder to the end of the play.[20]

There are four kinds of tragedy (for that number of parts has been mentioned): the complex, which consists wholly in reversal and recognition; the tragedies of suffering, for example, the *Ajaxes* and *Ixions* that have been written; the 1456a
tragedies of character, for example, the *Phthiotian Women* and the *Peleus*.[21] And a fourth type [the tragedy of spectacle],

[20] The text is in dispute here. Bywater, following a suggestion of Susemihl, translates the passage 1456a, 7-10, at this point in the text. Butcher, Hardy, and Kassel retain the traditional reading that I have followed in my translation.

[21] *The Phthiotian Women* and *Peleus,* neither now extant, were probably written by Sophocles. The *Lynceus,* mentioned above and at l. 7 in Ch. XI, is also no longer extant.

for example, is *The Daughters of Phorcis* and *Prometheus*[22] and those plays that take place in Hades. Now it is necessary to attempt, as much as possible, to include all elements in the play, but if that is not possible, then as many as possible and certainly the most important ones. This is especially so now, indeed, when the public unjustly criticizes our poets. For although there have been poets who were outstanding in regard to each kind of tragedy, the public now demands that one man be superior to the particular virtue of each of his predecessors.

It is correct to speak of a tragedy as different from or similar to another one on the basis of its plot more than anything else: that is, in regard to an action having the same complication and resolution. Many poets are skillful in constructing their complications, but their resolutions are poor. It is, however, necessary for both elements to be mastered.

The poet, as has frequently been said, must remember not to make a tragedy out of an epic body of incidents (by which I mean a multiple plot), [as would be the case], for example, if someone should construct a plot out of the entire *Iliad*. For, there, because of the length, the parts take on the appropriate magnitude, but the same plot used in the drama turns out quite contrary to one's expectations. A sign of this is that so many as have written about the entire destruction of Troy (and not of sections of it, as Euripides) or about the entire story of Niobe (and not just a part, as Aeschylus) either completely fail on stage or do badly, since even Agathon failed for this reason alone. But in their reversals and in their simple plots, these poets aim with marvelous accuracy at the effects that they wish for: that is, whatever is tragic and touches our human sympathy. This occurs whenever a clever but evil person is deceived, as Sisyphus, or a brave but unjust man is defeated. Such an event is probable, as Agathon says, because it is probable for many things to occur contrary to probability.

[22] *The Daughters of Phorcis* and *Prometheus* are both by Aeschylus; Bywater identifies them as lost satyr-plays and does not connect the latter play with the famous *Prometheus Bound*.

It is necessary to consider the chorus as one of the actors and as an integral part of the drama; its involvement in the action should not be in Euripides' manner but in Sophocles'. In the hands of our later poets, the songs included in the play are no more a part of that particular plot than they are of any other tragedy. They have been sung, therefore, as inserted pieces from the time Agathon first introduced this practice. And yet what difference does it make whether one sings an inserted song or adopts a speech or a whole episode from one play into another?

XIX

We have already spoken about other matters; it remains for us to discuss diction and thought. Concerning thought, let it be taken as given what we have written in the *Rhetoric*, for this is more appropriately a subject of that discipline. All those matters pertain to thought that must be presented through speech; and they may be subdivided into proof and refutation and the production of emotional effects, for example, pity or fear or anger or other similar emotions. Indi- 1456b
cations of the importance or insignificance of anything also fall under this heading. It is clear that we must employ thought also in actions in the same ways [as in speech] whenever we aim at the representation of the pitiable, the terrible, the significant, or the probable, with the exception of this one difference—that the effects arise in the case of the incidents without verbal explanation, whereas in the speech they are produced by the speaker and arise because of the speech. For what would be the function of the speaker if something should appear in the way that is required without being dependent on the speech?

Concerning diction one kind of study involves the forms of diction that are investigated by the art of elocution and are the concern of the individual who considers this his guiding art, for example, what a command is and what a prayer is, what a statement is, and threat and question and answer and any other such matters. For in regard to the knowledge or ignorance of these matters, no censure worth taking seriously can be made against the art of poetry. Why should any one accept as an error Protagoras' censure of Homer on the grounds that when he said, "Sing, O goddess, of the wrath . . ." he gave a command, although he really wished to utter a prayer. For Protagoras says to order someone to do something or not is a command. Let us, therefore, disregard such a consideration as being a principle of some other art, not the art of poetry.

XX

The following parts comprise the entire scope of diction: letter, syllable, connective, noun, verb, inflection and sentence. A letter is an indivisible sound; not every such sound is a letter, however, but only one from which a compound sound can be constructed. For I would call none of the individual sounds uttered by wild animals letters. The subdivisions of this category of "letter" are vowel, semivowel, and mute. A vowel is a sound that is audible without the contact of any of the physical structures of the mouth,[23] a semivowel

[23] I have followed Butcher and Hardy in seeing this passage as a reference to the physical means of producing speech. Bywater disputes this interpretation and argues that the ambiguous term *prosbole* does not refer to the impact of the

is a sound that is audible with the contact of some of the physical structures of the mouth, for example, the *S* and *R* sounds; and a mute is a letter produced by the contact of the physical structures of the mouth, but inaudible in itself, although it becomes audible when it is accompanied by letters that are sounded, for example, the *G* and *D* sounds. These letters differ in the positions taken by the mouth to produce them, in the places in the mouth where they are produced, in aspiration and smoothness, in being long or short and, furthermore, in having an acute, grave, or middle [circumflex] pitch accent. The detailed investigation concerning these matters belongs to the study of metrics.

A syllable is a nonsignificant sound constructed from a mute and a vowel. For, indeed, *GR* without an *A* is a syllable and also with it, for example, *GRA*. However, it is the business of the art of metrics also to investigate distinctions in this area.[24]

A connective is a nonsignificant sound that neither hinders
nor promotes the creation of one significant sound from many 1457a
sounds and that it is not appropriate to place at the beginning of a speech that stands independently, for example, *men, dē, toi, de*. Or it is a nonsignificant sound that is naturally able to make one significant sound from a number of sounds, for example, *amphi, peri,* and others like them. There is also a kind of connective that is a nonsignificant sound that shows the beginning, end, or division of a sentence and that may naturally be placed at either end or in the middle of a sentence.

A noun is a compound significant sound, not indicating time, no part of which is significant by itself. For in compound nouns we do not consider each part of the compound as being significant in itself; for example, in the name "Theodore" the root *dor* [gift] has no significance.

A verb is a compound significant sound indicating time, no part of which is significant by itself in the same way as

---

physical structures of the mouth but to the addition of one letter to another.

[24] The passage that begins here is corrupt and contains many difficulties of interpretation.

has been indicated in regard to nouns. For "man" or "white" do not tell us anything about "when"; but "He goes" or "He has gone" indicate the present and the past.

Inflection is a characteristic of a noun or verb signifying the genitive or dative relation, or other similar ones, or indicating the singular or plural, that is, man or men, or is concerned with matters that fall under the art of elocution, for example, questions and commands; for the phrases, "Did he go?" or "Go!" involve inflections of the verb in regard to these categories.

A speech is a compound, significant sound some of whose parts are significant by themselves. For not every speech is composed of verbs and nouns but it is possible to have a speech without verbs (for example, the definition of man). However, part of the speech will always have some significance, for example, "Cleon" in the phrase "Cleon walks." A speech is a unity in two ways. Either it signifies one thing or it is a unity through the joining together of many speeches. For example, the *Iliad* is a unity by the process of joining together many speeches, and the definition of man by signifying one thing.

XXI

Nouns are either simple, by which I mean constructed solely from nonsignificant elements, for example *gē* [earth], or compound. This latter category is divided into nouns that are constructed from both significant and nonsignificant elements (except that neither element is significant within the compound word itself) and nouns that are composed solely out of significant elements. Nouns may also be made up of three, four, or more parts, for example, many of the words in the Massilian vocabulary, such as Hermocaicoxanthus. . . .[25]

Every word is either standard, or is a strange word, or is a 1457b metaphor, or is ornamental, or is a coined word, or is lengthened, or contracted, or is altered in some way. I mean by standard, words that everyone uses, and by a strange word, one that foreigners use. Thus, it is apparent, the same word can be both strange and ordinary but not, of course, to the same persons. The word *sigunon* [spear] is ordinary for the Cyprians and strange to us.

Metaphor is the transference of a name from the object to which it has a natural application; this transference can take place from genus to species or species to genus or from species to species or by analogy. I mean by from genus to species, for example, "This ship of mine stands there." For to lie at anchor is a species of standing. An example of the transference from species to genus, "Odysseus has truly accomplished a myriad of noble deeds." For a myriad is the equivalent of "many," for which the poet now substitutes this term. An example of the transference from species to species is "having drawn off life with a sword" and also "having cut with unyielding bronze." For here to draw off is to cut and to cut is called to draw off, for both are subdivisions of "taking away."

I mean by transference by analogy the situation that occurs whenever a second element is related to a first as a fourth is to a third. For the poet will then use the fourth in place of the second or the second in place of the fourth, and sometimes poets add the reference to which the transferred term applies. I mean, for example, that a cup is related to Dionysus as a shield is to Ares. The poet will, therefore, speak of the cup as the shield of Dionysus and the shield as the cup of Ares. The same situation occurs in regard to the relation of old age to life and evening to day. A poet will say that evening is the old age of day, or however Empedocles expressed it, and that old age is the evening of life or the sunset of life. In some situations, there is no regular name in use to cover the

[25] There is a lacuna in the text here. Some editors accept Diel's conjecture, "praying to father Zeus," as the completion of this line.

analogous relation, but nevertheless the related elements will be spoken of by analogy; for example, to scatter seed is to sow, but the scattering of the sun's rays has no name. But the act of sowing in regard to grain bears an analogous relation to the sun's dispersing of its rays, and so we have the phrase "sowing the god-created fire."

It is also possible to use metaphor in a different way by applying the transferred epithet and then denying some aspect that is proper to it—for example, if one should call the shield not the cup of Ares but the wineless cup.[26] A coined word is one that is not in use among foreigners but is the invention of the poet. There seem to be some words of this type, for example, horns [*kerata*] called "sprouters" [*ernuges*], and a priest [*iereus*] called "supplicator" [*arētēr*].

A word may be lengthened or contracted. It is lengthened if it makes use of a longer vowel than is usual for it, or a 1458a
syllable is inserted in it; and it is contracted if any element is removed from it. An example of lengthening is *poleōs* to *polēos* and *Pēleidou* to *Pēlēiadeō;* an example of contraction is *krī* and *dō* and *ops* in *"mia ginetai amphoterōn ops."*

A word is altered whenever a poet utilizes part of the regular name for the object he is describing and invents part anew, for example, in the phrase *"deksiteron kata mazon"* the use of *deksiteron* in place of *deksion.*[27]

Nouns are subdivided into masculine, feminine, and neuter. Those are masculine that end in nu, rho, and sigma and in the two letters psi and ksi that are constructed in combination with sigma. Those nouns are feminine that end in the vowels that are always long, the eta and omega, and that end (in regard to the vowels subject to lengthening) in the lengthened alpha. Thus it turns out that there are an equal number of terminations for masculine and feminine nouns since psi and ksi are subdivisions of sigma. No noun ends in a mute nor in a short vowel. Only three end in iota, *meli,*

[26] Editors have noted that a definition of the term "ornamental word" belongs in the text at this point, although it is missing from the manuscripts.

[27] The phrase quoted comes from the *Iliad,* V, 393 and means "at her right breast." Two words meaning "right" are quoted to illustrate Aristotle's point here.

kommi, peperi, and five end in upsilon. Neuter nouns end in these vowels and in nu and sigma.

XXII

Diction achieves its characteristic virtue in being clear but not mean. The clearest style results from the use of standard words; but it is also mean, as can be seen in the poetry of Cleophon and Sthenelus. A really distinguished style varies ordinary diction through the employment of unusual words. By unusual I mean strange words and metaphor and lengthened words and everything that goes beyond ordinary diction. But if someone should write exclusively in such forms the result would either be a riddle or a barbarism. A riddle will result if someone writes exclusively in metaphor; and a barbarism will result if there is an exclusive use of strange words. For it is in the nature of a riddle for one to speak of a situation that actually exists in an impossible way. Now it is not possible to do this by the combination of strange words; but it can be done by metaphor, for example, "I saw a man who welded bronze on another man by fire," and other metaphors like this. A statement constructed exclusively from strange words is a barbarism.

It is therefore necessary to use a combination of all these forms. The employment of strange words and metaphor and ornamental words and the other forms of speech that have been mentioned will prevent the diction from being ordinary and mean; and the use of normal speech will keep the diction 1458b
clear. The lengthening and contraction of words and alterations in them contribute in no small measure to the diction's clarity and its elevation above ordinary diction. For because

such words are different they will prevent the diction from being ordinary through their contrast with the ordinary expression; and because they have a share in the customary word, they will keep the diction clear.

Thus, the criticism is not well-taken on the part of those who censure this way of using language and who mock the poet, as the elder Euclid did, on the grounds that it is easy to write poetry if you are allowed to lengthen forms as much as you want; Euclid composed a satiric verse in the very words he used, *Epicharēn eidon Marathōnade badizonta* and *ouk an g'eramenos ton ekeinou elleboron.*[28]

Now then, the employment of the technique of lengthening in excess is ridiculous, and moderation is a quality that is commonly needed in all aspects of diction. For, indeed, if one employs metaphors and strange words and other forms in an inappropriate way and with intended absurdity, he can also accomplish the same effect. When the ordinary words are inserted in the verse, it can be seen how great a difference the appropriate use of lengthening makes in epic poetry. If someone should also change the strange words and metaphors and other forms to ordinary words, he would see the truth of what we have said. For example, Aeschylus and Euripides wrote the same iambic line, but Euripides changed one word and instead of using a standard one employed a strange one; his line thus has an elegance to it, whereas the other is mean. For Aeschylus wrote in his *Philoctetes*:

phagedaina hē mou sarkas esthiei podos
[this cancerous sore eats the flesh of my leg].

Euripides in place of "eats" substitutes *thoinatai* [feasts upon]. A similar situation would occur in the line

nun de m'eōn oligos te kai outidanos kai aeikēs[29]

[28] This passage offers a number of difficulties in text and interpretation. The essential point is that the prosaic lines quoted can be technically turned into verse if enough licenses are allowed. The first phrase may be translated "I saw Epichares going to Marathon." The text of the second phrase is corrupt and does not have a clear meaning as it stands.

[29] A passage quoted from *Odyssey,* IX 515, meaning "someone small, worthless, and unseemly."

if someone should substitute the ordinary words

nun de m'eōn mikros te kai asthenikos kai aeidēs

or if we changed the line

diphron aeikelion katatheis oligēn te trapezan[30]

to

diphron moxthēron katatheis mikran te trapezan

or for *ēiones booōsin,* we substituted *ēiones krazousin.*[31] Furthermore, Ariphrades mocked the tragedians because no one would use their style in conversation; for example, the word order *dōmatōn apo* in place of *apo dōmatōn,* and the word *sethen,* and the phrase *egō de nin,* and the word order *Achilleōs peri* in place of *peri Achilleōs,* and many other similar 1459a
expressions. For he missed the point that the virtue of all these expressions is that they create an unusual element in the diction by their not being in ordinary speech.

It is a matter of great importance to use each of the forms mentioned in a fitting way, as well as compound words and strange ones, but by far the most important matter is to have skill in the use of metaphor. This skill alone it is not possible to obtain from another; and it is, in itself, a sign of genius. For the ability to construct good metaphors implies the ability to see essential similarities.

In regard to words, compounds are especially suitable for dithyrambs, strange words for heroic verse, and metaphors for iambic verse; in heroic verse all the forms mentioned are serviceable; but in iambic verse, because as much as possible it imitates conversation, only those words are appropriate that might be used in prose.

Of this nature are standard words, metaphors, and ornamental words.

Now, then, concerning tragedy and the imitation that is carried out in action, let what has been said suffice.

[30] A passage quoted from *Odyssey,* XX, 259 meaning "having set down [for him] an unseemly chair and a small table."

[31] A passage quoted from *Iliad,* XVII, 265 meaning "the shores cry out."

XXIII

Concerning that form of verse imitation that is narrative, it is necessary to construct the plot as in tragedy in a dramatic fashion, and concerning a single action that is whole and complete (having a beginning, middle, and end) so that, like a single integrated organism, it achieves the pleasure natural to it.

The composition of incidents should not be similar to that found in our histories, in which it is necessary to show not one action but one period of time and as many things as happened in this time, whether they concern one man or many, and whether or not each of these things is related to the others. For just as there occurred in the same period of time a sea battle at Salamis and a battle with the Carthaginians in Sicily, but these did not at all lead to a common goal, thus also in the sequence of time, occasionally one event happens after another without there being a common goal to join them.

However, almost all the poets commit this error. Also in this, then, Homer would appear to be of exceptional skill in relation to other poets, as we have already said, since he did not attempt to write about the complete war, although it had a beginning and end; for that would have been a very large subject and could not have been taken in easily in a single view; or even if its magnitude were moderate, the story still would be tangled because of the diversity of incidents. But note how although treating only one part of the war, he also introduces many of the other episodes in the war, for example, the catalogue of ships and others, by which he gives variety to his poem. Others write about one man and about one period
and one action with diverse parts, for example, the poet who 1459b
wrote the *Cypria* and the *Little Iliad*. Therefore from the 31
Iliad and *Odyssey* one or two tragedies apiece are constructed; but from the *Cypria* many tragedies are constructed and from the *Little Iliad* eight, for example, *The Award of the Arms, Philoctetes, Neoptolemus, Eurypylus, The Beggar, The La-*

conian Woman, The Sack of Troy, The Return Voyage, and a *Sinon,* and a *Women of Troy.*[32]

XXIV

Moreover, it is necessary for epic poetry to exhibit the same characteristic forms as tragedy; for it is either simple or complex, displays character or suffering, and is composed of the same parts, with the exception of song and spectacle. In epic, there is also a necessity for reversals, recognitions, and the depiction of suffering. Here too, thought and diction must be handled with skill. Homer used all these elements first and in a proper way. For each of his poems is well-constructed; the *Iliad* is simple and exhibits suffering, whereas the *Odyssey* is complex (for there is recognition throughout) and shows character. In addition to these matters, Homer outstrips all others in diction and thought.

Epic differs from tragedy in regard to the length of the plot, and the meter. The sufficient limit of length has been mentioned, for we have noted that it must be possible to take in the plot's beginning and end in one view. This would occur if the plots were shorter than those of the old epics but would extend to the length of the number of tragedies that are designated for one performance. For the purpose of extending its length, epic poetry has a very great capacity that is specifically its own, since it is not possible in tragedy to imitate many simultaneous lines of action but only that performed by the actors on the stage. But because of the narrative quality of epic it is possible to depict many simultaneous lines of action

[32] Butcher and Kassel bracket the names of the last two plays as being later additions to the original text of the *Poetics.*

that, if appropriate, become the means of increasing the poem's scope. This has an advantage in regard to the elegance of the poem and in regard to varying the interest of the audience and for constructing a diverse sequence of episodes. For the rapid overloading of tragedies with the same kind of incident is what makes tragedies fail.

The heroic meter has been found appropriate to epic through practical experience. If someone should write a narrative imitation in another meter, or in a combination of meters, we would feel it to be inappropriate. For the heroic is the stateliest and most dignified meter, and therefore it is especially receptive to strange words and metaphors, for narrative poetry in this regard is exceptional among the forms of imitation; the iambic and the trochaic tetrameter are expressive of motion, the latter being a dance meter and the 1460a
former displaying the quality of action. Furthermore, it makes a very strange impression if someone combines these meters as Chairemon did. Therefore no one has written a long poem in a meter other than the heroic; but, as we said, nature herself teaches us to choose the appropriate meter.

Homer deserves praise for many qualities and, especially, because alone of the poets he is not ignorant of the requirements of his craft. For it is necessary for the poet himself to speak in his own person in the poem as little as possible, because he is not fulfilling his function as an imitator when he appears in this way. Now the other poets are themselves active performers throughout the poem, and they perform their imitative function infrequently and in regard to only a few objects. Homer, on the other hand, when he has made a brief prelude immediately brings in a man or woman or some other character; and all his figures are expressive of character, and none lacks it.

Now then, it is necessary in tragedy to create the marvelous, but the epic admits, even more, of the irrational, on which the marvelous especially depends, because the audience does not see the person acting. The whole business of the pursuit of Hector would appear ridiculous on the stage with some men standing about and not pursuing and Achilles nodding at them to keep them back; but in the narrative description of epic, this absurdity escapes notice.

The marvelous is pleasant, and the proof of this is that everyone embellishes the stories he tells as if he were adding something pleasant to his narration. Homer has especially taught others how it is necessary to lie, and this is through the employment of false reasoning. For whenever one event occurs or comes into existence and is naturally accompanied by a second event, men think that whenever this second event is present the first one must also have occurred or have come into existence. This, however, is a fallacy. Therefore, if the first event mentioned is false but there is another event that must occur or come into existence when the first event occurs, we feel compelled to join the two events in our thought. For our mind, through knowing that the second event is true, falsely reasons that the first event must have occurred or have come into existence also. There is an example of this type of fallacy in the Bath Scene in the *Odyssey*.

The use of impossible probabilities is preferable to that of unpersuasive possibilities. We must not construct plots from irrational elements, and we should especially attempt not to have anything irrational at all in them; but if this is not possible, the irrational should be outside the plot (as in Oedipus' ignorance of how Laius died); it should not be in the drama itself, as occurs in the *Electra* concerning those who bring news of the Pythian games, or in the *Mysians,* concerning the man who has come from Tegea to Mysia without speaking. To say that without the use of such incidents the plot would have been ruined is ridiculous. For it is necessary, right from the beginning, not to construct such plots.

If the poet takes such a plot and if it appears to admit of a more probable treatment, the situation is also absurd,[33] since it is clear that even the improbable elements in the *Odyssey* concerning the casting ashore of Odysseus would not

[33] Butcher and Hardy, following a different punctuation of the text, interpret this passage to mean that it is possible to admit some element of the irrational to the plot; others feel that the Greek text does not make adequate sense as it stands. I have followed Bywater's punctuation and interpretation of this passage.

be bearable if a poor poet had written them. Here the poet conceals the absurdity by making it pleasing through his other skillful techniques. It is necessary to intensify the diction only in those parts of the poem that lack action and are unexpressive of character and thought. For too brilliant a diction conceals character and thought. 1460b

XXV

Concerning the number and character of the problems that lead to censure in poetry and the ways in which this censure must be met, the following considerations would be apparent to those who study the question. Since the poet is an imitator, like a painter or any maker of likenesses, he must carry out his imitations on all occasions in one of three possible ways. Thus, he must imitate the things that were in the past, or are now, or that people say and think to be or those things that ought to be. The poet presents his imitation in standard diction, as well as in strange words and metaphors and in many variations of diction, for we grant this license to poets. In addition to this, there is not the same standard of correctness for politics and poetry, nor for any other art and poetry. In regard to poetry itself, two categories of error are possible, one essential, and one accidental. For if the poet chose to imitate but imitated incorrectly through lack of ability[34] the error is an essential one; but if he erred by choosing an incorrect representation of the object (for example, representing a horse putting forward both right hooves) or made a technical error, for example, in regard to medicine or any other art, or introduced impossi-

[34] There is a lacuna in the text here that I have filled by translating Bywater's suggested reading, *hēmarte de di'*.

bilities of any sort, the mistake is an accidental, not an essential, one.

As a result, we must meet the criticisms of the problems encountered in poetry by taking these points into consideration. First, in regard to the problems that are related to the essential nature of art: if impossibilities have been represented, an error has been made; but it may be permissible to do this if the representation supports the goal of the imitation (for the goal of an imitation has been discussed) and if it makes the section in which it occurs, or another part of the poem, more striking. An example of such a situation is the pursuit of Hector in the *Iliad*. If, indeed, the goal of the imitation admits of attainment as well, or better, when sought in accordance with technical requirements, then it is incorrect to introduce the impossible. For, if it is at all feasible, no error should be committed at all. Further, we must ascertain whether an error originates from an essential or an accidental aspect of the art. For it is a less important matter if the artist does not know that a hind does not have horns than if he is unskillful in imitating one. In addition, the criticism that a work of art is not a truthful representation can be met by the argument that it represents the situation as it should be. For example, Sophocles said that he himself created characters such as should exist, whereas Euripides created ones such as actually do exist. If neither of the above is the case, the criticism must be met by reference to men's opinions, for example, in the myths that are told about the gods. For, perhaps, they do not describe a situation that is better than actuality, nor a true one, but they are what Xenophanes said of them—in accordance, at any rate, 1461a
with men's opinions. Perhaps the situation described by the artist is not better than actuality but was one that actually existed in the past, for example, the description of the arms that goes, "The spears were standing upright on their butt spikes"; for once this was customary, as it is now among the Illyrians. Now to judge the nobility or ignobility of any statement made or act performed by anyone, we must not only make an investigation into the thing itself that has been said or done, considering whether it is noble or ignoble, but we must also con-

sider the one who does the act or says the words in regard to whom, when, by what means, and for what purpose he speaks or acts—for example, whether the object is to achieve a greater good or to avoid a greater evil.

We must meet some kinds of criticism by considering the diction, for example, by reference to the use of a strange word, as in the phrase, *ourēas men prōton*.[35] The word oureas here could cause some difficulty because perhaps the poet does not mean mules but guards. Dolon's statement, "I who was badly formed," [36] has a similar difficulty involved in it; for he does not mean that he was misshapen in body but that he was ugly, because the Cretans use *eueidēs* [of fair form] to denote "handsome." A difficulty might arise in the phrase "mix the drink purer," [37] which does not mean stronger, as if for drunkards, but faster. Difficulties arise in thoughts that are expressed in metaphors, for example, "All the gods and men slept the entire night through," which is said at the same time as "When truly he turned his gaze upon the Trojan plain, and heard the sound of flutes and pipes." "All" is used here metaphorically in place of "many," since "all" is some division of "many." The phrase "alone, she has no share" [38] shows a similar use of metaphor, since the best known one is "alone." A problem may arise from the use of accent; Hippias the Thasian solved such a problem in the phrase, *didomen de oi* and similarly, in the phrase, *to men hoi katapythetai ombrō*.[39] Some difficulties are solved through punctuation, for example, in Empedocles' statement that "Suddenly things became mortal that had previously learned to be immortal and things unmixed be-

[35] Quoted from *Iliad,* I, 50. The phrase means "first of all, the mules."
[36] Quoted from *Iliad,* X, 316.
[37] Quoted from *Iliad,* IX, 202.
[38] Quoted from *Iliad,* XVIII, 489.
[39] The problem here is that words that are spelled the same way, when given different accents, change their meaning. In the first phrase quoted, *didomen* can be either a present indicative or an infinitive used as an imperative, depending on the way in which it is accented; in the second phrase, *ou* can be either a relative pronoun or a negative adverb, depending on the way in which it is accented.

fore mixed."[40] Some problems are solved by reference to ambiguities, for example, "more than two thirds of night has departed" because "more" is ambiguous here.[41] Some difficulties are met by reference to customary usages in our language. Thus, we call "wine" the mixture of water and wine; and it is with the same justification that the poet writes of "a greave of newly wrought tin"; and iron workers are called *chalkeas,* literally, copper smiths; and it is for this reason that Ganymede is called the wine pourer of Zeus, although the gods do not drink wine. This would also be justified through metaphor.

Whenever a word seems to signify something contradictory, we must consider how many different meanings it might have in the passage quoted; for example, in the phrase "the bronze spear was held there," we must consider how many different senses of "to be held" are possible, whether by taking it in this way or that one might best understand it. The procedure is opposite to the one that Glaucon mentions in which people make an unreasonable prior assumption and, having them- 1461b
selves made their decree, they draw their conclusions, and then criticize the poet as if he had said whatever they think he has said if it is opposed to their thoughts. We have had this experience in regard to discussions of the character Icarius.[42] People assume that he was a Spartan; but then it appears ridiculous that Telemachus did not meet him in Sparta when he visited there. Perhaps the situation is as the Cephallenians would have it, for they say that Odysseus married amongst them and that there was an Icadius involved, but no Icarius. Thus, it is probable that the difficulty has arisen through a mistake.

Speaking generally, the impossible must be justified in regard to the requirements of poetry, or in regard to what is

[40] The problem treated here is the effect that punctuation has on the meaning of a sentence. Thus, by means of different punctuations the word "before" in Empedocles' statement could be referred either to the phrase that precedes it, "things unmixed," or to the word that follows it, "mixed."

[41] The word "more" has a form in Greek that can also be translated as "full."

[42] In Homer, Icarius is Penelope's father.

better than actuality, or what, in the opinion of men, is held to be true. In regard to the art of poetry, we must prefer a persuasive impossibility to an unpersuasive possibility. Perhaps it is impossible[43] for the kind of men Zeuxis painted to exist; but they illustrate what is better than the actual. For whatever is a model must express superior qualities. The irrational must be justified in regard to what men say and also on the grounds that it is, sometimes, not at all irrational. For it is reasonable that some things occur contrary to reason.

We must consider contradictions in the same way as the refutation of arguments is carried on: that is, with reference to whether the same object is involved, and in the same relationship, and in the same sense, so that the poet, indeed, has contradicted himself in regard to what he himself says or what a sensible person might assume. There is justifiable censure for the presence of irrationality and depravity where, there being no necessity for them, the poet makes no use of them, as Euripides' handling of Aegeus in the *Medea* (in regard to the irrational) or in the same poet's treatment of the character of Menelaus in the *Orestes* (in regard to depravity). Criticisms of poetry, then, derive from five sources: either that the action is impossible or that it is irrational or that it is morally harmful or that it is contradictory or that it contains technical errors. The answers to these criticisms must be sought from the solutions, twelve in number, that we have discussed.

XXVI

The problem of whether epic or tragedy is the better type of imitation might be raised. For if whatever is less common

[43] Translating *kai ei adunaton,* suggested by Vahlen to fill a lacuna in the text at this point.

is better, that art would be superior that is directed at the more discriminating audience; and it is very clear that the art that imitates every detail is common. For on the grounds that the audience does not see the point unless they themselves add something, the actors make quite a commotion; for example, the poorer sort of flute players roll about the stage if they must imitate a discus throw and drag their leader about if they are playing the *Scylla*. Now tragedy is considered to be of the same character that our older actors attribute to their successors; for, indeed, Mynescus called Callippides an ape on the grounds of overacting, and such an opinion was also held about Pindarus. As these two types of actor are related to each other, so the 1462a
whole art of tragedy is thought to be related to epic by some people, who then conclude that epic is oriented toward a reasonable audience that does not at all require gestures, but that tragedy is disposed toward a less sophisticated audience. If, then, tragedy is directed toward a more common audience, it would be clear that it is the inferior art form.

Now then, first, this accusation is made against the art of acting, not poetry, since it is possible to overdo gestures both in epic recitations as Sosistratus did, and in song competitions as Mnasitheus the Opuntian did. Then, too, not every movement is to be rejected, if dancing indeed is not to be condemned, but only the movements of the ignoble, a point that was criticized in Callippides and now in others, since, it was charged, they were not representing free-born women. Further, tragedy even without action achieves its function just as epic does; for its character is apparent simply through reading. If, then, tragedy is better in other respects, this defect is not essential to it. We argue, next, that it *is* better since it contains all of the elements that epic has (for it is even possible to use epic meter in tragedy) and, further, it has no small share in music and in spectacle, through which pleasure is very distinctly evoked. Tragedy also provides a vivid experience in reading as well as in actual performance. Further, in tragedy the goal of the imitation is achieved in a shorter length of time (for a more compact action is more pleasant than one 1462b
that is much diluted). I mean, for example, the situation that

would occur if someone should put Sophocles' *Oedipus* into an epic as long as the *Iliad*. Further, the imitation of an epic story is less unified than that of tragedy (a proof of this is that a number of tragedies can be derived from any one epic). So that if epic poets write a story with a single plot, that plot is either presented briefly and appears to lack full development, or, if it follows the accustomed length of epic, it has a watered-down quality (I mean, for example, if the epic should be composed of very many actions in the same way as the *Iliad* and *Odyssey* have many such elements that also have magnitude in themselves). And yet these poems are constructed in the best possible way and are, as much as possible, the imitations of a single action.

If, then, tragedy is superior in all these areas and, further, in accomplishing its artistic effect (for it is necessary that these genres create not any chance pleasure, but the one that has been discussed as proper to them), it is apparent that tragedy, since it is better at attaining its end, is superior to epic.

Now then, we have expressed our view of tragedy and epic, both in general, and in their various species, and of the number and differences in their parts, as well as of some of the causes of their effectiveness or ineffectiveness, and the criticisms that can be directed against them, and the ways in which these criticisms must be answered. . . .[44]

[44] One of our manuscripts, Riccardianus 46, continues the text briefly at this point. The continuation seems to read, "Now as to iambic poetry and comedy. . . ."

A Commentary on

ARISTOTLE'S POETICS

by

O. B. Hardison, Jr.

Introduction: Bases of Interpretation

Aristotle's *Poetics* is generally regarded as the most important critical work of antiquity, perhaps the most important ever written. Its influence on critical thought and on drama has been enormous, and sooner or later every student of literature must come to terms with it. But this is not as simple as it seems. The *Poetics* is a complex, difficult document. In the first place, the Greek text, itself, is imperfect. Then there is the problem of translation. Readers who do not know Greek must depend on translations, but a translation is always a disguised commentary. Even the most conscientious and well-trained translator makes innumerable choices when rendering a passage of the Greek into English, and his choices depend heavily on assumptions he makes about the larger meaning of Aristotle's argument.

The reader of the *Poetics,* then, must be on guard against accepting uncritically a single text or a single translation. The present translation is based primarily on Bywater's text (1909) and its recent successor by Professor Rudolf Kassel of the University of Berlin, published in 1965; but other texts, particularly those of Gudeman and Rostagni, have been consulted. Unfortunately, no text can be called definitive, simply because many of the textual problems presented by the *Poetics* cannot be solved on the basis of present knowledge. The translation is as literal as possible, but the reader is urged to compare it with other translations in order to familiarize himself with the wide range of possibilities often inherent in the original Greek.

Interpretations of the *Poetics* are also affected by four non-textual problems. First, there is the problem of exactly what the Greek text represents. Should it be considered a set of lecture notes, or the rough draft of an essay intended ultimately for publication, or a finished work? Second, there is the problem of its relation to the works of Plato and to other works by Aristotle himself. Should it be interpreted as a reply to attacks on poetry made by Plato in the *Republic*? Should it be interpreted as continuous with Aristotle's other work, so that its terms and ideas can be explained by reference to more detailed comments in works like the *Rhetoric,* the *Politics,* and the *Nicomachean Ethics*? Or should it be interpreted as an independent, self-contained work whose key terms and ideas are best understood in context rather than by reference to other works? Third, there is the problem of Aristotle's method. Is the *Poetics* an empirical work, the result of Aristotle's observation of the practice of the Greek dramatists; or is it a deductive work in which the generalizations come first and the references to Greek literature are offered as illustrations of the points made? Last but not least, there is the problem of authenticity. Should everything in the *Poetics* be interpreted as Aristotle's own work, or is one justified in rejecting certain sections as interpolations by the scholars and scribes who copied Aristotle's manuscript in late antiquity? The positions taken in reference to these problems form what may be called the "bases of interpretation" of the *Poetics.*

(A) The Greek Text

There is no definitive Greek text of the *Poetics.* The most important twentieth-century editions are listed in the bibliography (pp. 297-99). They are the editions by Bywater (1909), Margoliouth (1911), Butcher (4th ed., 1923), Gudeman (1934), Rostagni (2nd ed., 1945), Montmollin (1951), Else (1957), and Kassel (1965).

The basic facts of the text are simple. It was written by Aristotle (or, perhaps, taken down by a student from his lectures) between 347 and 322 B.C., the year of his death. Assuming that the *Poetics* stems from Aristotle's manuscript, the work may be unrevised, or it may incorporate revisions and fresh material added by Aristotle at some time after the work was first written. Most authorities agree that the *Poetics* originally consisted of two books, the second devoted to iambic poetry, comedy, and (possibly) catharsis. After Aristotle's death the manuscript of the *Poetics* was altered in several ways. If Book II ever existed, it was lost. More important, corruptions were introduced into the part of the text that survived. Case endings were changed, words and phrases were confused or lost entirely, and explanatory notes (*scholia*), which had originally been separate from the text, were inserted in it so that they became indistinguishable from what Aristotle, himself, wrote.

Three manuscripts form the basis of all later editions of the *Poetics.* It is the differences among these manuscripts that permit scholars to make educated guesses about the history of the text. The earliest and most authoritative manuscript (Paris 1741) is from the eleventh century and is now at the *Bibliothèque Nationale* in Paris. One later manuscript, Riccardianus 46, has independent readings. Finally, there is an Arabic translation of the *Poetics* made in the tenth century, which goes back through a Syriac intermediary to a Greek manuscript of before the seventh century. As might be expected, the Arabic text is extremely unreliable. During the nineteenth and early twentieth century the important editions of the *Poetics* were based almost exclusively on Paris 1741. Contemporary editors have, however, tended to make greater use of Riccardianus 46, and several—most notably Margoliouth, Tkatsch and Gudeman—have placed considerable emphasis on the Arabic version.[1]

The textual question is complicated by conclusions forced on scholars in their efforts to interpret difficult passages. Montmollin has argued that the *Poetics* shows signs of revision and interpolation by Aristotle himself. He has attempted to distinguish between the "primitive" (original) version and the later text and has asserted that if we wish to understand the *Poetics* as a consistent, smoothly developing argument, we must base our analysis on the primitive version. Else has accepted Montmollin's theory (although by no means all his specific conclusions). In addition, Else has rejected a great many words, phrases, and even whole passages on the grounds that they are scribal interpolations and not by Aristotle. The arguments of Montmollin and Else are often very forceful; but, as reviewers of both pointed out, their approach has grave dangers. Evidence of later additions and interpolations is always indirect. An editor with a pet theory about what Aristotle said is sorely tempted to excise whatever does not agree with his theory.

[1] For more detailed discussion, see Lobel and Tkatsch in the Bibliography, p. 298.

The facts and conjectures concerning the history of Aristotle's text are presented in simplified form in Diagram I. Brackets and

Diagram I

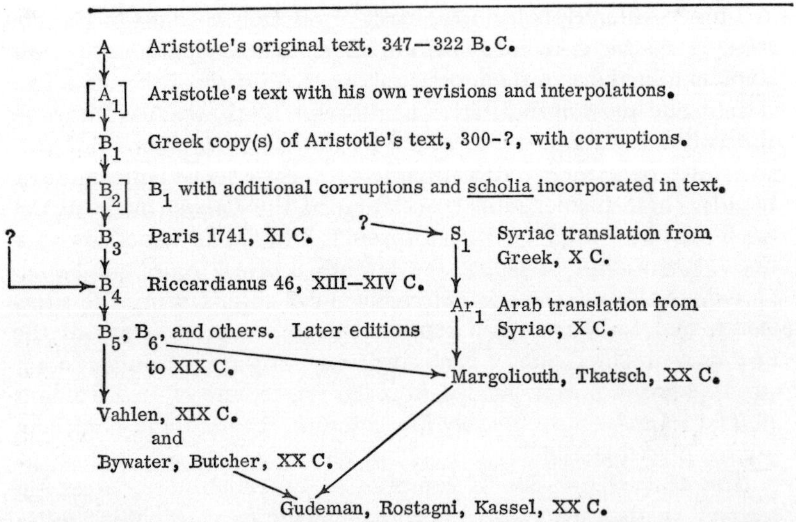

question marks indicate conjectural versions and relations. Note that the diagram is not a formal *stemma,* but a composite summary of the suggestions of several scholars.

(B) Bases of Interpretation

1. *The form of the text.* A long-standing tradition has it that the *Poetics* is a series of lecture notes made by Aristotle or (perhaps) taken down by a student. It is true that the Greek is laconic and often reads more like a rather full outline than a finished work. Gilbert Murray has made an experimental translation of Chapter I in the form of a lecture outline. His translation makes it clear why there are frequent puzzling gaps and abrupt movements from one topic to another. The text is not a formal essay, and what is omitted is often just what would be left out of a set of lecture notes—transitions, explanations, and illustrative material. On the other hand, in

order to make his translation conform fully to the "lecture note" form, Murray frequently must make his English even more compressed than the Greek.

A second theory as to the form of the text—the one adopted here—is that it is what scholars call an *esoteric* work by Aristotle. Aristotle evidently issued his works in two forms. Some works he developed sufficiently for publication. These are *exoteric,* since they were expected to circulate widely throughout Greece. Others he developed only far enough to be readily understood by pupils at the Lyceum (his "school"), who could be expected to be familiar with his system and terminology, and hence capable of following his ideas even in compressed form. Since these works were intended only for circulation among Aristotle's pupils and followers, they are called *esoteric.* The theory that the *Poetics* is an extremely curt esoteric work seems to fit the text better than the lecture note theory. Among other things, it explains why the *Poetics* is occasionally brief to the point of being enigmatic, but at other times relatively detailed and well-developed.

The one theory that no scholar accepts is the theory that the *Poetics* is a finished essay. Unfortunately, almost all translations imply this theory. In their efforts to make graceful English out of the Greek, translators add connectives, silently expand crabbed passages, and suggest nonexistent logical relations by transition phrases, punctuation and paragraphing. The plain fact is that a literal translation of the Greek is an impossible ideal; and the tendency of translators is to go to the opposite extreme by making the *Poetics* seem as much as possible like standard English prose. Yet this positively invites careless interpretation or misinterpretation. Since no simple solution to the problem is possible, the reader must compare translations frequently. The present translation attempts to be as literal as possible without being stilted, but no claim is made that it has avoided all the difficulties that have affected other translations. Among other translations that are useful for comparison are those by Butcher, Bywater, Else, Gilbert, and Telford, all listed in the Bibliography (pp. 297-99).

2. *Literary relations of the* Poetics. Since the Renaissance, it has been commonly assumed that the *Poetics* is best understood

as an answer to the charges made against poetry by Plato in the *Ion,* and in Books II, III, and X of the *Republic.* To interpret the *Poetics* as a refutation of another man's argument is quite different from interpreting it as an independent work that reaches conclusions often opposed to Plato. The importance of Plato to the *Poetics* is related to the question of when the *Poetics* was written. Aristotle was Plato's student for twenty years, until Plato's death in 347 B.C. The earlier the date of the *Poetics,* the more likely Platonic influence becomes. Conversely, a later date—say, after 330 B.C., when Aristotle had developed his own system of philosophy and was lecturing at the Lyceum—would suggest that the *Poetics* is best interpreted in relation to Aristotle's mature works rather than in relation to Plato. The works closest to the *Poetics* in subject matter are the *Rhetoric,* the *Nicomachean Ethics* and the *Politics.* In general, twentieth-century commentaries have given Plato credit for formulating some of the basic topics and problems dealt with in the *Poetics,* especially imitation and catharsis, but have dated the *Poetics* in the Lyceum period. The later date seems most probable. The *Poetics* is a positive analysis, not refutation, or "defense of poetry," and, in fact, Plato is never mentioned by name. The assumption that the *Poetics* is contemporary with or later than the *Politics* and *Ethics* also justifies use of these works to explicate its difficult passages.

A strikingly original approach to the literary relations of the *Poetics* has been taken by Richard McKeon. McKeon believes that the *Poetics* is a product of Aristotle's mature system. Furthermore, he argues that a basic characteristic of this system is that it divides human knowledge into several distinct compartments ("sciences"), each with its own special terminology and method. This means that the same Greek word may have quite different meanings in two different treatises. To understand the meaning of a technical term in Aristotle, one must determine its relation to the other terms within the specific "science" to which it is applied. Most important, to cite the definition of a word used in one "science" to explain the same word used in another "science" is to risk confusion rather than to clarify. Thus, according to McKeon, it is misleading to use Aristotle's discussion of catharsis in the *Politics* to "explain" the term as it occurs in the *Poetics.*

McKeon's position is useful in that it reminds us that Aristotle was a highly methodical thinker and that any adequate interpretation of his work must take his method into account. It is also extremely valuable as a reminder that many questions of interpretation of the *Poetics* are best answered by reference to the *Poetics* itself. On the other hand, it can be harmful if applied without tact. Aristotle's *Ethics,* for example, is clearly relevant to his discussion of character in the *Poetics.* The proper rule for interpretation would seem to be a commonsense one that uses the *Poetics* as far as possible but draws on other works, first, when Aristotle himself refers to them, as he does to the *Rhetoric,* and second, when there is a close and obvious correlation between them and the *Poetics.*

3. *Aristotle's method.* McKeon's theory concerning Aristotle's division of the sciences has already been mentioned. Briefly, McKeon believes that Aristotle divided his treatises into works on logic (the treatises comprising the *Organon*), works on "theoretical science" (for example, mathematics, metaphysics, astronomy, physics), works on "practical science" (basically, politics and ethics), and works on "productive science"—the sciences of "making" or "producing" things. The productive category is further subdivided into the "useful arts" (practical arts and crafts) and "fine arts," which operate by imitation. Needless to say, McKeon believes that poetics belongs in the "fine arts" category; its basic method is imitation and its products are poems. Many Aristotelian scholars disagree with this analysis, but no very satisfactory alternative has been offered.[2]

A different but equally important question concerns the logical method evident in the development of the *Poetics.* The older position, still evident in the twentieth-century work of Lane Cooper, for example, is that Aristotle based his treatise on a close empirical study of Greek poetry, especially drama, and most especially Sophocles' *Oedipus Rex.* This point of view justifies interpreting the *Poetics* by reference to the Greek theatre and the plays that Aristotle cites, as, for example, when *hamartia* is explained in terms of an empirical study by the commentator of the "flaws" exhibited by the protagonists of *Agamemnon, Oedipus, Hippolytus,* and *Medea.* It also occasionally has created the impression that the

[2] Bywater seems to consider the *Poetics* a subcategory of the practical sciences. See *On the Art of Poetry* (Oxford University Press, 1909), note on 1460^b 14.

Poetics is a useful handbook for interpreting Greek and Roman drama, but of limited use in reference to post-medieval drama.

The tendency of all recent commentaries has been to reject the empirical reading of the *Poetics.* For reasons that will appear in the discussion of Chapter I, the empirical reading is inadequate. Aristotle's generalizations are derived from the nature of the subject, not from a study of particular works. Typically, only after the generalizations does he cite specific works; and when they are cited they are almost always used as examples that confirm the theory. This does not mean that one can get along in the *Poetics* without a knowledge of Greek drama and dramatic conventions. It *does* mean that interpreting the *Poetics* is primarily a matter of close reading and careful analysis of the text itself. It also means that we can expect the *Poetics* to yield insights into literary problems of general significance instead of being restricted to Greek and Roman literature.

4. *The problem of authenticity.* This problem has already been touched on in connection with the text of the *Poetics.* Although Montmollin and Else have made a strong case for the notion that there are both "late additions" and scribal interpolations in the surviving manuscripts of the *Poetics,* there is almost no general agreement concerning which passages are late or spurious. For this reason the present commentary takes a conservative approach, accepting the whole text as authentic but pointing out important passages that have been questioned or rejected.

Chapter I

Chapter I of the *Poetics* is divided into three fairly distinct parts: (a) an introduction stating the subject, representative topics to be treated, and method (ll. 1-7); (b) a discussion of imitation and its elements (ll. 8-29, 49-55); and (c) a discussion of the chief false criterion of poetry, known in antiquity as the *ars metrica* (ll. 30-48). In part *b*, Aristotle asserts that there is a category of human activity based on imitation and that literature is a subcategory of it. "Literature" is a better term than "poetry" here, because Aristotle's discussion includes works in prose as well as works in verse. Note also that literature is a subcategory of imitative art and not equivalent to it, because imitative art includes painting, dance, and music as well as literature. Major emphasis in part *b* falls on "means" of imitation. Part *c* then discusses the metrical definition of poetry in order to expose its inadequacies. The last sentences of Chapter I (ll. 49-55) return to the subject of part *b* and should be recognized as a continuation of it.

So far so good. Difficulties arise, however, when we move from the content of the sections to the logical relations between them.

Introduction: The Placing of Poetic Art

The *Poetics* begins with the phrase, *Peri poietikes autes.* The first two words of this phrase can be (and have been) translated in all the following ways (with innumerable variations):

1. Concerning poetry (Bywater's translation is a variation of this)
2. Concerning the poetic art (Else; Golden)
3. Concerning making (Gilbert Murray)
4. Concerning the art of making (or "productive science") (Kenneth Telford) [1]

Each translation is possible; which is right? The answer hinges on the relation between the term *poietike* in section *a* and the term *imitation* (*mimesis*) in section *b*. Is *poietike* a broad term that includes *imitation* as one of its species; is it a synonym for *imitation;* or is it a term designating that group of the imitative arts that use language and, hence, a subcategory of imitation? Since no one has ever suggested equating *poietike* and *mimesis,* only the first and third positions need be considered.

[1] See Bibliography, pp. 297-98.

Translations beginning with "concerning poetry" or "concerning the poetic art" take the third position: *Poietike* refers to the literary subdivision of imitation. This is justified by the fact that *poietike* clearly means "poetry" (or "literature") in later sections of the *Poetics.* On the other hand, the Greek word has more than one meaning. To translate it here as "poetry" or "poetic art" would reverse Aristotle's normal practice in his introductions of moving from general to specific. Far more weight is given to this objection if we recall the scattered indications in Aristotle, principally in the *Metaphysics* and *Nicomachean Ethics,*[2] of a systematic division of human activities into three major compartments labeled "theoretic," "practical," and "productive." The Greek term for "productive science" is *poietike,* a usage based on the verb *poiein* meaning "to make." This meaning is enshrined in the many Elizabethan references to the poet as a *maker*. Aristotle's productive category includes "making" of all kinds, from the making of chairs to the making of poems and paintings. It is thus quite possible that in the introduction to the *Poetics* Aristotle means to "place" his discussion of literature within the productive category. Placing poetry within the productive category (the function of section *a*) distinguishes it from the theoretical and practical sciences. Placing it next within the imitative category (the function of section *b*) distinguishes it from the utilitarian branch of the productive arts that we would today call the "applied arts." "Concerning making" is therefore both a meaningful translation of *Peri poietikes* and one that provides a typically Aristotelian sequence of thought from "making" (most general) to "imitation" (less general) to "literature" (most specific). In the absence of equally strong arguments in favor of "concerning poetry," it is the better translation and will be provisionally adopted in the commentary, although the translation retains the more conservative reading.

The analysis of Aristotle's initial phrase needs one further extension. *Poietike,* as distinguished from *poiein* and *poiesis,* refers to the art or *techne* of doing something, not to the act or product.

[2] *Metaphysics,* 1025^b; *Ethics,* 1138-39; esp. 1140^a 1-28; *Topics,* 145^a 15; cf. Ross, *Aristotle* (London, Methuen & Co., Ltd., 1964), pp. 30, 216-18; and Elder Olson, "The Poetic Method of Aristotle," in *Aristotle's Poetics and English Literature* (Chicago: University of Chicago Press, 1965), pp. 175-81.

The force of the Greek is preserved in the English word *poetic* used as a noun to refer to rules or theories of poetry, as in the sentence, "Coleridge's *poetic* is superior to his poetry." To preserve this sense, Aristotle's *poietike* should be translated "the art of making" rather than "making." The *Poetics* is not an "appreciation" of a collection of poems, but a methodical philosophical investigation into the nature of literary art. The work differs from other classical and renaissance arts of poetry in that its principles are derived analytically, from the nature of the subject itself, rather than being presented as a miscellany of prescriptive rules for writing poems; the path followed, for example, in Horace's *Ars Poetica*.

Two corollaries follow from these observations. First, Aristotle's placement of poetry has some kinship with the aesthetic theory of poetry popularized in the nineteenth century by Coleridge and Croce, among others. Like aesthetic criticism, it draws a sharp line between art on the one hand, and utilitarian and moral activities on the other. It is, as Butcher insisted, a theory of "fine art." It cannot, however, be equated with modern aesthetic criticism. Coleridge and Croce have in common the fact that they begin with a theory of imagination—in some sense a psychology of art. Because of this they manifest a tendency toward absolute organicism in which genre distinctions and distinctions between the component parts of a successful work are irrelevant or even harmful. Aesthetic criticism tends to recognize only one category, beauty, and one criterion, variously labeled unity, coherence, fusion, tension, or some similar term. As will become clear during consideration of section *b* of Chapter I, Aristotle begins from the analysis of the materials of art rather than the mind of the poet or beholder. For this reason, his presentation abounds in precisely those distinctions between genres and between parts that aesthetic criticism rejects. In fact, in at least one instance, Aristotle's method leads him to define a category for which his contemporaries did not even have a name.

The second corollary is that whether by accident or design, Aristotle's theory is an emphatic answer to Plato's attack on poetry. In the *Ion* and again in the tenth book of the *Republic*, the basic objection to poetry is that it is a secondary kind of imitation. For every artificial object—a bed, for example, says Socrates—there is an absolute idea, which is the true form and essence of the object.

Next there is the material imitation of the object by a human craftsman. This imitation is only an approximation of the idea, and is therefore less real than the idea itself. Finally, the artist imitates the already imperfect copy. The artist's imitation is at a third remove from truth. If a skilled carpenter, for example, can only make an imperfect imitation of the ideal bed, the painter or poet, who has no training in carpentry, will produce an imitation more imperfect still. Since man's first duty is to seek truth, the artist's copy will necessarily be less valuable than the craftsman's. In some cases, it can actually be pernicious. The philosopher, for example, characterizes the gods as benign, whereas Homer teaches that they are jealous, vindictive, capricious, and oversexed. He thereby injures and corrupts impressionable readers.

If all human activities are placed on a simple linear scale ranging from absolute truth to falsehood, Socrates is right. If, however, there are different categories of human activity, each with its separate and distinct methodology, he is wrong. Socrates points out in the *Ion* that Homer has descriptions of battles, chariot races, and political systems, adding that the true seeker after knowledge would in each case do better to consult the experts rather than Homer—namely, the general, the chariot driver, and the politician. In reply, Ion protests that the artist is not to be judged on the basis of his knowledge of particulars, but on the basis of his combination of these particulars into an aesthetically pleasing art work; but Ion is never allowed to state his case fully. What Ion half-heartedly suggests is what Aristotle appears to be asserting in the introductory sections of the *Poetics*: there is a difference, and a fundamental one, between the applied and the imitative kinds of making. Socrates would have us judge a painting of a bed with the same criteria that we use to judge a bed made by a carpenter. Aristotle, conversely, would have us judge the carpenter's bed by one set of rules, a functional set, and the picture of the bed by an entirely different set, based on the painter's skill in combining forms and colors. Plato's position is echoed in the complaint we sometimes hear that works like Spenser's *Faerie Queene* or Picasso's *Guernica* are not "realistic"; Aristotle's position is found in the reply that the world of art is different from the world of material reality.

Introduction: The Method of the *Poetics*
(ll. 1-7)

We will, then, interpret the first two words of the *Poetics* as a placing of that work within the general scheme of the sciences. The third word, *autes,* is an intensive, having the force of "itself" or "in itself." That is, Aristotle will discuss *poietike* in itself, without a preliminary discussion of the reasons for the placement used. Chapters I-III constitute this discussion. They treat the basic principles of imitative art and the way that they operate and interact to create the major literary genres.

Following *Peri poietikes autes,* Aristotle gives a list of representative topics to be covered: the poetic species, the construction of plots, the parts of a poem, and "other matters." The list is obviously not inclusive. It gives the reader a rough outline of what to expect, but it is not intended as a complete index. Plot, it may be observed, is the only one of the constituent parts of a poem to be mentioned by name. This is the first hint of Aristotle's well-known preoccupation with plot, which he later calls the "soul" of the literary work. The closing phrase is simply a catch-all to take care of whatever has not been specified earlier—"as many other matters as are relevant."

The first sentence performs the function of an introduction, stating subject and representative divisions. The second sentence is also recognizably part of a formal introduction. In a modern rhetoric textbook, it would be called Aristotle's statement of method. Literally translated, it reads, "Let us proceed according to nature with firsts." The phrase "according to nature" (*kata phusin*) is central. It loses its force when translated "naturally." Aristotle does not mean "Let us proceed in the easiest [or most obvious] way," but something closer to "Let us proceed according to the way [or "order"] of Nature herself." In the *Physics,* and again in the *Generation of Animals,*[3] the "order of nature" is to begin with certain fundamental principles operative on matter. These act and interact, causing increasing ramification and specification, until they have produced the myriad particularities of the natural world.

The order of nature is also the order of the philosophical critic.

[3] *Physics,* I-II; *Gen. An.,* 736^{a-b}, 778^{a-b}.

The philosophical critic does not begin like the craftsman with customs inherited from tradition, or habits learned by trial and error. Rather, he begins with those first principles or causes that are the starting point of Nature herself. His treatise is a kind of map of the process whereby the first principles have produced the various types and species considered. If the inductive method is to begin with particulars and to move backward to ever larger generalizations, Aristotle's method must be labeled deductive. And if induction is the method that untutored man "naturally" takes to arrive at truth, the method "according to the order of nature" is the opposite of "natural." By corollary, the word "firsts" (*proton*) in Aristotle's sentence should not be translated in the rather inane sense of "Let us begin at the beginning"; nor should it be rendered by the phrase "primary facts," which inevitably suggests the inductive approach. "Let us follow the order of nature, beginning with first principles" is the proper translation. There are three first principles. They are the means, object, and manner of imitation explained in Chapters I-III, and they combine to produce the famous definition of tragedy at the beginning of Chapter VI.

The validity of this interpretation of Aristotle's second sentence can be demonstrated by reference to the structure of the *Poetics* as a whole. Before moving to structure, however, we need to consider sections *b* and *c* of Chapter I in detail.

Imitation: Means of Imitation
(ll. 8-29, 49-55)

"Imitation" is the key word in section *b*. It is introduced in two sentences whose function can easily be misunderstood. Today we are used to definition by term, genus, and differentia, as in the sentence, "Man [term] is an animal [genus] that thinks [differentia]." So standard is this form of definition that we tend to forget that there are other perfectly satisfactory methods of definition, as, for example, definition by synonym, by contrast, and by enumeration of parts. The opening sentences of section *b* are, in fact, a definition of imitation by enumeration of parts. Instead of giving its genus and differentia, Aristotle enumerates the parts (or species) that it includes, and then in the next sentence, he adds that the parts differ among themselves by means, object, and manner of imitation. Epic, comedy, tragedy, and dithyramb are parts of imitation; and to remind us that there are nonliterary parts as well, Aristotle adds flute-playing, lyre-playing, and painting.

After the definition, Aristotle concentrates on means of imitation. As used here, "means" refers to the elements from which the work is created. In the applied arts, the means are material, but this is not true of the fine arts. The carpenter makes his chair out of wood, and this material influences the design of the finished product. The poet, on the other hand, describes the chair in artistic language; and the characteristics of language rather than the characteristics of wood must influence his description. Here, incidentally, we are again reminded of the difference between Aristotle's aestheticism, beginning as it does with the means of artistic creation, and modern aestheticism, beginning with a theory of imagination. Aristotle, we might say, begins with the material cause of art; modern theory, with the efficient.

The means of imitation listed in sentence four are form, color, and sound. Sound is further analyzed into rhythm, harmony, and speech, used separately or in combinations. Painters imitate with form and color. (One can hazard the guess that if Aristotle had mentioned sculptors, he would have said they imitate with form. Although Greek statuary was frequently painted, form is essential to sculpture, whereas color is accidental.) That Aristotle does not consider paints or plaster walls as the "means" of the painter emphasizes the gap separating the applied and fine arts: paints are material substances; form and color are qualities.

The parenthesis in sentence four is also important. Artists are divided into two groups, one working by "art"—that is, *techne*—and the other working by "habit." This echoes the distinction, already touched on in connection with section *a,* between the philosophical and the pragmatic approaches to artistic creation. The painter or poet who imitates "by art" is what we would call the "conscious artist," who knows his craft in terms of its inner principles. The artist who works from custom or habit is an artisan working by rules of thumb acquired from his teachers or his own experience. He does not know why he uses such-and-such a technique; he only knows that it "works." The difference is roughly that between an architect and a contractor. Introduced parenthetically in Chapter I, this distinction will become central in

Chapter IV, where Aristotle describes the slow emergence of tragedy and comedy from the trials and errors of artisan poets from pre-Homeric times through the Age of Pericles.

The arts depending on sound are far more important than those using color and form. They employ "rhythm and speech and harmony . . . separately or in combination" (ll. 19-20). The term "rhythm" should evidently be understood as the repetition of stress at regular intervals, as in a drum beat. Since *ruthmos* also means "measured motion" in Greek and is explicitly associated with dance by Aristotle (l. 24), the term may imply "bodily movement" as well as repeated stress. If so, there is a difference between using rhythm and using poetic meter. This would explain why later in Chapter I Aristotle appears to say that certain types of metrical poetry lack rhythm. Rhythm by itself is the basis of the art of dance (ll. 24-26).

The next element of imitation using sound is harmony (*harmonia*). Unlike rhythm, harmony—a relation between tones—cannot exist by itself. It must be combined with rhythm, and the combination produces melody (*melos*). Therefore, the second category of imitative arts is that using "rhythm plus harmony," as exemplified in flute and lyre music.

Speech (*logos*) is the highest element of imitative arts using sound. All literary art falls within this category. The initial differentiation among the various literary arts depends on whether they use "words alone" (l. 27) or words plus the other elements of sound. The first category is called by Aristotle "the nameless art," because he knows of no Greek word that fits it. Today, we would probably call it fiction. It is further subdivided (l. 27) into works in prose and works in verse (that is, meter). Mention of works in verse is puzzling, because Aristotle's phrase "words alone" appears to mean "words without rhythm or harmony." The puzzle can be solved in two ways. Most commentators assume that the phrase "words alone" is ambiguous and really means "words plus rhythm." The trouble with this assumption is that the nameless art includes prose as well as metrical poetry. If the formula for the nameless art is "words plus rhythm," then prose must employ rhythm. In fact, Gerald Else suggests that Aristotle considered even Plato's dialogues rhythmic prose. This, one feels, is a rather desperate expedient. The alternative is to accept the suggestion that rhythm, as used in Chapter I, implies bodily movement as well as repeated stress. Since narrative poetry consisting of "words in verse," unlike drama and dithyramb, has no historical associations with dance, this latter alternative seems most acceptable.[4]

After dividing the nameless art into the categories of prose and verse, Aristotle further subdivides the verse category into works using one meter throughout and works using a variety of meters. Only after this long chain of distinctions, arrived at solely on the basis of deductive analysis, does he cite specific works and authors. In the course of discussing them, he moves to section *c* of Chapter I, which both extends the list of examples and also attacks the use of meter as the basic criterion for distinguishing between poetry and nonpoetry. Not until the closing paragraph of Chapter I does Aristotle further extend his own scheme of differentiation. There he considers forms using all three elements of imitation. Dithyramb and nome use all three simultaneously, whereas tragedy and comedy use them separately; that is, the episodes of a Greek drama use speech alone, whereas the choral parts require singing and ballet-like movements by the chorus.

The complex but methodical scheme developed in section *b* in the *Poetics* is represented visually by Diagram II (p. 72). Because the interpretation of *poietike* as a reference to the productive category is conjectural, the first level of differentiation on the diagram is bracketed. The diagram makes it evident that two techniques are involved in Aristotle's method. First, the analysis moves "from left to right"; second, as we move to the right, the categories tend to become more complex. That is, the arts using sound begin with rhythm only, then harmony plus rhythm, then speech plain, and finally, rhythm plus harmony plus speech.

[4] This is not consistent, however, with the comment in Chapter IV, ll. 21-23: "Since imitation is given to us by nature, as are harmony and rhythm (for it is apparent that meters are parts of the rhythms). . . ." The passage may simply be a slight inconsistency. Or one may suspect the sort of interpolation that Else finds so frequently in other parts of the Greek text, since the passage in question is grammatically parenthetical and obviously serves as a gloss on the term *meter*. If the passage is genuine, Aristotle may be thinking ahead to his observation (Chapter IV, ll. 69-71) that the trochaic meter was originally a dance meter: "For the poets first used the trochaic tetrameter because their poetry was satyric and very closely associated with dance." If so, the passage simply asserts that meters share ("are parts of") certain forms derived from dance music ("the rhythms"). See below, pp. 95-6.

Diagram II[5]

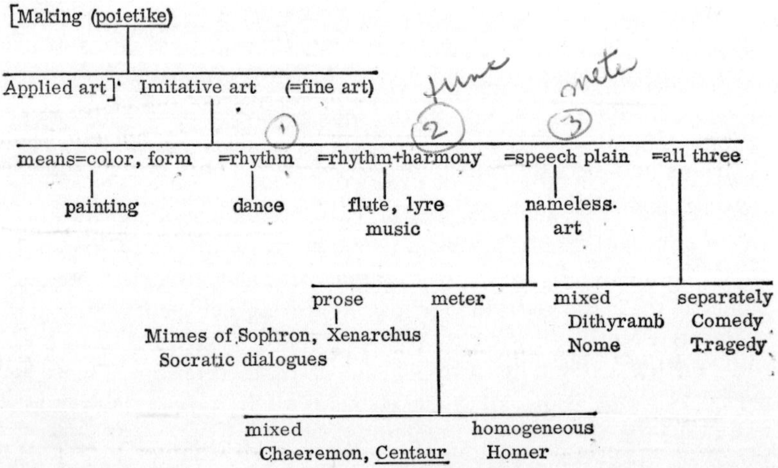

Another point that should not be overlooked is the inclusion of the "Socratic dialogues" in the "nameless art" category. Almost all commentaries agree that "Socratic dialogues" means the dialogues of Plato, particularly the early, highly dramatic ones in which Socrates is individualized instead of appearing as a transparent mask for Plato himself, as in the later dialogues. Aristotle classified the dialogues as a form of poetic art because they use imitation; but the reference is surely also an ironic gesture toward the philosopher who had banished poets from his ideal republic. To be consistent, Aristotle seems to be suggesting, Plato should have banished himself!

Finally, there is a definite limit to the degree of differentiation possible on the basis of means of imitation. The mimes of Sophron are brief satirical sketches. They are lumped together with the lengthy and very serious dialogues of Plato. Still more obvious, no differentiation is made between tragedy and comedy. A further criterion is needed in these cases, but it is not supplied until the consideration of "object of imitation" in Chapter II.

[5] For a somewhat different analysis, assuming Aristotle's use of a bipartite (diacritic) method of procedure, see Gerald Else, *Aristotle's Poetics,* p. 67.

The *Ars Metrica* (ll. 30-48)

What has been called section *c* of Chapter I appears to be a digression. It extends from sentence eight through sentence thirteen. While discussing the nameless art, Aristotle observes (l. 34) that people commonly use the name of the meter for the genre of the poem. He is thinking of a critical system taught by ancient grammarians and usually called the *ars metrica*. This system involves two assumptions: first, that the difference between poetry and nonpoetry is whether or not the composition is in verse. And second, that there is an essential relation between the kind of meter used and the nature of the poetry resulting. On this assumption, for example, any work written in dactylic hexameter (the meter of the *Iliad*) is automatically "heroic"; and any poem using the elegiac distich is automatically either sad or amorous.[6]

Aristotle disagrees strongly on both counts and attacks the *ars metrica* on several occasions in the *Poetics*. In Chapter I, he points out that a work is not necessarily poetry just because it is in verse. The defining quality of poetry is the use of imitation; the use or rejection of meter merely serves to differentiate kinds of imitation. Plato's dialogues are imitative. They use a means (language), imitate actions with agents, and employ the dramatic manner of Chapter III. Therefore, they are poetry, even though written in prose. Conversely, Empedocles wrote natural philosophy. Even though he versified it, it belongs in the theoretic rather than the poetic category. The fact that the adherents of the *ars metrica* claim the reverse, making Plato the philosopher and Empedocles the poet, shows the wrongness of their system and the pernicious confusion that results from using it. That the *ars metrica* encourages lumping Homer and Empedocles together merely because they used the same meter makes the point all the clearer.

Evidently, section *c* is more digressive in appearance than in fact.

[6] Compare Horace, *Ars Poetica*, ll. 73-98: "Homer has shown us in what meter may best be written the deeds of kings and great captains. Verses of unequal length were first used for laments, later also for the sentiment aroused by love granted. . . . The Muse has given to the lyre the celebration of the gods . . . the victorious boxer . . . the loves of youth. . . . If I do not know and cannot observe the conventions and forms of poems, why am I called by the name of poet?"

It seems digressive on first reading because there is no clear transition to it from section *b*. On the other hand, the main subject of section *b* is differentiation according to means of imitation. The *ars metrica* also attempts a kind of differentiation according to means, but uses superficial differences rather than substantive ones derived from "first principles." It is empirical rather than deductive according to "the order of nature." Aristotle exposes its defects to prevent it from being confused with his own theory. Rhetorically speaking, section *b* is the demonstration of his theory; and section *c*, the refutation of an influential countertheory.

Coda to Chapter I: "The Order of Nature" and the Organization of the Poetics

Let us now return to the first two sentences of the *Poetics*. Reduced to its essentials, and with "making" used to translate *poietike*, the first sentence is as follows:

> Let us discuss the art of making itself, and its species,
> describing the character of each of them,
> and . . . plots, and . . . parts . . . ,
> and . . . other matters.

If the first sentence is taken as a rough outline of the *Poetics*, its relation to the chapters of the work is as follows:

Diagram III

	Sentence I	Section	Content
BOOK I	Making (poietike):	I.	Criteria of Making (Chs. 1-3)
	Species (eidos):	II.	Genres
			a. History of evolution of genres (Ch. 4)
			b. Comedy (Ch. 5); Tragedy (Ch. 6)
	Plot (muthos):	III.	Plot and parts (Chs. 7-10)
		IV.	Complex plot (Chs. 11-14)
	Other parts:	V.	Character (Ch. 15)
		VI.	Thought (Ch. 19)
		VII.	Diction (Chs. 20-22)
		VIII.	Epic (Chs. 23-24)
	Other matters:	IX.	Technical questions and Solutions (Chs. 25-26)
? BOOK II		? X.	a. Iambic
			b. Comedy
			c. Catharsis

Sentence two promises to follow "the order of nature, beginning with first principles." It suggests that there is a method embodied in the outline derived from sentence one. To bring out this method, we can represent the outline schematically:

Diagram IV

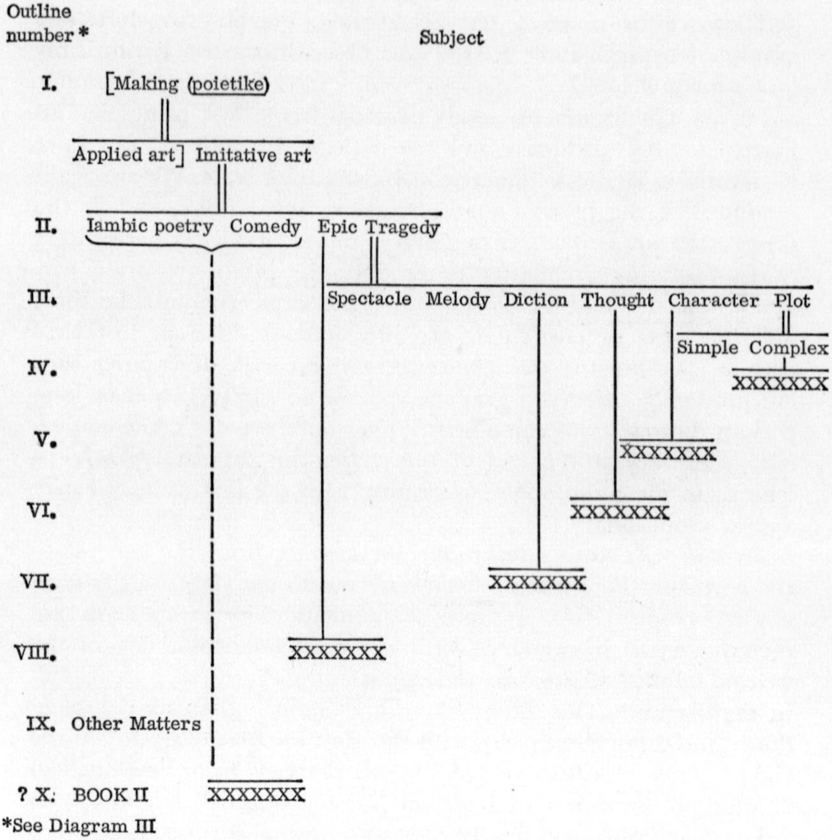

*See Diagram III

In Diagram IV, the Roman numerals on the left are the numbers of the sections of the *Poetics* as defined in Diagram III. A double vertical line indicates the dominant movement of Aristotle's thought, as, for example, in Chapter I he moves directly from making in general to imitation, and from imitation to parts or species of imitation. A short horizontal line with "X's" beneath indicates a terminal discussion—a discussion after which there is no significant new subdivision. Although the diagram is simplified and intentionally omits important passages in the *Poetics* (most obviously, Chapters XVI-XVIII),[7] it represents accurately the general movement of Aristotle's thought and serves better than a more detailed scheme to bring out his method. We may conclude our examination of Chapter I with four observations concerning Aristotle's method.

First. The argument clearly proceeds from "first principles" to particulars. It is deductive and schematic, and it follows "the order of nature" as Aristotle understood Nature to operate. We are again reminded of the pattern that emerges in the *Physics,* and in the *Generation of Animals* of a small number of highly generalized causes operating on matter to produce the infinitely varied particulars of the natural world. Since the causes operate in time, different sorts of particulars are produced at different historical periods. Because the particulars interact on each other after they are produced, there is a gradual increase in complexity over long periods. Lower forms come first; higher ones, later. To the empiricist, beginning at the end of the chain, the pattern looks teleological; to the philosopher, beginning with the first causes, it may appear evolutionary.

Second. Aristotle's technique for moving from the general to the particular is to move "downward and to the right." Each term is analyzed into two or more components. The components are then presented in sequence with the most important last in the written form of the treatise, the equivalent of "farthest to the right" in the diagram. This "most important" term is then itself broken down into component parts, with the most important again "on the right." Thus, the first line of analysis proceeds from "making" to "imitation" (section 1 of Diagram III) to "tragedy" (section 2) to "plot" (section 3), and finally ends with "complex plots, their characteristics, and virtues" (section 4).

Third. When the last item on the right—complex plots—has

[7] Gomperz, Bywater, Montmollin, and Solmsen, among others, argue that Chapters XVI-XVIII are late additions, or a kind of appendix to the discussion of plot.

been discussed—the method is reversed. We move "to the left" and, if necessary, up. The next item after complex plots is simple plots, but evidently Aristotle feels that enough has been said about these in connection with the discussion of plot itself. Aristotle therefore moves not only to the left, but upward to the next level of generalization. Here the movement "one to the left" of plot brings him to character, which is accordingly given a chapter of discussion (outline, section 5). The next movement to the left brings him to thought (section 6), and after that comes diction (section 7).

In general, the order of discussion follows the order of importance Aristotle assigned to these parts. Plot is most important and comes first; then character, then thought, then diction. Neither spectacle nor melody interested Aristotle greatly, and neither is accorded separate discussion. Therefore, the next movement to the left requires moving upward to the major genres and over from tragedy to epic. The movement is appropriate because epic is the ancestor of tragedy in the evolutionary line of development sketched out at the beginning of Chapter IV. Consideration of epic (section 8) completes the first unit of material in the *Poetics.* The next step to the left brings us to comedy; but according to Chapter IV, the evolutionary line of comedy is distinct from that of epic and tragedy. Book I of the *Poetics* is therefore rounded off with two chapters on general critical questions about tragedy and epic, particularly the question of which is the more excellent of the two forms (section 9).

The second of the two lines of development mentioned in Chapter IV is the line moving from iambic (that is, satiric) poetry to comedy. We would expect this line to be treated by Aristotle and would not be surprised if it were treated in a second book. Most commentators accept the tradition that a second book of the *Poetics* existed in antiquity, although some remain skeptical. If such a book existed, it dealt at least with comedy, probably with iambic poetry, and possibly with catharsis. Reinforcing the tradition of a second book dealing with comedy, one of the three primary manuscripts of the *Poetics,* Riccardianus 46, ends with an almost illegible phrase, usually rendered, "Now as to iambics and comedy. . . ." If we accept the evidence of this phrase, Aristotle evidently completed his plan by moving "to the left" of epic (the hypothetical section 10). If Book II included a discussion of catharsis—a possibility suggested by the comment on catharsis in the last book of the *Politics*—after considering comic and iambic poetry, Aristotle may have again moved "up and to the left," since catharsis is an aspect of the effect of imitative art in general. The evidence for this is so tenuous, however, that it has little value. Even if Book II is discounted, the text of Book I is sufficient to reveal Aristotle's method. It is, as Diagram IV shows, a rigorous method, elegantly developed according to "the order of nature, beginning with first principles."

Fourth. It is because of this method that Aristotle inverts historical order. The *Poetics* is a *techne* of literary art, not a literary history. When Aristotle sketches the history of literature in Chapter IV, he shows that the highest forms are historically the last to emerge. Epic, for example, precedes tragedy by several centuries. Yet in the *Poetics* the chapters on tragedy precede the chapters on epic. The strategy is appropriate in philosophical criticism because the highest form produced by the first principles is also the most nearly perfect manifestation of their working. Because higher forms include lower ones—tragedy includes all the parts of epic, as Aristotle remarks in Chapter V—inversion of historical order has the incidental value of greatly increasing the economy of the discussion. For example, many of the points made in connection with tragedy apply equally well to epic and, therefore, do not need to be repeated in the chapters devoted to epic.

Chapter II

Chapter II treats "object of imitation," which is the second element of imitative art mentioned in Chapter I (l. 12). As we have seen, the first element ("means") is insufficient to differentiate between literary forms using the same means, such as the mimes of Sophron and the Socratic dialogues, or comedy and tragedy.

"Object" is the most important of the elements of imitative art. In Chapter VI it is said to give rise to three of the six parts of tragedy—plot, character, and thought; and plot, the part most obviously generated by object of imitation, is called the "soul" of the tragic poem (Chapter VI, l. 81).

Chapter II begins by introducing terms related to object of imitation. These are action, agent, and "noble and base." These terms are mentioned in the first sentence, but they are not developed fully until later chapters. The basic function of the chapter is to show how "object of imitation" differentiates among works of art using the same means.

Differentiation by Objects of Imitation

After sentence one, Aristotle asserts that "the objects imitated are either better than, worse than, or like the norm." The sentence is often taken as a statement that the artist can idealize a character or debase him or present him realistically. This is unsatisfactory. Aristotle is speaking here of qualities contributed to the art work by the object of imitation (action with agents), not by the artist, whose contributions are considered in Chapter III under "manner of imitation."

The "better than, worse than, or like" phrase is ambiguous. However, if we bypass this problem for the moment, the remainder of the chapter goes smoothly. Painting is the art mentioned first in Chapter I. Aristotle now points out that the different kinds of painting can be distinguished on the basis of the painter's object. Polygnotus imitates men "better than"; Pauson, "worse than"; and Dionysius, "like." Dancing and music are the arts that followed painting in Chapter I. Accordingly, they are mentioned after painting in Chapter II, although no specific examples are given. After music came the "nameless art," which is accordingly treated next in Chapter II. Homer treats men "better than," Cleophon, men "like," and Hegemon and Nicochares men "worse than." Finally, at the end of Chapter I, Aristotle treated the arts using all means. Dithyramb and nome used the means "mixed." The Greek text of the sentence in Chapter II illustrating the different objects used by writers of these forms is extremely confused. Probably the references to nome writers have been lost. Timotheus is known to have written dithyrambs, and the *Cyclops* of Philoxenus was certainly a dithyramb. The two poems mentioned by Aristotle were probably both about Polyphemus, the Cyclops in Homer's *Odyssey*. Else argues that Timotheus emphasized his noble traits—presumably those revealed in his dealings with Ulysses—while Philoxenus, selecting another episode in his life (his love for Galatea), treated him as a comic figure and used him to satirize the tyrant Dionysius I of Syracuse and his mistress. If so, the two poems provide neat illustrations of the "better than" and "worse than" forms of dithyramb. The last forms mentioned in Chapter I are tragedy and comedy. They are picked up again at the end of Chapter II. Tragedy makes its figures "better than" and comedy, "worse than."

The close parallel between Chapters I and II illustrates the rigor of Aristotle's method. Notice, too, that the order of the chapters is logically necessary. Only after the basic genre distinctions have been made in terms of means of imitation is the second set of distinctions in terms of object appropriate.

One problem needs to be mentioned as we turn from the organization of Chapter II to its underlying concepts. Else has argued on the basis of both textual and historical evidence that the body of the chapter is corrupted by a systematic set of interpolations. He believes that Aristotle recognizes only two categories—"better than" and "worse than"—and that the "like" category and the artists illustrating it were added by Hellenistic scholars as notes that were later copied into the text. Else's arguments are persuasive, especially the fact that, as he remarks, Aristotle generally ignores the "like" category in his later discussion, for example, the history of poetic forms in Chapter IV.

The problem is important because it affects our answer to the question, "Better than, worse than, or like what?" In the *Nicomachean Ethics,* where Aristotle presents his theory of moral character, he asserts that actions form character and that they tend either to the good or the bad: "It is from playing the lyre that both good and bad lyre players are produced. . . . This, then is the case with the virtues also; by doing the acts that we do in our transactions with other men we become just or unjust" (1103^b 8-21). If this is true, the actions and agents that are the object of imitation are always either good or bad; there is no middle category, only a dividing line between them. To say that the poet imitates actions and men "better than, worse than, or like ourselves" is meaningless because the actions of men "like us" are themselves either "better than" or "worse than" the line (or norm) separating virtue from vice. The first sentence in Chapter II appears to make this point: "All of us [are] different in character because of some quality of goodness or evil" (ll. 3-4).

Else's argument presents the translator with something of a quandary. A conservative translation must follow the Greek text without omitting passages that are generally accepted. The present translation approaches the problem by preserving the third category but completing the comparison with the word "norm": "the objects imitated are either better than, worse than, or like the norm" (l. 5); and the objects of Dionysius and Cleophon are "like the norm" (ll. 8, 15). Those who reject Else can interpret "like the norm" to mean "like the average man" or "like ourselves." Those who find his arguments persuasive but reject his textual changes can interpret it in the sense of "tending to" or "not far from" the dividing line between good and evil.

Object of Imitation Defined

Let us now return to the underlying concepts of Chapter II. These are all presented in the first sentence of the chapter.

Sentence one has two parts. First it asserts that artists imitate men involved in action, and second that these men must of necessity be either noble or base. To follow this we need to examine the logic of the sentence and its key terms, which are "men involved in action" and "noble and base." Actually, we have already considered the logic underlying the idea that men in action are necessarily either noble or base when considering Else's theory about the text of Chapter II. Aristotle asserts that in human life, action determines the quality of a person's character. All actions tend either to the good or the bad. In the *Ethics* this is a general concept, so that at any given point in a man's life we can say that his "character" is the sum of his past actions and, in turn, determines the way he will act in the future. Since human beings perform many actions, they are usually a complex mixture of goods and bads. In the *Poetics* the notion of action is much more limited. In Chapter VII Aristotle insists that a tragedy should include one and only one action; and in Chapter VIII he adds that "There are many actions in the life of a single person from which no over-all unity of action emerges" (ll. 4-6) and that the poet should select a single action from the many that occur in a man's life. Considered by itself, a single action with a beginning, middle, and end will clearly fall on one side of the dividing line or the other; and its agent will *of necessity* be characterized by it. This explains why two poets, Timotheus and Philoxenus, can treat the same figure, Polyphemus, and yet produce two quite different types of poems. One has selected an action in the fictional life of Polyphemus that is "better than," and the other, an action that is "worse than" the norm.

Turning now to the basic terms of Chapter II, "men involved in action" is an inadequate translation of the Greek participle *prattontas,* from the verb *prattein,* to act. In the Greek, the emphasis is on action, not on the men performing the action. There is no question but that the Greek emphasis is correct. Tragedy is defined in Chapter VI as an "imitation of a noble action" (l. 5); and we are later explicitly told that "Tragedy is not an imitation of men *per se* but of human action and life. . . . Both happiness and unhappiness consist in a kind of action" (ll. 48-50). Action comes first; it is the object of imitation. The agents who perform the action come second.

Agent (*pratton*) should be carefully distinguished from character (*ethos*), for agents—people who perform actions—are necessary to a drama; but character in the technical Aristotelian sense is something that is added later and, in fact, is not even essential to successful tragedy, as we learn in Chapter VI (l. 59). Unfortunately, the translation of *prattontas* as "men involved in action" can lead an unwary reader to assume that Aristotle is primarily concerned with depiction of character. One should guard against this assumption. Aristotle's emphasis on action is fundamental to his thought about literature. It is one of his most significant and valuable insights, but it is a difficult insight to appreciate at first. Modern readers often assume that the chief interest of a fictional work lies in its creation of fascinating characters or its psychological revelations. Aristotle does not assume this. The implications of his approach will emerge as we proceed.

The other terms that need comment in sentence one are *spoudaios* and *phaulos,* here translated *noble* and *base.* The Greek words have several possible meanings. They can be translated *good* and *bad, noble* and *base,* or *serious* and *trivial.* First, it should be noted that they are qualities inherent in agents by virtue of the actions in which they are involved. If tragedy always imitates actions with agents who are "noble" (Chapter II, l. 2), and if tragedies can be written without character (Chapter VI, l. 59), then nobility and baseness cannot, strictly speaking, be part of character at all. If they do not stem from character (the second "part" of tragedy), they must stem from action, the first "part."[1]

Each of the various translations has merit, and each has weaknesses. *Good* and *bad* are probably the most common translations. They are appropriate because Aristotle seems to have moral qualities in mind. We have cited the moral theory of the *Ethics* in commenting on the "better than" and "worse than" categories of art. In addition, the last phrase of sentence one ("all of us being different in character because of some quality of goodness or evil") is in some sense an explanation of *spoudaios* and *phaulos;* and the terms that Aristotle uses for "goodness or evil" (*arete, kakia*) are explicitly ethical. *Good* and *bad,* however, cause two difficulties. First, they can lead to a false moralizing of the *Poetics.* Aristotle never suggests that dramas should teach moral lessons. Second and more serious, the protagonists of Greek drama are seldom "good"

[1] It can be argued, however, that "actions" become "noble" because they involve noble agents. This is the position taken by Leon Golden, "Is Tragedy the Imitation of a Serious Action?" *GRBS,* VI (1965), 283-89. Golden's position is strengthened by the fact that in Chapter XV, which is explicitly concerned with character (*ethos*), Aristotle's first requirement is that character be "good" (*chrestos*). The position taken in the commentary, conversely, is that an agent is noble because of his involvement in a noble action and that this quality is therefore independent of those features added to the agents by the poet as "characterization." In Chapter VI (l. 5) Aristotle defines tragedy as "an imitation of a noble and complete action," making no reference to character. Because "nobility" occupies a kind of "no-man's land" between plot and character, differences of opinion are both legitimate and—perhaps—inevitable. See also the comment on *chrestos* below in Chapter XV, pp. 200-202.

in a simple moral sense. Ajax, Prometheus, Medea, and Oedipus amply illustrate the point.

Serious and *trivial* have the advantage of pointing to the most general distinction separating Greek tragedy from comedy. As Chapter XIII shows, Aristotle is quite willing to call a play with a happy ending (for example, *Iphigenia in Tauris*) a tragedy, although the modern tendency would be to call it comic on the basis of its structure. If structural considerations are invalid, the difference between the two forms must stem from their different qualities. The actions and agents of tragedy are obviously "serious"; while those of comedy (especially Greek comedy) may be characterized as "base" or "trivial." This is another way of saying exactly what all of Chapter II is designed to demonstrate—that the differences between comedy and tragedy are the result of their different objects of imitation. The translation has the added advantage of conforming to Greek practice. Although Medea may not be "good," she is certainly serious and involved in a serious action. On the other hand, *serious* and *trivial* are morally neutral. They convey one part of Aristotle's meaning at the expense of another, more important part.

The terms *noble* and *base* were popular during the Renaissance when it was thought that tragedy should present kings and princes, and comedy, figures of the middle and lower classes. This is clearly not what Aristotle has in mind. However, if the terms *noble* and *base* are understood in their larger sense, they are probably the best compromise possible. *Noble* can mean "larger than life," "majestic," or "having grandeur," and *base,* the opposite. We generally consider that which is noble to be good, but the terms are not synonymous. Greek tragedies drew their "actions" from myths and legends that embodied far more primitive concepts of good and evil (for example, the codes of revenge and blood loyalty) than Aristotle's *Ethics*. These primitive concepts are only partly rationalized in the dramas of Aeschylus, Sophocles, and Euripides, although the actions are noble—even awesome—and the protagonists are heroic in stature. The feelings embodied in them also have certain overtones that probably come from religious influences on primitive Greek drama. They are serious, elevated, and also in some sense "good," without being amenable to neat moral classification. *Noble* catches this combination of qualities most effectively, and since Aristotle's labels in Chapter II are antithetical, *base* is appropriate for *phaulos*. On the other hand, no translation is entirely satisfactory. This may be because Aristotle himself had no terms adequate to cope with the complex mixture of qualities embodied in Greek tragedy. Lacking an adequate terminology, he had to be satisfied with an approximate description. We will return to this problem in connection with *hamartia* and *catharsis*.

Chapter III

Chapter III is divided into a consideration of manner of imitation and a second, digressive section on the Dorian claim to having originated drama.

Manner of Imitation (ll. 1-15)

Having discussed means and object, Aristotle now moves to manner of imitation. Manner of imitation is up to the poet. It is not inherent in his materials (means) or objects, and the same object can be treated in different manners. Three manners of imitation are introduced at the beginning of Chapter III, two "pure" and one mixed. The mixed kind, illustrated by Homer, is formed of the other two. The first pure manner is used when the poet speaks in his own person throughout the poem. Today one thinks of lyric poetry as an example of this type, but modern "lyric" is too narrow for Aristotle's meaning. The second pure manner is dramatic. The poet never speaks in his own person. Rather, the characters do their own "imitating."

In the third book of the *Republic* (III, 392-94) Socrates discusses manners of imitation. He seems to deny that the form in which the poet speaks in his own person is imitative at all (393). This is the least pernicious form of poetry but also the least moving. Drama, in which the characters carry on the imitation and the poet disappears, is pure imitation and the most moving of literary forms. Since Plato distrusts emotionalism, it is also the most pernicious. The mixed form exemplified by Homer is therefore the best compromise and the form that Socrates advocates—with reservations—for his ideal state.

Aristotle clearly draws on these ideas but makes significant changes. In the first place, all three of his "manners" are imitative, a fact that follows from his concept of imitation itself. In the second place, because he is interested in artistic effectiveness rather than morality he considers the dramatic manner the best rather than the most pernicious of the three.

In spite of these differences, Plato's discussion clarifies several points in the *Poetics*. When discussing epic imitation Socrates points out that Homer's method is a union of two simple forms (which he calls "narration" and "imitation"). He illustrates the assertion with the following remarks.

> You know the first lines of the *Iliad* in which the poet says that Chryses prayed Agamemnon to release his daughter. . . . Now as far as these lines —"And he prayed all the Greeks, but especially the two sons of Atreus, the chiefs of the people"—the poet is speaking in his own person; he never leads us to suppose he is anyone else. But in what follows he takes the person of Chryses, and then does all he can to make us believe that the speaker is not Homer, but the aged priest himself. And in this double form Homer cast the entire narrative of the events which occurred at Troy and in Ithaca and throughout the *Odyssey*.

In other words, when the poet is using third-person narration he is speaking "in his own person" just as much as when he speaks in the first person (modern "lyric"). Only when he is composing dialogue in which the characters "speak for themselves" is he using what Plato calls simply "imitation," and Aristotle, the third manner of imitation. In a particularly interesting passage, Plato indicates that the form in which the poet characteristically speaks "in his own person" is dithyramb:

> Poetry and mythology are, in some cases, wholly imitative—instances of this are supplied by tragedy and comedy; there is likewise the opposite style, in which the poet is the only speaker—of this the dithyramb affords the best example; and the combination of both is found in epic.

If we turn back now to Aristotle and add dithyramb to the examples cited in Chapter III, we have the following three "manners":

1. Mixed (Epic: Homer)
2. Narrative-Lyric (Dithyramb)
3. Dramatic (Comedy, Tragedy)

Normally, we would expect an ascending scale from simple to mixed to dramatic. There are several possible reasons for Aristotle's order. One is the fondness for parallelism that we have already observed in the parallels between Chapters I and II. In Chapter I, the most complex of the "nameless arts" was Homeric epic. Dithyramb and nome came next, and comedy and tragedy last (see Diagram II, p. 72). The order of "manners" simply follows the order of forms established in Chapter I—moving from narrative to dithyramb to drama. Another, perhaps more important reason, is that Aristotle believed dithyramb to be the starting point of tragic drama (Chapter IV, l. 57). His movement from Homer to dithyramb to drama anticipates the brief history of drama in Chapter IV: Homer came first and discovered a dramatic method (dialogue) but presented his work by recitation. A little after Homer, dithyrambic poets (l. 57) wrote "in their own persons," but their compositions were adapted to performance by a chorus. Drama is the last and highest form to emerge. It is the result of combining Homeric dialogue technique with the manner of presentation of the dithyramb.

This point leads to one further observation concerning the dramatic "manner." The operative concept in it is whether or not the poet appears in his own person. When he disappears entirely, the result is drama. In other words, the definition of drama depends on what the poet does, not on the performers (an idea also suggested by Aristotle's observation that a tragedy does not have to be acted to produce its pleasure [Chapter XXVI, l. 36]). A skillful poet will adapt his text for performance; but the text, not the actors or the staging, is central. This means that when we come to *spectacle,* the part of tragedy that is caused by manner of imitation, we will need to explain it in terms of the poet's text and not—as is often done—in terms of *mise en scène.*

After the definition of manner of imitation, Aristotle summarizes the discussion so far, listing the three elements of imitation and showing how they can be used to differentiate among various poets. This passage contains the only reference in the *Poetics* to Aristophanes. For reasons that first become apparent in Chapter IV, Aristotle must have considered Aristophanes a rather primitive dramatist. After mentioning him, Aristotle remarks that he and Homer represent men "acting and dramatizing." He uses two participles in his phrase, the first from the Attic (Athenian) verb *prattein* (to act) and the second from the Dorian verb *dran* (to do). This leads to a digression that is very probably a late addition of the type discussed by Montmollin. It adds nothing to our understanding of the official subject of the chapter ("manner of imitation"); and insofar as it relates to Aristotle's larger argument, it would seem most appropriate not in Chapter III, but in Chapter V, which discusses the history of comedy.

The Dorian Claims to Having Originated Drama (ll. 15-36)

The excuse for the digression is the fact that the Greek word *drama* is derived from Dorian *dran*. Since the generic term came from Dorian dialect, Dorian Greeks could claim that their ancestors must have discovered both tragedy and comedy.

To follow the additional arguments used by the Dorians, the reader needs to know that the Dorians were a far-ranging, active ethnic group in ancient Greece with important settlements at Megara (near Corinth; the Peloponnesian Dorians), and on Sicily. The Dorians felt a keen cultural rivalry with the Attic-speaking (especially Athenian) Greeks. Not being a native of Athens, Aristotle may have sympathized with the Dorians. At any rate, he goes on to point out that the inhabitants of Megara claim to have originated comedy "when democracy was established among them." Megara "became a democracy" in the seventh and the early sixth century B.C., well before there are records of comedy in Athens. Reinforcing the somewhat nebulous claim of the Megarians is the historically specific claim of the Dorians in Sicily to Epicharmus. Epicharmus is a fairly solid historical figure who lived at some time between the sixth and the fifth century B.C. The Dorians naturally date him as early as possible. According to them he "far antedates" two early Athenian comic poets, Chionides and Magnes (fifth century B.C.).

We now turn from the claims of the Megarians and their colonial relatives in Sicily to the claims of the "Dorians in the Peloponnesus" (who may or may not be a third group) that they originated tragedy and comedy. Their claim for tragedy (ll. 25, 34) simply repeats the *dran, drama* argument cited earlier. Their claim for comedy introduces another etymology, and one that is now recognized to be false. The Greek word *komodia* is made up of two words *kom-* and *ode* (song). The Athenians correctly traced *kom-* to the Attic verb *komazein* (to revel). The Dorians, however, insisted the term comedy refers to the fact that early comedians were kept out of the city, rather than to the religious festivals (revels) to which the Athenians traced comedy. This being so, they argued that *kom-* must come from *komai* the word for "outlying villages." That *komai* is a Dorian word (the applicable Attic word is *demoi*) reinforces the argument for the Dorian origins of comedy.

One wonders why Aristotle devoted so much time to the Dorian claims. Parts of the passage may be corrupt, but in general, it is probably authentic. One possible answer is that the Dorian tradition is linked to the invention of plot in Chapter V (ll. 18-22). As we will see, this associates it with the development of New Comedy (exemplified for the modern reader by Menander's plays), which Aristotle felt superior to the Old Comedy, exemplified by the works of Aristophanes, and which is fairly definitely an Athenian form.

Chapter III ends with another summary sentence referring to the three elements of imitation thus far treated.

Chapter IV

Chapter IV is one of the more complex chapters in the *Poetics*. Generally speaking, it is historical, but Aristotle uses his historical materials in three ways.

A. In discussing the origins of imitation in human nature, Aristotle touches on its purpose or function. This adds a fourth basic element to the three previously considered, thus rounding out the first logical unit in the *Poetics*, the discussion of "elements of imitative art." At the same time it traces the mimetic impulse to a fundamental human trait. Since Aristotle knew nothing of primitive society, he could not discuss the historical origins of poetry as modern anthropologists have. The alternative was to derive poetry from a universal psychological trait presumably constant in human nature at all periods of history. Thus, in addition to rounding out the discussion of elements of imitation, the first section of Chapter IV is the foundation on which the following historical section rests.

B. The historical section that follows discusses the evolution of poetry from two primitive "kinds," encomium and lampooning verse, to sophisticated tragedy and comedy. The section contains a good deal of solid historical evidence, but its outlines are deductive rather than inductive. The historical evidence is generally used to confirm the theory. This explains why the historical section is not strictly chronological but includes two distinct historical lines of development, with traces of a third.

The first line of development is in terms of "object of imitation" and extends to the question about tragedy's "formal development" (l. 51). The second traces the history of the dramatic "manner" of imitation and contains at least brief glances at the history of the tragic meters—that is, "means" of imitation. This history (or mixture of histories) extends naturally into Chapter V, which summarizes the development of comedy. Chapter IV is thus continuous with Chapter V. Since tragedy and comedy result from the confluence of all three imitative elements, the histories are not entirely separate, and there is some overlapping and repetition.

C. Considered in its larger outlines, Aristotle's history illustrates the distinction made in Chapter I (l. 16) between artists who work by habit or custom and those who work by art. The early poets were artisans. They could not see, with Aristotle, the whole pattern of literary forms; and by definition, they had no way of knowing the direction in which their work was leading. They knew from experience what "worked," and they discovered new techniques by experimenting. The result is a very gradual development of literary forms beginning before Homer (that is, about 1000 B.C.) and not ending until Aristotle's day. Indeed, Aristotle seems to imply in Chapter IV (ll. 51-54), and again in Chapter IX (in his comment about the validity of the fictional tragic plot, ll. 30-37), that tragedy is capable of evolution beyond the point that it had reached in his day. The history both illustrates literary evolution—the tendency of the first principles to combine and recombine in ever more complex and sophisticated forms—and helps us to appreciate the difference between the artisan poet and the poet who understands the whole range of his art in terms of its theory, its *techne*.

The Origin and Function of Imitation
(ll. 1-20)

Chapter IV begins with the assertion that poetry results from two "natural causes." There is disagreement about what the two causes are. Butcher, for example, identifies them as (1) man's proneness to imitation (ll. 2-3), and (2) man's instinct for harmony and rhythm (ll. 21-23). Telford and Bywater prefer to identify them as (1) man's proneness to imitation (ll. 2-3), and (2) man's delight in imitation (ll. 5-6). To decide which position is preferable, we need to note that Aristotle is here talking about poetry in the sense of literary art, not in the sense of "productive science," as the term was used in Chapter I. This is clear from the content of the chapter (a history of literary forms) and also from the fact that "productive science" is a larger category than "imitation," whereas the "poetry" of Chapter IV is something generated by imitation and hence must be subordinate to it. Poetry in this narrower sense is impossible without "means," and the means include the rhythm and harmony of ll. 21-22, which constitute Butcher's second cause. We will therefore tentatively follow Butcher.

Man's proneness to imitation is first established by an empirical observation: Man is the most imitative of animals and children first learn by imitation, in the sense of copying. This is a very functional type of imitation and also personal since it is done for one's self rather than for others. It explains how men learn but not why they invented the "art of poetry" mentioned in sentence one. The first cause of works of art—of works produced to bring delight to others—is that "all men find pleasure in imitations" (l. 6). That is, "imitation" has two sources—instinct and pleasure—but "poetry" in the sense of works of art arises from only one of these—the pleasure it brings. Mentioning man's instinct for imitation may be useful as evidence that man has the capacity to imitate (if such evidence is really needed); and it has the more important value of establishing that the origin of imitative art was a universal human characteristic, a characteristic as typical of primitive man as of children of Aristotle's day.

But the main point of the passage is to explain why poetry is produced. As we have seen, the reason is pleasure. This being the case, "pleasure" must be considered a basic element of imitative art. It is the last basic element mentioned by Aristotle, and so the complete list of elements is (1) means, (2) object, (3) manner, and (4) purpose (*i.e.*, pleasure). We will return to this point later.

Aristotle now analyzes and defines imitative pleasure. First he offers an empirical observation. Normally we shun ugly animals and dead bodies, but these can be enjoyable when they are represented in paintings. The point is still valid today. Aristotle's examples may have been chosen simply because they are striking and extreme, but it should be noted that both involve a paradox that is closely related to tragedy—the paradox of pleasure resulting from things that would be painful if experienced or witnessed in real life.

Having stated his idea and confirmed it with an example, Aristotle now explains it. The pleasure derived from imitative works is not sense-gratification but a type of pleasure associated with learning. This learning, in turn, comes from observing "that this particular object is that kind of object" (ll. 16-17). According to Aristotle (for example, *Metaphysics,* 1036ᵃ 28; 1059ᵇ 29), "learning" occurs when we come to know universals or perceive the relation of the specific to the universal. Without going into this concept in detail, we can see that in a general sense it is being used in the *Poetics*. It is a key concept, for it emphatically differentiates Aristotle's "imitation" from the Platonic notion of imitation as copying. There is a certain pleasure to be derived from comparing a good likeness to the original. We refer to this pleasure when, for example, we say, "That photograph is a fine likeness of John." Clearly, this is *not* the pleasure Aristotle has in mind. Rather, he is referring to the fact that imitative works, if they are well done, reveal generic qualities—the presence of the universal in the particular—and that the spectator or audience learns as a result of this. This learning takes place even if we have never seen the original. If, for example, we say, "That photograph is a fine likeness of John; it catches his character beautifully; and he should use it for the application form," we are echoing the *Poetics*. What we are saying is (a) that the photograph communicates the fact that John possesses certain general traits (warmth, strength, sense of humor, and so on); and (b) that it will reveal these traits to *someone who has never seen John*—the recipient of the application form. Obviously, a painting communicates a great deal more than a photograph. We have never seen the "originals" of Rembrandt's portraits, but we know the kind of men they were, better, perhaps, than we know all but our closest friends. Note that viewing a Rembrandt portrait not only enables us to learn that "this particular man is that kind of man"; it is also extremely pleasurable. As a final example, consider Audubon's paintings of birds. Audubon was a naturalist and his pictures were intended primarily as a contribution to science and only secondarily as works of art. In other words, their original purpose was to inform. They do this by revealing in the image of a single bird qualities that define its class. Even if we have never been to the seashore, we can learn a great deal about the seagull from looking at Audubon's illustration. At the same time, as everyone knows, Audubon's paintings are works of art. They give pleasure and the source of the pleasure according to Aristotle is their communication of the universal in the particular.

This point is central to Aristotle's theory of art. It does not mean that art is allegory—that artists simply present general concepts in particular examples—but we will postpone more precise definition, pausing only to note that the idea of art as an embodiment of universals recurs in Chapter IX when Aristotle discusses the relation of poetry to history and philosophy. The parallels are summarized in the table below.

PAINTING (CHAPTER IV)	POETRY (CHAPTER IX)
Model (source of portrait)	"Singulars" of history (source of poem)
Portrait	Poem
"Kind" or "type"	"Philosophic universals"

Chapters IV and IX agree that aesthetic pleasure does not come from the comparison of the portrait to the model (or the poem to its historical source) but from the sense of the "kind" (or the universal) in the work itself. In *Republic* X, Socrates says that imitation is basically copying, and he complains that it falsifies the things being copied. Aristotle denies that imitation is copying and maintains that we learn from it.

The second half of the sentence under consideration (ll. 17-20) is both a proof of the first half and a further explanation of it. Aristotle has said that the pleasure of imitation comes from the perception of the universal in the specific. The proof that he now adds is that we gain pleasure from works whose originals we have not seen. (The parallel point in Chapter IX is that a fictional plot—one for which there is no historical source—can have true tragic effect.) The phrase "imitation *qua* imitation" (l. 18) is ambiguous in Greek as well as English, but the meaning is fairly obvious: "If one has not happened to see the object previously, he will not find any pleasure in the imitation *qua* copy but rather in the workmanship or coloring or something similar."

The last part of the sentence tells us how the artist communicates his "sense of the generic." Obviously, he does it by means of his technique—"workmanship" (although this is a little weak for the Greek *apergasia,* which has the sense of "a perfect execution")—and his materials. The truth of this is so plain that it is usually missed. When we see a painting we see *only* forms and colors—the "means" of Chapter I, and correlative to "workmanship or coloring" [2] in the present passage—and when we read a poem we have

[2] "Workmanship" is roughly parallel to "form" in the "color-form" equation for painting in Chapter I. For Aristotle, "form" is a means but must be de-

only, we might say, "workmanship and words." If the painting or poem communicates anything at all, it must do so with what it has. The clause under discussion is not an afterthought. Aristotle is not saying, "True imitative pleasure comes from comparing the copy to the original; but if you can't do that you still have the consolation prizes of workmanship and coloring." His sentence has precisely the opposite meaning. It says that the pleasure of imitation comes from learning, not from comparison to the original; that the proof of this is that we get the pleasure even if we have not seen the original; and that the learning and pleasure are caused by the artist's skill (his mastery of his *techne* and his materials). The point becomes clear when we recall that artists often intentionally deviate from the individual models before them to make their pictures communicate more clearly. This always happens, for example, in botanical and zoological art like Audubon's bird paintings.

The first section of Chapter IV ends with a reference to man's instinct for rhythm and harmony, which Butcher considers the second cause of poetic art. Since rhythm and harmony are identified as means in Chapter I, it is really not a new cause. The only problem is the parenthetical remark, ". . . it is apparent that meters are parts of the rhythms." In Chapter I, we saw that there was good reason to suppose that the phrase "words alone" means "language without rhythm or harmony," in spite of the fact that the category includes Homer (l. 41). The present passage seems to contradict this. In fact, a slight inconsistency is possible. Probably, however, Aristotle is consistent. In Chapter I the basis for interpreting "words alone" as "language without rhythm" was the observation that Aristotle and his contemporaries associated rhythm with bodily movement, that is, dance. Homer has meters but his poems certainly do not involve dance as do the choral sections of Greek tragedies. Here in Chapter IV, Aristotle says only that meters are parts (*morion,* a small piece, portion) of rhythms. They may

termined by object of imitation. *Apergasia* may also take in "manner of imitation." In this case the sentence refers to all four elements of imitation. Its purpose is to explain "pleasure" (element four). It does so by asserting that pleasure is the result of the proper use of object and manner (*apergasia*), and means (color). The parallel between painting and poetry is continued in Chapter VI (ll. 82-85). There the outline of the painter (his form) is compared to plot, and color to character.

have originated in rhythmic compositions involving dance (see, for example, l. 70, on trochaic meter), and if so, they may be understood as detached pieces—"parts"—of the original rhythms.

Overview of Chapters I-IV (to IV, l. 20)

Before we come to the historical section of Chapter IV, it will be useful to summarize the first logical unit in the *Poetics*. Aristotle predicts in Chapter I that he will proceed "according to the order of nature, beginning with first principles" (ll. 6-7). As we saw, this is a statement of method; and the method is based on Aristotle's concept of the way Nature operates. Four "first principles" have emerged: (1) means, (2) object, (3) manner, and (4) function. Means is to imitative art what material is to applied art. That is, the painter "makes" a bed out of form and color; the carpenter makes it out of wood. Object of imitation—action—gives the poem its form, its plot, which is also called its "soul" (Chapter IV, l. 80). Manner is entirely determined by the artist himself. Both artist and artisan have "manners," the one imposing them on "means," the other on material. Likewise, both imitative and applied art have purpose. As we noted in discussing Chapters I and IV, the general purpose of imitative art is pleasure; of applied art, utility.

It is very tempting to extend these observations one step further. Aristotle believed that four causes cooperated to produce each phenomenon, natural or artificial. The causes are (1) material, (2) formal, (3) efficient, and (4) final. It seems possible that first logical unit of the *Poetics* presents the four causes of poetry; and we might therefore amend our translation of sentence two of Chapter I to read: "Let us proceed according to the order of nature beginning with first causes." In tabular form, the causes of imitative art and poetry are as follows.

Cause	*In Art Generally*	*In Poetry*
Material:	Means of Imitation	Language, Rhythm, Harmony
Formal:	Object of Imitation	Actions with Agents
Efficient:	Manner of Imitation	Lyric-Narrative, Epic, Dramatic
Final:	Pleasure	Pleasure

The Historical Sections of Chapter IV: History by Object of Imitation (ll. 21-50)

Having established imitation as something instinctive, Aristotle is on solid ground when he asserts that "Men, having been naturally endowed with these gifts from the beginning and then developing them gradually . . . finally created the art of poetry from their early improvisations." The instinct provides him with a starting point. He could not prove his point by historical evidence (he had none); he therefore had to establish it indirectly by reference to qualities that are innate to man and, presumably, to be found among the most primitive peoples. Starting from this "prehistoric" condition, the sentence surveys the history of poetry from its origin to its emergence as a well-defined form. The fact that the process was "gradual" and resulted from "early improvisations" is a reminder that the pattern illustrates the trial-and-error methods of the early artisan-poets.

Primitive poetic "improvisations" soon divided into two rudimentary genres of poetry. The division is based on the ideas of Chapter II concerning object of imitation. They are here said to operate in complementary ways. The dispositions of early poets were "of greater dignity" or "less dignified" and the poets were led by their dispositions to noble or base objects. We notice, by the way, that there is no mention of a middle ("like") category, and apparently not even the possibility of one, a fact that strengthens Else's theory concerning the spuriousness of the "like" category in Chapter II.

The better poets imitated the actions of heroes, and the genres that they produced were hymn and "encomium" (a song of praise). The baser sort produced "invectives," or satires of base men. Notice that the existence of "invectives" before Homer cannot be demonstrated. Aristotle confesses, "We know of no 'invective' by poets before Homer, although it is probable that there were many who wrote such poems" (ll. 32-34). In other words, the existence of "invectives" before Homer is deduced from the theory; it is not established by empirical evidence. The case for "hymns and encomia" is a little more solid. Aristotle is probably thinking of the hymns and panegyrics to heroes and noble citizens that Plato admitted to his *Republic* (X, 607) and that are represented in surviving Greek literature by the "hymns" of Orpheus and the odes of Pindar.

The next stage in the evolution of poetry in terms of object of imitation is the emergence of formal literary types. Here we encounter a name for the first time in the history. Homer not only stands at the head of Greek poetry, he is the first writer to assume even shadowy form in the history of Greek poetry. According to a tradition accepted by Aristotle and his contemporaries, Homer wrote three poems: the *Iliad,* the *Odyssey,* and the *Margites.*

Margites means literally *The Fool's Epic.* The poem was a rather crude burlesque poem with a fictional plot and in hexameters mixed here and there with lines in iambic meter. It has not survived, and it most certainly was not by Homer. Aristotle doubtless mentions it because it is the earliest poem known to him illustrating fictional invective. He does not appear disturbed by the fact that attributing it to Homer gives Homer a character that is both noble and base.[3]

Having cited the *Margites,* Aristotle digresses briefly. The subject of the digression is the *ars metrica* familiar from Chapter I. Aristotle remarks that iambic meter is a fitting one for invective and was therefore adopted very early by the "base" writers. Since the Greek verb for "to satirize" is *iambizein,* he observes that the name of the meter comes from the subject-matter of the poetry that originally used it. This undercuts the claim of the *ars metrica* that there is an essential connection between meter and subject-matter. According to Aristotle iambic meter received its name because it was first used for satire, not because it is intrinsically "satirical." The most important fact about iambic meter for Aristotle is that it is close to the rhythm of normal speech. This fact may explain why the iambic writers used it and makes clear why iambic eventually came to be used in tragedy (Chapter IV, ll. 69-76), in spite of the fact that tragedy is more closely related to the epic than the satiric tradition. By the same token, because dactylic hexameter was used for epic, it became known as "heroic" meter. Thus, ". . . of our earliest writers some were heroic and some iambic poets" (l. 39).

[3] Else rescues Homer from this schizophrenia by emending l. 28 to read "differences of character in the poetry itself" instead of "dispositions of the poets."

The third stage in the evolution of poetry is the emergence of tragedy and comedy from epic and the type of satiric epic illustrated by the *Margites*. Homer is the central figure in the discovery of ways to treat the "noble actions" appropriate for tragedy. As is clear from other references, especially Chapter VIII, Homer's excellence stems from his ability to present materials in a consistent, well-developed, and above all, unified plot.

Homer also made another decisive contribution, mentioned by Aristotle in the parenthesis of line 41. He not only handled actions well, he also "made his imitations dramatic." This observation anticipates the history of the evolution of the dramatic manner traced in the next paragraph. Evidently, Aristotle means here what he states more explicitly in Chapter XXIV (ll. 45-49)—that Homer allows his characters to speak for themselves and minimizes his own part in the poem. The observation also accords with the point made in Chapter III that Homer employs the "mixed" manner of imitation.

Aristotle now returns to the main subject. In addition to converting simple hymns and encomia into well-articulated plots, Homer pointed the way for the writers of comedy. He did this by changing the bitter ridicule of early invective poetry into an image of the ridiculous. Since Old Comedy, of the type represented today by Aristophanes, includes a great deal of bitter personal invective, and since its plots are poorly articulated by Aristotle's standards, he is evidently suggesting that Homer pointed the way for Middle and New Comedy.

An immense historical gap now opens in Aristotle's scheme, a gap best understood as the result of a deductive rather than an inductive approach. Greek tradition placed Homer in the eighth century B.C. or earlier. Tragedy and comedy, however, did not emerge until the sixth century. Aristotle skips over the intervening centuries without a word. It does not really matter to him here when tragedy and comedy emerged. The point is that they are the most highly developed literary forms. When they *did* appear, the noble poets naturally turned from epic to tragedy, and the base, from "epic satire" to comedy. Aristotle concludes the section with a brief note suggesting that tragedy may still not be fully "developed in its formal elements" (l. 52) but adds that the question "belongs to another discussion."

What we have, then, is a three-stage scheme for the evolution of poetry "by object." Since "object of imitation" can be noble or base, the scheme has two lines, and because "object" gives form to the literary work, the points of interest in the development of literature are those marking the emergence of new forms. Encomia and invectives are "noble and base" but topical. They lack well-developed plots. (Incidentally, being topical, they are the forms that come closest to history, hence to being imitations in the sense of copies; and the whole tendency of Aristotle's treatment here is to show how poetry *moves away* from the idea of copying.) Homer's compositions have well-developed plots, but they are "mixed" compositions, and his serious epics use meters that are not suited to speech. Tragedy and comedy derive in part from Homer, but only in part. Their manner is purely dramatic, and their meter ("means") is iambic. A history of poetry in terms of object of imitation can note their emergence but cannot explain it fully. To explain it we need a history of manner and means. The schema developed so far may be summarized as follows:

DATE	NOBLER FORMS	BASER FORMS	CHARACTERISTIC
Pre-historic	*Imitative improvisations*		
C. 1000 B.C.	Hymn, encomium	Invective	Close to History; Pure Narrative Manner
C. 800 B.C.	*Iliad, Odyssey*	*Margites*	Unified Fictionalized Plots; Mixed Manner
C. 550 B.C.	Tragedy	Comedy	Unified Fictionalized Plots; Pure Dramatic Manner
347-322 B.C.	Modern Tragedy (Are new developments possible?)	Middle Comedy	

History by Manner and Means
(ll. 51-80)

Aristotle now returns to the "improvisations" mentioned earlier. He specifies two particular kinds of improvisation, dithyrambs and phallic songs.[4] Both these literary forms are associated with primitive religious rites, and both were "performed" rather than read or recited. The ancient Greeks recognized that their theater originated from rites associated with the worship of the god Dionysus. Modern anthropologists have speculated that these rites involved the death and rebirth of the god and were celebrated originally by human sacrifice.[5] Dithyrambs were chanted antiphonally by a chorus dressed as satyrs and a leader. They were serious religious compositions originally concerned with the exploits of the god (hence possibly related to the "hymns" of l. 31). As they developed, their narrative element became more important. The dithyrambic chorus is retained in the chorus of Greek tragedy. Phallic songs were related to the Saturnalian phase of worship. They were licentious rather than serious and celebrated the renewal of fertility that Dionysus was believed to bring to the community. Almost certainly Aristotle felt that there was a close connection between phallic rituals and the practice of equipping the actors of Old Comedy with phallic emblems.

Having named the literary kinds from which the tragic and comic manners originated, Aristotle devotes the rest of Chapter IV to tragedy, reserving comedy for Chapter V. Presumably Aristotle believed that the dithyramb was an ancient form, perhaps predating Homer. He asserts that tragedy "gradually" developed out of it as poets improved on the experiments of their predecessors. For reasons that are not entirely clear, Aristotle leaves out a tradition preserved in his (lost) dialogue *On the Poets* concerning the development of tragedy before Aeschylus. According to this tradition, dithyramb remained static until the seventh century B.C. At that time the half-legendary poet Arion formalized the dithyramb by stationing the chorus in a circle around an altar and assigning a definite text. Next came a still more important figure, Thespis, who supposedly lived in the middle of the sixth century and was generally credited with the invention of formal tragedy (in, for example, Horace, *Ars Poetica,* ll. 275-77). He did this by introducing a figure with a set speech who impersonated not the god Dionysus

[4] A few editors read "songs of the phauloi"—the base men—rather than "phallic songs."

[5] See Gilbert Murray and F. M. Cornford, Bibliography, pp. 300, 301.

but a legendary or historical character. This innovation created the basis for the plot, characters, and dialogue of formal tragedy.[6]

Instead of referring to this tradition, Aristotle places the satyr-play in the intermediate position between dithyramb and tragedy (l. 67). The satyr-play is a rather crude form of drama resembling tragedy. It frequently dealt with heroes (Hercules for example), but the chorus dressed as satyrs, and the plot was usually grotesque. It formed the fourth in the group of four plays presented by poets at the Greek dramatic contests. Given the crude form of the satyr-play, the fact that the chorus (like the dithyrambic chorus) dressed as satyrs, and Aristotle's evolutionary bias, it is understandable that he should have regarded the satyr-play as an intermediate stage between dithyramb and tragedy. In this, however, he is probably wrong. The modern tendency is to regard tragedy and satyr-play as independent lines of development.

Whatever its prehistory, tragedy began to take final shape in the fifth century. Three kinds of development occurred, all representing a movement away from dithyramb. First, the number of actors was increased. Aeschylus (525-456 B.C.) increased the number of actors from one to two, and Sophocles (495-405) increased it to three. This has the effect, Aristotle points out, of increasing the importance of the dialogue and diminishing the importance of the tragic chorus. Homer's influence is important here. Although the *Iliad* and *Odyssey* are not intended for performance, they are highly dramatic. Specifically, they have many passages in which the characters speak for themselves—many passages, that is, of monologue and dialogue. The Homeric influence is confirmed by the prominence of Homeric subjects (for example, the *Oresteia*; *Iphigenia in Aulis*) in Greek drama. As dramatic poets drew their plots from Homer, they also discovered the possibilities of dialogue. The more they exploited these possibilities, the further into the background they pushed the choral parts. In terms of the criteria of means of imitation of Chapter I, they emphasized the "words alone" part of drama at the expense of the part using words and rhythm and harmony. The clear implication of this passage is that the chorus is an undramatic relic of the early history of drama and may eventually

[6] See especially Pickhard-Cambridge, Bibliography, p. 301.

disappear, as it already was doing in the Middle and New Comedy. The introduction of scene painting by Sophocles (l. 65) may be considered a corollary of the development of the dramatic element in drama. Scene painting is not the work of the poet and hence not really part of the art of poetry. The more dramatic the compositions, however, the greater the incentive to bring out the implications of the poet's text through the techniques of dramatic production.

Complementing the addition of more actors and the increased emphasis on dialogue, we have the discovery of improved techniques of plotting. If, as Aristotle believes, the satyr-play preceded Aeschylean tragedy, it follows that at some point prior to Aeschylus, the poets must have abandoned the "short plots" and grotesque incidents of the satyr-play in favor of longer, more dignified compositions. In Chapter V, Aristotle says that when the new plots first appeared, they were of epic dimensions (ll. 31-32). This comment makes it fairly certain that the change in dramatic plots discussed in Chapter IV is due to—or heavily influenced by—Homer. Homer's epics have unity and great magnitude. Aeschylus and his contemporaries evidently learned from them how they might advance beyond the sketchy presentation of actions characteristic of the satyr-play. In fact, they were too heavily influenced by Homer at first. Their plots were "epic" in size (perhaps an allusion to the Aeschylean trilogy), and only later did they discover the ideal magnitude for tragedy. Near the end of Chapter VI (l. 76) Aristotle adds, "Moreover, the number of episodes was increased." This is consistent with the idea of increasing the magnitude of the plot at the expense of the chorus, since in Greek drama an episode is simply a section of dialogue between two choral odes. To increase the number of episodes is to increase the proportion of dialogue to choral chant.

The third way in which tragedy developed was by the discovery of an appropriate meter. The dithyramb and the lines of the tragic chorus were in a variety of meters. Aristotle does not even mention them. As we have seen, he is interested in dialogue. The satyr-play advanced beyond dithyramb in that it included speeches, but its meter was trochaic tetrameter. The reason for this is that like its ancestor the dithyramb, the satyr-play involved dancing; and trochaic meter has a dancelike rhythm (l. 71). On the other hand, iambic meter "is the most conversational of the meters," and we frequently speak iambs unconsciously (l. 74). Iamb thus has a natural fitness for poetry that purports to present dialogue between characters. As soon as tragic poets became conscious of what they were doing, they changed from trochaic to iambic meter. Aristotle's remark that in conversation we used "few [dactylic] hexameters" (l. 75) may simply be an illustration intended for emphasis. However, since Homer (a) provided the chief model for dramatic dialogue, and (b) wrote in dactylic hexameter, it may be something more. If so, it reminds us that when they turned to Homer for inspiration, dramatic poets imitated his technique but found his meter just as unsuitable as the trochaic meter of satyr-play. They needed a conversational meter; and they took this from satiric (iambic) poetry and comedy.

The chapter ends with the observation that to treat all the special embellishments of tragedy would be "an enormous task." For Aristotle, it is unnecessary since he has covered the history of the essentials: object, manner, and means.[7]

Chapter V

Chapter V completes Aristotle's historical survey of drama and ends with a general comment on a subject treated in Chapter IV, tragic magnitude.

History of Comedy (ll. 1-22)

The discussion of comedy begins with a summary definition of the comic object ("baser men"). It then differentiates comic base-

[7] For an outline of the history of tragedy as given in Chapter IV, see Diagram V, p. 107.

ness from out-and-out depravity, and comic humor from abuse. Comic baseness is said to be a form of the ridiculous (*geloion*), which in turn is not "every kind of vice" but a subdivision of "deformity." More specifically, it is an "error" (*hamartema*) that produces no painful or harmful effects (l. 5). On the one hand, this sounds like an answer to Plato, who had claimed (*Republic*, X, 606, and elsewhere) that comedy (1) corrupts the passions by showing images of depravity, and (2) engages in malicious and painful abuse. Plato probably has Aristophanes in mind and perhaps *The Clouds*, Aristophanes' outrageous satire of Socrates. On the other hand, Aristotle is refining points made in Chapter IV concerning the history of comedy. There he had observed that comedy originated in invectives of base men. He explicitly says, however, that in the *Margites* Homer broke away from this tradition by presenting "not invective but the ridiculous" (l. 43), and by doing so in a dramatic way. We have already noted that the *Margites* is more closely related to Middle and New Comedy than to Aristophanic Old Comedy. Aristotle's definitions in Chapter V, then, should probably be understood in relation to the type of universalized satire of men and mores found in New Comedy rather than in relation to the bitter personal invective of Old Comedy. A proper comedy should amuse, not cause pain. Finally, we can note in passing that the comic error (*hamartema*) is paralleled by the tragic flaw (*hamartia*, Chapter XIII, l. 29), and comic laughter by tragic pity and fear.[1]

Curiously enough, in spite of his fairly detailed comments on Dorian comedy in Chapter III, Aristotle begins his history of comedy by admitting that its early stages are unknown. He is doubtless referring to its "phallic song" period rather than to the age of Epicharmus (sixth-fifth century); and his reference to the granting of the chorus by the archon, an event that occurred in 486 B.C., does not mean that the comic chorus originated at that date—merely that this is the first record of a performance of comedy in Athens. Aristotle adds that the inventors of masks and prologues, and the arbiters of numbers of actors are also unknown. In fact, he mentions only three specific names, but two of these are quite

[1] On the basis of this passage and hints in Aristotle's *Rhetoric*, the late-classical *Tractatus Coislinianus*, and other works, Lane Cooper has attempted to construct an Aristotelian theory of comedy comparable to the theory of tragedy in the *Poetics*. See Bibliography, p. 297.

significant. Epicharmus, the Dorian poet of Chapter III (l. 22), is identified as the inventor of comic plots. This can only be a reference to the movement from the topical, formless satire of invective to the fictional technique of the *Margites*. Aristotle, then, is saying that the Dorians in Sicily developed a proper comic form well before the Athenians. Only somewhat after Epicharmus, according to Aristotle's chronology, do we find an Athenian, Crates (fifth century), who follows the Sicilian's lead. Crates "departed from iambic [or invective] poetry and began to write speeches and plots of a more universal nature" (ll. 20-2).[2]

We are now in a position to understand Aristotle's curious silence in Chapter V concerning Aristophanes. He considers the true line of comedy to be that of fictional comedy—of Middle and New Comedy. He begins this line with Epicharmus the Sicilian who followed Homer's lead and shifted from comic invective to fictional presentations of the ridiculous. As early as the fifth century Crates was doing the same thing in Athens. Aristophanes, on the other hand, employed the personal invective of Old Comedy even though he wrote after Crates. To Aristotle, he must have seemed something of an anachronism, an evolutionary throwback to a phase of comedy corresponding, perhaps, to the satyr-play phase of tragedy. He receives no place in a history stressing new evolutionary developments.

Aristotle's history of poetry is now complete. It is a complex one, theoretical in outline, and involving the tracing of three separate but interrelated lines of development that converge in tragedy and comedy—the history of object, of manner, and of means. These are summarized in Diagram V.

Comparison of Epic and Tragedy; Unity of Time (ll. 23-38)

The last section of Chapter V begins (l. 23) with a summary description of epic and tragedy that resembles the summary descrip-

[2] The key phrase here is "plots of a more universal nature." This does not mean that Epicharmus and Crates invented New Comedy, merely that they discovered one of the elements (universal plot) that characterized it when it emerged in the fourth century and that differentiated it from Old Comedy.

Diagram V

Forms not mentioned by Aristotle are in parentheses

Evolution of Tragedy

Date	Object	Manner	Means
Prehistoric	Improvisations	The Improvised Dithyramb (antiphonal chants; chorus of satyrs)	Circular choral dance; rhythm, harmony, speech; "mixed"
Pre-Homeric	Hymns, encomia (nonfiction)		
c. 800 B.C.	Homer, *Iliad*, *Odyssey*		
		(Formal Dithyramb: ?Arion)	
c. 550		(Dithyramb with actor: ?Thespis)	
		Satyr-Play (chorus plus dialogue)	Choral parts plus dialogue (speech plain) in trochaic meter
525—456		Aeschylus	Chorus plus dialogue in iambic trimeter*
496—406		Sophocles (Additional actor; scene painting; less chorus; Euripides)	
?350 B.C.	Modern epic	Complete?	

Evolution of Comedy

Date	Object	Manner	Means
Prehistoric	Improvisations		
Pre-Homeric	Bitter invective (nonfiction)	Phallic songs	Iambic meter
c. 800 B.C.	Homer, *Margites*		
		? Old Comedy** (Aristophanes, 448–380 B.C.)	
6th to 5th Centuries		Epicharmus, Phormis (Dorians; invented plot)	
		Crates (Athenian, c. 450 B.C.)	
		Middle Comedy	
		New Comedy (began c. 336 B.C.)	
?350 B.C.	Modern Satire	(Menander, 342–292 B.C.)	

* Iambic trimeter. From comic tradition?

** This is the logical position of the Old Comedy, *not* the chronological position. Aristophanes logically belongs here; chronoligically, of course, he is after Crates. Note that Old Comedy is to Middle and New Comedy roughly what satyr-play is to tragedy.

tions in Chapter III (ll.9-15). In this sense, it rounds off the historical chapters as the earlier comparisons had rounded off the discussion of means, object, and manner. It is more limited, however, in that it considers only the forms that imitate noble subjects, saying nothing about satire and comedy. The limitation points forward to the discussion of tragedy that is initiated in the next chapter and forms the bulk of Aristotle's first book.

The similarities of the two forms need not detain us long. We are familiar with the fact that epic and tragedy imitate the nobler kinds of subjects and do so in verse. Some editors make the Greek (which is corrupt here) read "imitation of noble subjects in meter," omitting the word "elevated." This has the effect of emphasizing Aristotle's rejection of the theory of the *ars metrica* that there is a fundamental kinship between heroic meter and heroic subject-matter. The position may, however, be too extreme, and the present translation preserves the word "elevated."

Two of the differences between epic and tragedy arise from means and manner of imitation. Epic uses "words alone" and a single meter throughout, while tragedy uses words plus rhythm and harmony and employs a variety of meters in the choral sections. Epic also uses the "mixed" narrative manner of Homer, whereas tragedy uses the third or "dramatic" manner.

A third difference relates to the size and constituent parts of the two forms. Although both imitate the same object (noble actions), the fact that they do so using different means and manners affects the way in which they present their material. Tragedy is intended for stage presentation (manner) and has parts not found in epic (means).

Aristotle's comment on the length of tragedy gave rise during the neoclassic period to the doctrine of unity of time. According to this doctrine, which became literally a critical dogma in seventeenth-century France and in Restoration England, when Aristotle asserts that "tragedy attempts, as far as possible, to remain within one circuit of the sun" (ll. 27-28), he is referring to the time covered by the dramatic action of the play. This interpretation accords with the rationalist bias of neoclassic critics. Spectators, they argued, would not believe in the reality of an action that compressed several days (or, in the case of Shakespearean drama, several years) into a three-hour drama. And if the spectators did not believe in the reality of the action, the tragedy would not have its proper effect. The idea was carried to absurd extremes. In England Shakespeare and his Elizabethan contemporaries were severely criticized, or even rejected as barbarous, for their indifference to unity of time. In France, the controversy took a bizarre turn when critics began debating in earnest as to whether "one circuit of the sun" meant a twenty-four hour day (*jour naturel*) or the twelve-hour period of daylight (*jour artificiel*). The melancholy results of this ingenuity can be seen in the documents relating to the controversy over Pierre Corneille's drama *The Cid,* which used a thirty-hour period. Ideally, of course, the neoclassicists believed that there should be an exact correspondence between the time of the dramatic action and the time of the events being imitated, so that a play lasting three hours would depict historical events that took only three hours to work themselves out.

Unity of time is one aspect of a larger neoclassic concern for what is called verisimilitude—likeness to truth. This concept is based equally on a highly rationalistic theory of what audiences will and will not believe, and a Platonic (not Aristotelian) theory of imitation as copying. It underlies all three "unities" attributed to Aristotle by neoclassic critics—unity of action, unity of time, and unity of space—and also has important implications for characterization, language, and even versification.

The tendency of twentieth-century critics has been to reject the notion that Aristotle formally advocated unity of time in the *Poetics.* In the first place, not all Greek tragedies confine their action to a "single circuit of the sun" in this sense. The *Agamemnon* and *Eumenides* are well-known examples of plays that cover several days. In the second place, neoclassic verisimilitude is a demonstrably false doctrine and one that is inconsistent with Aristotle's explicit rejection of the theory that poetic imitation is (or should be) a "copying" of history.

The most common solution to the problem is summed up in Bywater's observation, "What Aristotle actually says is not a precept, but only an incidental recognition of a fact in the practice of the theatre of his age." This may be satisfactory, for it is true that Greek tragedy has a general tendency to limit the time of the dramatic action, in spite of the exceptions already mentioned. An alternative solution proposed by Else is, however, more in keeping with the context of the passage. We have noticed that Aristotle is discussing how manner and means affect the ways that epic and tragedy present actions. The most obvious influence is manner: Epic is recited in the mixed manner, whereas tragedy is written to be presented by the agents, that is, for performance on the stage. The reference to the length of tragedy, then, may very well be to its length as determined by its manner and not to the imaginary time that elapses between the beginning and the end of its plot. If this is so, the meaning of Aristotle's comparison is both clear and simple. Since Greek theaters had no artificial illumination, a tragic text had to be written so that it could be performed during the daylight, or at least "not depart from this by much" (l. 29). This is not the typical length of a tragedy; it is the maximum length, as determined by the manner. In practice, Greek dramas were much shorter, taking an average of perhaps two hours. Epic, on the other hand, has no theoretical limit. An epic is like a novel in this respect. Some epics can be read (or recited) at one sitting, but the *Iliad* is some 15,000 lines long; and there is nothing *in the epic manner of imitation* to prevent an epic of 30,000 or even 100,000 lines, a point corroborated, for example, by Spenser's *Faerie Queene*.

The fact that there is an inherent limit to the length of tragedy but not of epic is consistent with Aristotle's general tendency to consider the most complex—that is, the most fully determined—form the highest manifestation of the working of first principles. It is also consonant with the fact that epic is more primitive than tragedy in the evolutionary history of Chapter IV. The interpretation has the added merit of clarifying the observation that "At first the poets proceeded in tragedy in the same way as they did in epic" (ll. 31-32). Aristotle states in Chapter IV that the satyr-play was the precursor of tragedy and that the satyr-play used "short plots" and "absurd diction" (l. 67). As Diagram V shows, the satyr-play represents a stage in the development of the tragic manner between dithyramb and formal tragedy. Before tragedy could emerge, poets had to learn how to put together "long plots" and write elevated dialogue. They learned this from Homer, who is the only epic poet to achieve unified plots (Chapter VIII) and also pre-eminent for his use of the dramatic part (dialogue) of the mixed narrative manner. Aristotle does not mention any writers of tragedy before Aeschylus. Evidently, he felt that Aeschylus led the way in incorporating Homeric techniques into tragedy. If we ask in what sense the plays of Aeschylus and his contemporaries are longer than those of later Greek dramatists, the answer is that they are not longer in dramatic time but in the time required to perform them. At the dramatic contests, Greek tragedians presented three tragedies followed by a satyr-play. During the first era of tragedy—the age of Aeschylus—the three tragedies were sometimes combined in single overplot to form a unified trilogy. Evidence is scarce, but what there is indicates that the unified trilogy became increasingly rare in the later era of tragedy. At any rate, the only unified trilogy that has survived is the *Oresteia* of Aeschylus. It is probably significant that the *Oresteia* continues the *Iliad* by telling of the murder of Agamemnon by Clytemnestra (*Agamemnon*); the slaying of Clytemnestra by her son Orestes (*Chœphoroe*); and the cleansing of Orestes by the Athenian tribunal (*Eumenides*). The *Oresteia* is Homeric in size and content. Although far from requiring "one circuit of the sun" for performance, it points toward this maximum limit, in contrast to the rather brief "separate" play. As tragic poets assimilated the Homeric influence more fully, the trilogy lost popularity and was replaced in the contests by three separate tragedies, each requiring about two hours to perform.

The last contrast in Chapter V between epic and tragedy anticipates Chapter VI. There Aristotle demonstrates that there are six "parts" or constituent elements in tragedy: three derived from object of imitation, two derived from means, and one from manner. Epic has only four "parts." Tragedy uses one additional means, song (using rhythm and harmony), and employs spectacle (derived from the dramatic manner). According to Aristotle, we judge a poem in terms of its parts. A reader of tragedy can judge an epic also because he understands all the parts of epic from his exposure to them in tragedy. The reverse, on the other hand, is impossible. A judge of epic can only evaluate four of tragedy's six parts. Hence, Aristotle treats tragedy before epic in spite of the fact that epic preceded tragedy in history. Tragedy includes epic. Most of the important concepts related to epic can be brought up in connection with tragedy. Thus, the discussion of epic can be rather brief without being superficial.

Chapter VI

Chapter VI makes the transition from poetry in general to tragedy. It consists of three major sections: (1) a definition of tragedy, (2) a derivation of six "parts" from this definition, and (3) a discussion of the ranking of the parts. Chapters VII-XXII extend this discussion of the parts. Although it will be necessary to make some preliminary definitions of the parts in the comment on Chapter VI, extended definition is neither necessary nor desirable. The most famous and controversial term to appear in Chapter VI is *catharsis* (l. 10). An interpretation of this term is offered in the course of the commentary. For interested readers, an interchapter is added as an appendix to the commentary. This interchapter offers a brief survey of the problems related to interpreting catharsis and an outline of two lines of interpretation that differ from the line taken in the commentary.

When considering Aristotle's definition of tragedy, the reader will do well to keep in mind the difference between the Greek and modern concepts of what a tragedy is. Today, we usually think of tragedy as a story with an unhappy ending and conforming to the so-called Freytag pyramid, that is, having a rising action,. a climax-reversal, a falling action, and a final catastrophe for the protagonist. The Greek theater-goer, on the other hand, had no such preconceptions. Etymologically, *tragedy* means "goat song" (*tragos,* goat; *ode,* song). The term was traced by Hellenistic critics to the practice of awarding a goat to the winner in dithyrambic contests honoring Dionysus. Later, the term tragedy came to be used as the label for plays performed at the dramatic contests that replaced the dithyrambic contests. On each day of a dramatic festival, four plays were performed, three generally serious in tone and one satyr-play. Tragedy, then, simply meant "one of three plays presented before a satyr-play at a dramatic festival." This definition presupposes no definite tragic structure. Greek tragedies were serious in tone in contrast to the satyr-plays and comedies; but many of them had happy endings. Many, in fact, could be considered romances or even comedies by modern standards, as, for example, *Oedipus at Colonus* and the *Eumenides.* It is clear that Aristotle did not consider tragedy from the modern point of view. In *Poetics* XIII, two of the four possible tragic plots move from "misery to happiness"; and one of Aristotle's favorite plays, *Iphigenia in Tauris,* has a happy ending. It is essential that the reader keep the distinction between the Greek and modern concepts of tragedy in mind as he proceeds beyond Chapter VI.

The Definition of Tragedy
(ll. 1-17)

Sentence one postpones the discussion of hexameter poems (epic) and comedy for a later discussion. Epic is discussed in Chapters XXIII-XXV. Comedy is never discussed in detail. Consequently the present sentence is strong evidence in favor of the contention that Aristotle wrote a second book of the *Poetics* (now lost) dealing at least with comedy.

The formal definition of tragedy is preceded by a promise to formulate the definition "from what we have already said." This is another reminder of the generally deductive tendency of the *Poetics.* Aristotle's definition is not based on the examination of a great many individual tragedies; it is derived from the larger theory of literature found in the preceding chapters. All commentators agree that his definition fulfills this promise, with the single exception of the clause relating to catharsis. Only one recent commentator (Golden) discovers anticipations of the catharsis clause, but Golden's observations are important.[2]

The first part of the definition presents no problems. "Tragedy is . . . an imitation of a noble . . . action" (l. 5) simply repeats

[2] See below, pp. 114-117.

Chapter II. Note that "action" in Aristotle's sense is not "activity," or what the performers do on the stage, but something closer to "process." A play contains a great deal of activity, but as we learn in Chapter VIII, it is based on a single action. This action is, essentially, the process of change that takes place between the beginning and end of the play.

The words "complete" and "having the proper magnitude" add the qualification, already touched on in Chapter IV (l. 66) and at the end of Chapter V, that there is a normative length for tragedy. "Completeness" is further explained in Chapter VII, but it is implicit in the earlier discussion of action. "Language . . . enhanced by each of the kinds of linguistic adornment" alludes to the analysis of means in Chapter I. The "linguistic adornments" are further explained immediately after the definition of tragedy. They are rhythm and harmony, which combine with speech to produce song. They are said to be "applied separately" because they are used only in the choral sections of a tragedy. "In dramatic, not narrative form" alludes to the distinction between the epic and dramatic manners of imitation in Chapter III.

This leaves us with only the catharsis clause: ". . . and achieves, through the representation of pitiable and fearful incidents, the catharsis of such pitiable and fearful incidents." The clause refers to the function of tragedy—what tragedy is supposed to do. Aristotle's Greek is ambiguous, and the translation given here is one of several possible renditions. Like all other translations, it is related to a theory of what the word *catharsis* means. This theory will be explained in the paragraphs that follow. Alternative translations and the theories to which they lead are discussed below in the interchapter.

The most important hint that Aristotle gives regarding how the clause should be interpreted is his statement that his definition of tragedy is based on ". . . what we have already said" (l. 4). If we take this statement seriously, we must begin our analysis with comments found in Chapters I-V. If we can find no relevant comments, we will be forced to conclude that catharsis is not inherent in the broad theory of literature already developed. Because catharsis is generally considered a central Aristotelian idea, this would represent a serious defect in method. Catharsis would have to be considered an afterthought—a key idea that is not implicit in what has gone before.

When we recognize that the catharsis clause in Chapter VI is a brief definition of the function of tragedy, the problem begins to resolve itself. Aristotle has not discussed the function of tragedy previously, but he *has* discussed the function of imitative art in general. At the beginning of Chapter IV, he asserts that imitative art produces pleasure. He then states that the pleasure produced is associated with learning and that it is a pleasure enjoyed by men in general, as well as by philosophers. His examples are significant: They are pictures of corpses and of ugly animals (l. 10). The paradox of pleasure being aroused by objects that are painful or repellent in everyday life anticipates the paradox involved in tragedy. Tragic incidents are pitiable and fearful. They include such events as a man blinding himself, a wife murdering her husband, or a mother slaying her children. When we read of similar events in the daily newspaper, they sadden or repel or outrage us. Yet it remains as true for modern audiences as for audiences of Aristotle's day that when such events are presented in great drama, they produce pleasure.

At the beginning of Chapter IV "pleasure" emerges as the fourth basic element of imitative art, comparable to the Aristotelian final cause. Since Aristotle's formal definition of tragedy in Chapter VI incorporates the first three basic elements (means, object, manner), we would expect him to incorporate the fourth one also. He evidently does this in the catharsis clause. Catharsis should therefore be understood as the tragic variety of the pleasure associated with imitation in general, and equated with the function (*ergon*) of tragedy mentioned at the beginning of Chapter XIII (l. 3). That catharsis is a variety of pleasure is clear from Aristotle's warning in Chapter XIV, "We should not seek every pleasure (*hedone*) from tragedy but only the one proper to it. Since the poet should provide pleasure from pity and fear through imitation, it is apparent that this function must be worked into the incidents" (ll. 12-17). Just as the pleasure produced by imitation is the cause that first impelled men to produce imitative "improvisations," tragic pleasure is both the function of tragedy and the reason why men write, present, and witness tragedies.

Most translations of the catharsis clause in Chapter VI relate catharsis not to the incidents of the play but to the emotions of pity and fear. Bywater's translation is typical: ". . . with incidents arousing pity and fear, wherewith to accomplish its catharsis of such emotions." Such translations relate catharsis to the psychology of the spectator rather than to what happens in the tragedy itself. But the *Poetics* is a *techne*—a technical treatise concerned with the nature of tragedy, not the response of the audience. The present translation reflects this fact by relating catharsis to incidents rather than to emotions. It is supported by Aristotle's statement, already quoted from Chapter XIV, that the tragic pleasure "must be worked into the incidents" (l. 17).

To understand what "catharsis of incidents arousing pity and fear" means, we need to recall two points. First, the Greek word *katharsis* can mean "clarification" as well as "purgation" or "purification."[2] Second, in Chapter IV Aristotle insists at some length that imitation does not produce "pleasure in general" but only the sort of pleasure that comes from learning. He further states that this learning comes from discovering a relation between the object represented and certain universal elements embodied in it. Painting is used to illustrate the idea in Chapter IV; but there is a point-for-point correspondence between what Aristotle says about painting and what he says about literature in Chapter IX, where he tells us that the poet is quite different from the historian in spite of the fact that he may use historical source material. The difference is that the poet orders his plots in terms of probability and necessity —in terms of what "might be" rather than what is. Because of this, "Poetry . . . is more philosophical and more significant than history, for poetry is concerned more with the universal and history more with the individual" (ll. 11-14).

As early as Butcher we find the suggestion that catharsis has something to do with an enhanced understanding of the events depicted in tragedy. The tragic poet presents them free of accidents that obscure their larger meaning, leaving the spectator "face to face with universal law" (Butcher, p. 271). We can now extend Butcher's suggestion. The tragic poet begins by selecting a series of incidents

[2] See Leon Golden, "Catharsis," *TAPA*, XCIII (1962), 55-58.

that are intrinsically pitiable or fearful. He may derive them from history or legend (the usual Greek practice); but he can also follow the lead of Agathon (Chapter IX, l. 33) and make them up, as do most modern writers. He then presents them in such a way as to bring out the probable or necessary principles that unite them in a single action and determine their relation to this action as it proceeds from its beginning to its end. When the spectator has witnessed a tragedy of this type, he will have learned something—the incidents will be clarified in the sense that their relation in terms of universals will have become manifest—and the act of learning, says Aristotle, will be enjoyable.

This interpretation of the catharsis clause in Chapter VI was first proposed by Leon Golden. It has many virtues. In the first place it makes the clause a reference to the *techne* of tragedy, not to the psychology of the audience. Second, it relates catharsis both to the theory of imitation outlined in Chapters I-IV and to the discussion of probability and necessity in Chapter IX. Moreover, it coincides with much current aesthetic theory. This is not to say that the "clarification theory" of catharsis is right because it makes Aristotle agree with modern writers, but rather to say that Aristotle and modern aestheticians both attempt to define the same thing and that one need not be surprised to find parallels in their conclusions. The modern aesthetician might say that a work of art is successful insofar as it achieves "coherence" and that the discovery of this "coherence" is the essential aesthetic pleasure. Francis Fergusson considers "perception" the third and climactic stage both of the tragic action and of the spectator's experience; James Joyce uses the term "epiphany" (a vision of truth) to describe the effect created when a series of apparently disparate events suddenly assume coherence in the mind; and Austin Warren uses the phrase "rage for order" to describe both the object of the poet's quest and the need in the reader that is satisfied by poetry. What these critics have in mind is what depth psychology calls an "insight experience." Aristotle's comments in Chapters IV, VI, and IX indicate that he considered the experience of tragedy a kind of "insight experience": (1) The experience is pleasurable, not painful as the same events would be if experienced in "real life"; (2) the pleasure is the kind that results from learning; (3) the learning is related to the discovery of the relation between the particulars of the plot *via* the universals that make the particulars coherent; and (4) the term designating the tragic function is catharsis—something like "clarification."

We can conclude our examination of the catharsis clause with a few observations concerning "pity and fear." Although in the present interpretation catharsis is not a "purgation" of pity and fear, if the tragic incidents are initially pitiable and fearful and if the end result is "pleasure that comes from learning," the pity and fear must somehow have been eliminated along the way. In Book II, Chapter V, of the *Rhetoric,* Aristotle says that fear is caused "by whatever we see has great power of destroying us, or of harming us in ways that tend to cause us great pain" (1352^a 27). Later in the same chapter, he adds, "Speaking generally, anything causes us to feel fear that—when it happens to or threatens others—causes us to feel pity." In Book II, Chapter VIII, of the *Rhetoric,* he further remarks, "Pity may be defined as a feeling of pain caused by the sight of some evil, destructive or painful, which befalls one who does not deserve it, and which we might expect to befall ourselves . . ." (1385^b 13). In other words, pity and fear are reciprocal. What we pity in others we fear for ourselves, and vice versa. The events of tragedy presumably are pitiable because they seem "undeserved" and fearful because we (the spectators) fear that they may happen to us.

If we limit ourselves strictly to what Aristotle says, he claims only that at the end of a tragedy we learn how the events depicted "might have been," acording to probability or necessity. There is no concept of poetic justice or amelioration here. Oedipus and Hamlet suffer agonies far in excess of what they may have deserved, and the spectator cannot leave their plays with the fatuous observation, "God's in his heaven, all's right with the world." Strictly speaking, his pleasure in learning "how these things came about" has simply displaced his pity and fear of the events themselves—in the same way that his pleasure in learning about, for example, the human body, might displace his disgust for the "pictures of corpses" cited in Chapter IV.

But this interpretation is too narrow. The fact that Aristotle insists in Chapter XIII on a tragic error (*hamartia*) suggests that in a tragedy the spectator can learn something about the relation between character and destiny, no matter how vague the definition of the tragic error in the *Poetics* may be. If so, the spectator may not decide at the end of a fatal tragedy that the hero "deserved what he got," but will at least perceive a coherent relation between the hero's character and his end. This will alleviate (if not eliminate) his pity and by the same token reduce his fear for himself. Note that the alleviation is a byproduct of the learning that produces the tragic pleasure, not its chief object. The point needs to be stressed because Aristotle is often sentimentalized. During the Renaissance, catharsis was often taken to be a moral doctrine requiring the tragic poet to show that bad men come to bad ends, or, alternately, a kind of theological relief arising from the discovery that God's laws operate invisibly to make all things (even suffering) work out for the best. This theological catharsis can be seen, for example, in Milton's *Samson Agonistes,* where Samson's death is presented as a heroic triumph. It persists in Butcher to some degree; and it is still evident in the familiar notion that tragic figures like Lear or Hamlet gain a "nobility" or "self-knowledge" that compensates for their suffering.

Aristotle's concept of catharsis is certainly not didactic. Nor is it theological, although it may have a residual theological element. This element is perhaps traceable—like the problems associated with the term *spoudaios*—to the fact that Aristotle is attempting a rational explanation for something that goes beyond reason. The prototype of tragedy is religious ritual; and the prototype of catharsis is the theophany, or joyous sense of rebirth and communion, that follows the sacrifice and rebirth of the god. The complexity of this experience will be apparent to anyone who attempts to "explain" the experience of communion at the end of the Catholic Mass. Certainly learning is an element. Communion incorporates the worshiper in the divine; he experiences a transcendent sense of the coherence of things. At the same time, he feels a oneness with other men (communion) and a profound renewal (rebirth). If anthropological critics such as Gilbert Murray and Northrop Frye are correct, some of this ritual experience is duplicated in the experience of tragedy. Because Aristotle was a philosopher, not an anthropologist, he treated the experience in intellectual terms—in terms of learning—and many connotations of the experience are necessarily excluded from his treatment. On the other hand, his treatment has the virtue of probing deeper into the experience and coming closer to defining its essential quality than didactic and theological explanations.[3]

The Parts of Tragedy
(ll. 18-46)

In the second paragraph of Chapter VI, Aristotle derives six "parts" of tragedy from his initial definition. In order of importance, they are plot (*muthos*), character (*ethos*), thought (*dianoia*), diction (*lexis*), melody (*melos*), and spectacle (*opsis*). These parts are produced by the basic principles of imitation, manner, means, and object.

Since the dramatic manner requires that the agents, not the poet, perform the imitation, drama includes an element that Aristotle calls spectacle. Note that spectacle is produced by the poet, not by the costume designer or actors. Therefore, "spectacle" refers first and foremost to the way that a dramatic text is written. The text of a play by Shakespeare, for instance, is worked out in a way quite different from the text of a novel. The dramatist cannot describe —he must rely entirely on dialogue; he must adjust dialogue to the actions that he imagines the characters performing; he must provide minor characters such as messengers to relate matters beyond the ken of his major figures; he must avoid actions that are impossible or palpably ridiculous; he must limit the number of characters and avoid placing the same character in two locations at the same time; and so forth. Noteworthy as they are, these adjustments contribute little to the tragic pleasure. Moreover, costumes, masks, stage sets, and actors are not actually spectacle. They merely "realize" the possibilities inherent in the tragic text as written. At the end of Chapter VI, Aristotle observes that tragedy can produce its proper pleasure without being acted and that spectacle is the "least artistic and least essential" element, because "for the realization of spectacle, the art of the costume designer is more effective than that of the poet" (l. 108). We are far more aware of spectacle when seeing a

[3] The interested reader can proceed immediately to the interchapter on alternative theories of catharsis, below, p. 133.

tragedy performed than when reading it, and this awareness comes primarily from the art of production. Aristotle does not dismiss spectacle, but he feels that it is a minor part of the poetic art. This surely explains why he does not devote a chapter to it later in the *Poetics.*

After manner, Aristotle considers means. Means are responsible for two parts of tragedy—melody and diction. Melody is later called "the greatest of the linguistic adornments" (l. 104); but like spectacle, it is an adornment rather than an essential. Because Greek tragedians composed the choral sections of their dramas, and these sections were to be chanted, melody is a part of "the poetic art." It is implicit in the meters used in the choral sections. However, it only achieves its full effect in performance. The reader of a dramatic text will sense the rhythm of the choral odes but not necessarily the harmony, and the formula for melody is rhythm plus harmony. Like spectacle, then, melody is a minor element and must be "brought out" by the performer's art. Aristotle does not discuss it separately.

Diction (*lexis*) is involved in both the choral and dialogue parts of a tragedy. The choral odes were written in a variety of meters a bit like complex stanzas. The dialogue was written in one meter, iambic trimeter, which Aristotle identifies in Chapter IV (l. 73) as being close to the rhythm of everyday speech. Note that Aristotle treats diction as an active concept and relates it closely to the poet's command of the meters. It is not "metrical composition" but "the act . . . of making metrical compositions" (l. 23). This narrow definition is later expanded (Chapters XX-XXII) to include not only metrical composition but also word usage and imagery. On the other hand, Aristotle never broadens his definition to include the expression of concepts in language. Concepts are part of character and thought. This approach is difficult to grasp at first because we usually consider words as vehicles for the expression of concepts, and when reading, we are aware of words before we are aware of concepts. The words seem to "cause" the concepts. Aristotle, on the other hand, is thinking in terms of "the poetic art"—that is, the process of *making* a literary text. This is why he speaks of diction as "the act . . . of making metrical compositions." From Aristotle's point of view, the tragic poet begins with the largest concept (plot), and then proceeds to character and thought. Only after he has worked out these elements does he begin composing the speeches and choral odes. From this point of view, diction is the fourth step in the process, whereas from the reader's point of view it is the first. From either point of view, however, diction is an important element. Accordingly, Aristotle devotes three long chapters to it, Chapters XX-XXII.

Aristotle now comes to the most important of the three basic principles that produce the parts of tragedy—object of imitation. The object of tragic imitation is an action involving agents. The agents, in turn, have two qualities, character and thought (*ethos* and *dianoia*). Since the equivalent in a literary composition to an action in "real life" is plot (*muthos*), object of imitation accounts for plot, character, and thought.

Before proceeding, Aristotle adds an important parenthetical note: "It is, indeed, on the basis of these two considerations that we designate the quality of actions, because the two natural causes of human action are thought and character. It is also in regard to these that the lives of all turn out well or poorly. For this reason we say that the tragic plot is an imitation of an action" (ll. 27-32). Notice that in this passage Aristotle turns momentarily from literature to life. When we consider human actions, we think of them as the outcome of the character and intelligence—the "personalities"—of the individuals who perform them. Character and thought are the "natural causes" of actions. When we read a tragedy, we carry this preconception with us. That is, we think of the actions of Hamlet or Macbeth as the results of the personalities of these two dramatic figures. A little consideration, however, will show that this is false reasoning. Hamlet and Macbeth do not have "personalities" in the sense that living people do. Hamlet and Macbeth exist only as words on a printed page. They have no consciousness, and they do whatever the dramatist requires them to do. The feeling that they are living people whose personalities determine the actions they perform is an illusion. A skillful dramatist like Shakespeare will encourage this illusion by preserving a necessary or probable relation between character and action; but the result is an illusion nonetheless. As soon as we move from the reader's point of view to that of the dramatist creating the tragedy, the illusion vanishes.

The dramatist assigns character to the agents on the basis of the actions they perform.

Aristotle's note thus differentiates between the parallel realms of nature and art. In nature, personality causes action and hence success or failure. In art, action is objectified by plot; and plot can thus be said to "cause" character and thought. If the literary work is skillful, the reader has the illusion that it embodies the cause-effect sequence of real life. We are conscious here of the influence of Aristotle's understanding of the "art of poetry" on his definition of the parts of a drama. His approach, it may be added, is a valuable antidote to naïve criticism. It encourages seeing a literary work from the poet's point of view as a problem in the creation of an illusion. (The alternative is impressionistic criticism in which the critic simply tells "how he felt" when he experienced the work under consideration, or the silly sort of criticism that assumes, for example, that Hamlet had a childhood and then speculates on how his childhood experiences may have affected his psychology.)

Having derived the six parts of tragedy, Aristotle now ranks them in order of importance and offers further comments. Plot is defined as "the arrangement of the incidents" (l. 33). We have turned from action, which is the thing imitated, to plot, which is the artistic objectification of action. Notice, too, that plot is defined (like diction) in active terms. It is not "the story" but the way that the poet arranges the incidents that make up the story. A naïve critic asked to "tell the story" of a work like *Paradise Lost* might begin with the War in Heaven, then move on to the debate of the Fallen Angels in Hell, and then to the temptation of Adam and Eve in the Garden of Eden. This is not the plot of Milton's poem, however. Milton begins *in medias res* with the Fallen Angels in Hell; only at a later point does he narrate the prior action that led to their being in Hell. His plot is *the way he has arranged the incidents,* not the story. A dramatist can arrange the incidents in a story in a great many ways. He can treat some in detail and barely mention or even omit others, as Sophocles omits everything that happened to Oedipus before the plague in Thebes. He can observe chronological sequence, he can distort it, he can use messengers or flashbacks, and so forth. Each arrangement produces a different plot, and a great many plots can be made from the same story. Aristotle's point is an important one that if observed, would greatly improve the general quality of criticism.

Next comes character (*ethos*). We learned in Chapter II that actions necessarily involve agents, and that the agents are "noble or base" (*spoudaioi, phauloi*) as a result of the sorts of actions in which they are involved. Character is now defined, in Chapter VI, as ". . . that element in accordance with which we say that agents are of a certain type" (ll. 34-35). Aristotle's phrasing reminds us that in every age there are certain general categories or "types" whereby human characters are classified. Today, for example, we are familiar with a whole array of "type characters" in popular literature such as the Western or the detective story, as well as with certain allegedly more scientific type concepts such as the extrovert-introvert categories of psychology or the endomorphic, mesomorphic, and ectomorphic categories of popular anthropology.

"Character" is discussed in detail in Chapter XV. For the present, it can be understood as "moral predisposition" based on such factors as age, sex, occupation, and nationality. The term "moral" enters the definition for the simple reason that most of what would now be called psychology was included by ancient and renaissance thinkers under the heading of "moral philosophy." Aristotle's term *ethos* has obvious and intimate relations to his major essay in moral philosophy, the *Nicomachean Ethics*. It has been translated by such terms as *mores* (Latin for "moral customs"), *costumi* (Italian for "customs" or "habits"), and *moeurs* (French for *mores*). All these terms are better, because less amorphous, than English *character*.

While moral philosophy is the general source of Aristotle's concept of character, the popularized formulas for various character types found in classical rhetoric are equally important, if not more so. Book II, Chapters XII-XVII, of Aristotle's *Rhetoric* includes lengthy sketches of various character types divided according to age and social status. Another source of type concepts that Aristotle does not treat but that was important for late classical and renaissance authors is the medical theory according to which one's disposition is established by the preponderance of one or another of the four humours. Ben Jonson is perhaps the most obvious example of a dramatist who bases characterization on the humours theory.

Note one significant but often overlooked point about "character." In literature, or at least in literature as understood by Aristotle, the poet begins with action. Action involves agents, and the key traits of the agents are determined before "character" is added. For example, the most essential trait of Macbeth is determined by the fact that he murders Duncan. He can approach the murder timidly; he can be eager to perform it; he can be merciful; or he can sadistically prolong his victim's agonies. Regardless of the chosen alternative, he must be capable of committing murder, and the murder is determined by the action. Moreover, because the tragic action is what determines that the agents are of the "nobler" sort, Macbeth's elevated stature is not, strictly speaking, part of character at all. Character must therefore be considered a secondary element. To "characterize," the poet adds to the agents the type traits suggested in works such as the *Ethics* or the *Rhetoric*. In general, he should maintain a probable or necessary relation between the agent and the type characteristics assigned. If the agent happens to be a young man (Romeo, for example), the poet will draw on the rhetorical formulas for the "youthful type." Doing this will enhance the reader's or spectator's illusion that the literary work reproduces the causal pattern of real life. Occasionally, of course, the dramatist will vary the formulas by assigning, perhaps, a young man's traits to an old man, as Shakespeare did with Falstaff. This sort of variation can enhance the interest of the drama by creating agreeable surprises.

"And by thought (*dianoia*) I mean that which is found in whatever things men say when they prove a point, or, it may be, express a general truth" (ll. 35-37). Nothing could demonstrate more obviously the difference between modern "character" and Aristotelian *ethos* than the fact that *ethos* is so emphatically distinguished from thought. In what sense are a person's thoughts distinct from his character? The answer is, "In no sense," if by "character" we mean something like "personality." Aristotle's distinction is clear, on the other hand, if we think of character as related to moral type. It is a "given" for the dramatist. Once he has chosen the type traits appropriate to a specific agent, these traits remain constant throughout the drama. A young man remains "youthful"; a warrior remains "military"; a woman remains "feminine." In general, then, character is a constant while thought is related to contingencies and varies from speech to speech. Aristotle's remark near the end of Chapter VI confirms this general interpretation: "Thought is . . . the ability to say whatever is pertinent and fitting to the occasion" (ll. 88-89).

Thought is specifically related to logic in the observation that it is present whenever agents ". . . prove a point, or, it may be, express a general truth" (l. 37). The Greek word translated as "general truth" is *gnome,* a proverb or maxim. Because the *Rhetoric* discusses both methods of proof and the use of maxims, it seems clear that thought, like character, is a concept borrowed from (or at least indebted to) rhetoric. This is confirmed later in Chapter VI when Aristotle states that thought is related to "the arts of politics and rhetoric" (l. 91). In Book II of the *Rhetoric,* Chapters XIX-XXIV, Aristotle discusses the ways that thought manifests itself in speeches. The three most important are by maxims (Chapter XXI), by enthymemes (XXII), and by general "lines of argument" (XXIII) that can be applied to any subject.

Although it is clear how dramatic speeches can use rhetorical techniques, the reference relating thought to "the art of politics" is less clear. Evidently, Aristotle is thinking of the kind of social philosophy embodied in his *Politics,* and the reference may well include an allusion to the *Ethics* as well. Given the problems typically confronting the characters in a tragedy, social philosophy can obviously supply lines of thought appropriate for dramatic speeches. Toward the end of Chapter VI, Aristotle observes that "Our earlier poets made their characters speak like statesmen and our contemporary ones make them speak like rhetoricians" (ll. 92-93). Since "political art" is a subject with a definite content while rhetoric involves general techniques of argument that can be used for any subject, this statement suggests a movement of drama away from emphasis on content and toward emphasis on technique. At any rate, insofar as thought is derived from "political art"—the art drawn on by "statesmen"—it involves general truths; and insofar as it is derived from rhetoric, it involves forms of argument—enthymemes, "lines of argument," and maxims. The truths of "political art" and the arguments of rhetoric are independent of character, but when faced with problems the dramatic personage draws on truths and lines of argument to solve them. The result is speeches "pertinent and fitting to the occasion."

The remainder of the paragraph is summary. The six parts are listed, and their relation to means, manner, and object again pointed out. The paragraph ends with the observation that many poets have used all six parts for "every drama [theoretically]" has them (l. 45). The only problem here is the phrase "every drama." "Theoretically" is a gloss added by the translator but is necessary, for in the next paragraph, Aristotle remarks that tragedy without character is quite possible (l. 59). The idea seems to be that tragedy does not achieve its full potential without all six parts, although tragedies that exploit less than the full potential can be written.

The Ranking of the Parts: Plot and Character (ll. 47-87)

We are now ready to consider the relative importance of the six parts. Establishing this requires further discussion of plot, and especially of the relation between plot and character. Aristotle will not compromise on the primacy of plot. Indeed, he begins his ranking with the assertion that "The most important of these parts is the arrangement of the incidents; for tragedy is not an imitation of man, *per se,* but of human action and life and happiness and misery" (ll. 47-49). The "arrangement of incidents" is the plot. Plot is the analogue in literature to action in life; thus plot can be described as an "imitation of life." Also, a plot embodies change. If its beginning is "happiness," the change will be to "unhappiness," and vice versa. In this sense, plot is an imitation of "happiness or misery."

To explain this concept further, Aristotle turns from literature to life. There is no question concerning his belief that human life is basically process. We are all constantly changing, and the changes that we experience tend toward happiness or unhappiness. This is clear from the *Ethics* as well as from the present passage in the *Poetics.* Since life is a dynamic process, it is possible to say that the "end" of life is action, not stasis. Aristotle's division of modes of human life into "active" and "contemplative" does not contradict this idea, because even the contemplative man seeks to change the quality of his understanding. Character, on the other hand, is a static concept. At a given point in his life a man's character conforms to a certain "kind" (again the reference is to the concept of moral types, not to personality), but the larger action in which he is involved determines his "happiness or misery." This argument is slightly different from the earlier discussion of causality in art and life (l. 29), but its conclusion is similar. In the earlier discussion, Aristotle pointed out that in life character causes action, whereas in art action causes character. Here he adds that even in life, if we judge life in terms of its final results (as we do, for example, when reading a biography), action is the determining factor. A man's character causes individual actions. These in turn contribute to a larger process in which factors other than character also play a part. The larger process is an action; and the result of this action is success or failure, "happiness or the opposite."

We now return to poetry. If action is more important than character in life itself, poetry must preserve this ranking. Action comes first, and "character is included on account of the action." Plot, then, is the "end" or goal of drama, and "The end is . . . the most significant of all" (l. 57).

Having demonstrated the primacy of plot, Aristotle pauses for four additional "confirmations" of his position:

1. His first confirmation is that tragedy is possible without character but not without action. The impossibility of having a tragedy without action is almost self-evident. We have already seen that Aristotle's action means "process," not "activity." A play without action, in his sense, would be a play in which nothing happens —in which there is no difference between the beginning and the end. The episodes in a play are there to bring out the steps in the process that is taking place, so a play without action would provide no basis for the selection and arrangement of the episodes. Episodes could be added or subtracted at will, and presented in any order. The result would be a series of disparate units—a collection of brief sketches rather than a drama. On the other hand, a play with action has a definite form and agents that perform the action. The poet will add "character" if he wishes to achieve the best possible effect, but this is not absolutely necessary.

The point is confirmed by two examples. "Modern poets," says

Aristotle (l. 61), generally write tragedies that are "characterless." The possibility of tragedies without character is proved by the fact that such tragedies exist. The secondary meaning of the sentence is less clear. Many translators use "younger poets" rather than "modern poets" on the assumption that inexperienced dramatists fail to give their characterization the refinements found in the work of more experienced writers. Perhaps. We have seen, however, that "character" is not a matter of refinements but of the use of general type concepts found in "political art" and rhetoric. Actually, a youthful writer is likely to depend on stereotype more than an older man (as, for example, the young Shakespeare's *Comedy of Errors* or *Romeo and Juliet,* which abound in stereotype, in contrast to *Hamlet* or *Lear*). Moreover, to translate the Greek as "younger writers" blurs the relation between this passage and the later one (l. 79) in which Aristotle says that the early writers of tragedy learned diction and character before plot. The second reference is clearly historical. In Chapter IV, we learned that early writers were slow in discovering the art of constructing plots. Satyr-plays used "short plots"; Aeschylus added a second actor; and Sophocles added a third. The pattern in Chapter IV is a movement from the inadequate plots of early poets to the sophisticated plots of later ones. If we extend this pattern to Euripides and Agathon, the inventor of the fictional tragic plot (Chapter IX, l. 33), Aristotle's meaning is plain. It is not "younger poets" but "modern poets" who stress plots heavily. Who the "modern poets" are remains ambiguous. They may be poets of Aristotle's own generation whose work has not survived. What is plain is that they have simply carried the evolutionary tendency apparent in the history of drama from dithyramb to Sophocles to its logical conclusion. Their preoccupation with plot is so great that their dramas can be called "characterless."

A second example is now cited from painting. Polygnotus includes character and action in his pictures; Zeuxis omits character. The existence of the paintings of Zeuxis—like the existence of the tragedies of the moderns—proves that imitation is possible without character.

2. Having shown that drama is possible without character, Aristotle observes that character without action ". . . will not . . .

achieve the end of tragedy" (l. 68). We have already touched on this idea in connection with action. A group of "speeches that show character" is not, in itself, a drama. Unless the speeches are incorporated into a plot, they remain "set pieces," no matter how interesting they may be individually. "Ten great soliloquies" chosen from six plays by Shakespeare, for example, would make extremely entertaining reading, but no one would think of calling them a drama. Even the poorest melodrama has greater unity than ten soliloquies from six plays.

3. The third confirmation introduces two terms that are new to the *Poetics*. These are reversal (*peripeteia*) and recognition (*anagnorisis*). These terms are defined in Chapters X and XI. Aristotle believed that they are the most powerful means of securing the tragic effect. Because they are parts of the plot rather than the characterization, they confirm the idea that plot is more important than character.

4. The fourth confirmation is historical. It is based on Chapter IV. Aristotle says that "Those who attempt to write tragedies are able to perfect diction and character before the construction of the incidents, as we see, for example, in nearly all our early poets." The reference is clearly to the slow evolution of manner of imitation. The first form in the dramatic manner, the dithyramb, emphasized song and dance rather than plot. The satyr-play was an improvement, but its plots were "short" (Chapter IV, l. 67). Only at a rather late date did the dramatic poets discover the technique of "long" plots; and they learned this technique from Homer, not their immediate predecessors.

The discussion of plot and character and the arguments for the primacy of plot are now complete. Aristotle summarizes his conclusions with the statement, "The first principle, then, and, to speak figuratively, the soul of tragedy is the plot, and second in importance is character" (ll. 80-81). In the *De Anima* soul (*psyche*) is defined as "the cause or source of the living body" (415^b 7). It is the formal cause in that it is the principle that determines the harmony of the material parts of an animal or man; and it is the efficient cause in that it is the inner principle of motion. Aristotle is careful to point out that the parallel between the soul and the plot of a drama is an analogy, and we should not, perhaps, push the analogy too far since it implies an organicism somewhat foreign to the *Poetics*. The main point of the analogy is that plot is the form of drama. Aristotle turns to painting for an illustration: "If someone should paint by applying the most beautiful colors but without reference to an over-all plan, he would not please us as much as if he had outlined the figure in black and white" (ll. 82-85). Plot, in other words, is to character what design is to color. Colors splashed on a surface without design produce something incoherent; but a sketch in outline is pleasing even without color. Incidentally, the example may hold true for nonobjective art as well as for the type of painting familiar to Aristotle. In some nonobjective painting the formal element is emphasized almost exclusively, as witness the paintings of Piet Mondrian.

The Ranking of the Parts: Thought, Diction, Song, Spectacle (ll. 88-110)

Only a few observations need to be added to what has already been said concerning the four remaining parts. Thought is related to "political art" and rhetoric, and the point is made that early poets drew on the political art, whereas the moderns draw on rhetoric. To distinguish between thought and character, Aristotle asserts that "Character is that part of tragedy that shows an individual's purpose by indicating . . . what sort of things he chooses or rejects" (ll. 94-96).

We have seen that "character" is a type concept. When the dramatist decides what general traits he will assign an agent, he has decided "what sort of things [the agent] chooses or rejects." A young man, for example, will be more interested in love and honor than security; an old man will avoid unnecessary danger, preferring money and power to adventure. These are the "sorts of things" that each type tends to choose. By definition, speeches that reveal these traits will manifest "character," and speeches involving choice will manifest character with particular clarity. Thought, on the other hand, does not involve character traits. As we have seen, it is related to lines of argument and general truths that exist independently of character: "Thought we find in those speeches in which men show that something is or is not, or utter some universal proposition" (l. 99). A character draws on political and rhetorical truisms and modes of reasoning when attempting to answer questions such as, "What is the truth of this situation?" or "What should I do?" Two corollaries seem justified: (a) Just as there should be a necessary or probable relation between action and character, so there should be a necessary or probable relation between character and thought; and (b) most speeches will involve character and thought simultaneously.

Diction, melody, and spectacle are treated summarily. Diction is the verbal expression of thought. It is "the same whether in verse or prose," because diction as a subject includes all phases of the use of language. This does not, of course, mean that Aristotle believed that a tragedy in prose was possible or desirable, in spite of his coolness toward the *ars metrica*. Melody is mentioned as "the greatest of the linguistic adornments." The term "adornment" emphasizes the fact, evident in the gradual decay of the chorus throughout the history of tragedy, that melody is not essential. Spectacle is dismissed as the "least artistic and least essential" part (l. 106). It is present in the text of a tragedy, but its effect is brought out in performance. It depends on the actors and "costume designer" (l. 109), whose arts contribute as much or more than the art of poetry to its realization. The relative insignificance of spectacle is clear from Aristotle's remark, "the power of tragedy is felt even without dramatic performance and actors" (ll. 107-108).

Summary

In spite of its length and complexity, Chapter VI is relatively simple in outline. It offers (1) a definition of tragedy, (2) a derivation of six parts with brief definitions, and (3) a discussion of the relative importance of each part with emphasis on plot and character. The discussion of plot and character is perhaps the most difficult of the sections because it introduces concepts unfamiliar to the modern reader and because, for the purpose of contrast, plot and character are treated together rather than separately. The reader should formulate working definitions of the six parts from Chapter VI, but each of the four most important parts is examined later in more detail, and their full import will emerge naturally as the discussion proceeds.

Interchapter: The Catharsis Clause of Chapter VI

The catharsis clause in Chapter VI can be translated in several different ways. Each translation is related to a prominent theory of catharsis. In this interchapter, we will consider two traditional theories—the purgation theory and the purification theory. The present text translates the catharsis clause as ". . . through the representation of pitiable and fearful incidents [tragedy achieves] the catharsis of such incidents" (ll. 9-11). This results in the "clarification" theory presented in the commentary proper.

Two other more traditional translations are as follows:

1. ". . . through pitiable and fearful incidents [tragedy achieves] the catharsis of these emotions."
2. ". . . through pitiable and fearful incidents [tragedy achieves] the catharsis of such emotions."

These translations themselves vary according to the translator's interpretation of Greek *katharsis*. *Katharsis* can mean "clarification," "purification," or "purgation."

In general, texts using the first translation interpret catharsis as "purgation," and translations using the second, as "purification." Because the immediate context of the catharsis clause offers no evidence as to which alternative is preferable, each is supported by reference to passages in Aristotle's other works that seem to explain the *Poetics*. "Purgation" is supported by a passage in the *Politics* discussing musical catharsis, and "purification" by passages in the *Nicomachean Ethics*. Each interpretation has a long history, and each still finds favor among readers of the *Poetics*.

The first translation ("catharsis of these emotions") makes catharsis a reflexive process. Tragedy arouses pity and fear and then somehow drives them out. Since Plato had specifically castigated tragedy for arousing pity and making spectators timid (*Republic*, X, 605), this is an attractive solution. It makes Aristotle's theory a direct answer to Plato. Tragedy *does* arouse pity and fear, says Aristotle, but only to drive them out. Here the passage from the *Politics* becomes important. In the last chapter of Book VIII of this work, Aristotle discusses the place of music in the ideal state. Among the benefits, he mentions *catharsis*. When he first uses the term he seems to refer explicitly to the *Poetics,* a fact that has led to speculations that the lost second book of the *Poetics* discussed not only comedy but catharsis as well.[4] Usually *katharsis* is translated "purgation" in the *Politics*. The passage is as follows:

> But we maintain further that music should be studied . . . with a view to . . . purgation (the word "purgation" we use at present without explanation, but when hereafter we speak of poetry we will treat the subject with more precision) . . . in listening to the performances of others we may admit the modes of action and passion also. For feelings such as pity and fear, or, again, enthusiasm, exist very strongly in some souls, and have more or less influence over all. Some persons fall into a religious frenzy, whom we see as a result of the sacred melodies—when they have used the melodies that excite the soul to mystic frenzy—restored as though they have found healing and purgation. Those who are influenced by pity and fear, and every emotional nature, must have a like experience . . . and all are in a manner purged and their souls lightened and delighted. (*Politics,* 1341^b37-42^a17)

The concept of arousing a passion in order to "purge" it is quite emphatic here. The only question is, how does this curious "purgation" operate?

As early as the Renaissance, commentators on the *Poetics* suggested that the mechanism Aristotle has in mind is the ancient homeopathic theory of medicine. According to this theory, "like drives out like"—for example, one applies heat to reduce a fever and cold to cure chills. The theory can be found in Galen. John Milton's preface to *Samson Agonistes* expresses the theory succinctly:

> Tragedy [is] . . . said by Aristotle to be of power, by raising pity and fear, or terror, to purge the mind of those and such-like passions. . . . Nor is Nature wanting in her own effects to make good his assertion; for so in physic things of melancholic hue and quality are used against melancholy, sour against sour, salt to remove salt humours.

The homeopathic theory of catharsis, although it never disappeared, lost ground in the eighteenth century, only to be revived by Jacob Bernays in 1857. Since then it has become the most common theory. Needless to say, it gained immeasurably in popularity with the advent of Freud. Freud and Breuer discovered that by

[4] Possibly, however, the reference is to a later (lost) book of the *Politics*.

helping patients to recall painful childhood experiences under hypnosis, they could alleviate neurotic symptoms. They originally called their treatment "the cathartic method." Freud later abandoned hypnotism, but his mature method of psychoanalysis still involves the reconstruction and "purgation" of painful childhood experiences. Freud believed that the most basic cause of adult anxiety is the Oedipus complex, and he felt that the power of *Oedipus* and *Hamlet* derives from the fact that both plays express this complex in symbolic form. He believed that all great tragedy has some cathartic effect. Freud, then, seems to confirm the notion that catharsis is a purgation, providing a scientific substitute for the inadequate homeopathic explanation on which Aristotle (in this interpretation) relied.

One objection to the homeopathic theory is that it makes Aristotle too reliant on Plato. Plato believed that the emotions ("passions") are threats to the intellect, and his ideal man (as well as the guardians of his republic) must fight constantly to reduce them to a minimum. Aristotle rejected Plato's view. For him, the emotions are as much a part of the human being as the intellect. They are not bad; they are merely capable of harm if not properly controlled. Therefore they must be trained and conditioned. This line of thought gives rise to the purification theory.

Because the advocates of the purification theory think of catharsis as a general principle applying to emotions in general, they prefer to translate the catharsis clause as "catharsis of such [rather than "these"] emotions." This translation transforms pity and fear into representative examples of the whole range of emotions that can be harmful if not properly "purified." The purification theory is attractive because it does not involve "driving out" emotions. After all, pity is usually considered a "good" emotion, and fear—in its proper place—is healthy. They should be controlled, but not "driven out."

The purification theory is usually supported by reference to the argument found in the *Nicomachean Ethics* that mental health is a mean between two extremes. The following passage is typical:

> . . . virtue must have the quality of aiming at the intermediate. I mean moral virtue, for it is this that is concerned with passions and actions, and in these there is excess, defect, and the intermediate. For instance,

> both fear and confidence and appetite and anger and pity and in general pleasure and pain may be felt both too much and too little, and in both cases not well; but to feel them at the right times, with reference to the right objects, toward the right people, with the right motive, and in the right way, is what is characteristic and best, and this is characteristic of virtue. (*Ethics*, 1106b8-23)

In the light of this passage, catharsis is a kind of moral conditioning. When witnessing a tragedy, the spectator learns the proper use of pity, fear, and similar emotions. Like the purgation theory, the purification theory can be considered an answer to Plato, but it is one based on Aristotle's understanding of emotions, not on Plato's.

There are a great many varieties of the purification theory. During the Renaissance Robortello and Castelvetro suggested that tragedy helped to harden or "temper" the emotions. Castelvetro, for example, compared the experience of spectators at a tragedy to the experience of soldiers. Just as the soldiers overcome their fear of death after seeing it frequently on the battlefield, so spectators become hardened to the pitiable and fearful events of life by witnessing them in tragedies. A more liberal version of the purification theory is suggested in Milton's definition in *The Reason of Church Government* of the function of epic: ". . . to calm the perturbations of the mind and set the affections in right tune." In the eighteenth century, critics such as Batteux and Lessing argued that tragedy purifies the spectator by increasing his sensitivity—still purification, but almost the opposite of the kind of purification found in Castelvetro.

The purification theory involves the idea of moral instruction and moral learning. Consequently it underlies various purely didactic theories of catharsis even though they use the word "purgation" to translate catharsis. Thus Giraldi Cinthio wrote in the sixteenth century that tragedy "presents things that involve vice, making them horrible and pitiable . . . [and] purges our spirits of similar passions, and stimulates us to virtue, as in Aristotle's definition of tragedy." This makes tragedy homiletic. We learn from the terrible fates of evil men to avoid the vices they manifest. It is far from Aristotle. A variation on the notion of moral purification is found in Thomas Taylor's introduction to the *Poetics*, published in 1818:

> . . . according to the modern commentators on this treatise, the meaning of Aristotle is that the terror and pity excited by the tragedy purify the

> spectator from terror and pity. . . . This cannot be the meaning of Aristotle, as it contradicts what he asserts in his *Ethics*. . . . Aristotle meant to say, that *the terror and pity excited by tragedy purify the spectator from those perturbations which form the catastrophe of the tragedy*. Thus in the *Ajax* of Sophocles, the terror and pity excited by the catastrophe purify the spectator from anger and impiety toward divinity; and in a similar manner purification is effected in other tragedies.

After Bernays the purification theory lost ground among scholars. However, Butcher's interpretation of catharsis, while paying lip service to purgation, actually leans to purification. Butcher says, "Let us assume, then, that the tragic *katharsis* involves not only the idea of emotional relief, but the further idea of purifying the emotions so relieved." He ends with the statement: "The poets found out how the transport of human pity and human fear might, under the excitation of art, be dissolved in joy, and the pain escape in the purified tide of human sympathy."

As pointed out in the commentary, the trouble with both the purification theory and the purgation theory is that they wander off into speculations (often tenuous) about the psychology of the audience. It will bear repeating that Aristotle is writing about the art of poetry, not psychology. In spite of the attractions of purgation and purification, the best translation for the catharsis clause is "catharsis of these incidents." This translation has recently been defended by Else—who argues that catharsis is related to the tragic *hamartia* on the one hand and the tragic discovery on the other—and by Golden, who proposes the clarification theory found in the commentary.

Chapter VII

Chapters VII-XIV form an extended discussion of plot. They move in a simple path from most general to most specific considerations. Chapter VII discusses wholeness and magnitude. Chapter VIII discusses unity. Chapter IX carries this discussion forward to a consideration of the sources of poetic unity, the principles of probability and necessity. Chapters X-XI treat types of plots and the two basic elements of plot, recognition and reversal. Chapter XII lists the "quantitative parts" of plot. Chapter XIII considers the question of which type of plot most fully realizes the potential of the tragic form; and Chapter XIV deals with two subsidiary questions —plot versus spectacle, and the nature of the "tragic deed."

Chapter VII begins with a transition sentence: "Now that we have defined these terms, let us discuss . . . the arrangement of incidents." Aristotle then repeats the first part of the definition of tragedy in Chapter VI as a convenience to the reader: "We have posited that tragedy is the imitation of a complete and whole action which has a proper magnitude." This sentence gives him the two subjects of the chapter. It is also the first reference to what neoclassic critics called unity of action. As will become apparent, unity of action is a truly Aristotelian concept, unlike unity of time and place. The neoclassic tendency to equate unified action with action centering around a single individual and the neoclassic rejection of subplots in the name of unity of action are, however, questionable extensions of the Aristotelian concept. Aristotle clearly assumed that most actions center around a single protagonist, and he had no experience of subplots. On the other hand, his concept of action is not biographical, and a social "action" involving the interrelation of several important figures is quite possible given the framework that he establishes. In fact, he appears to recognize this possibility in Chapter VIII. Although the *Iliad* involves many conflicting characters and groups, he explicitly praises it (l. 19) for its unity of action.

Wholeness (ll.3-17)

The phrase "complete and whole action" reminds us of the difference between Aristotle's action (*praxis*) and "activity." Action does not refer to the various things that characters "do" in the course of a play and much less to the movements of the actors, which if they enter the *Poetics* at all, do so in relation to spectacle. The characters in a play "do" a great many things, but the sort of action Aristotle has in mind is single and complete. Used in this sense, action must be a comprehensive concept referring to the movement of the entire play from its beginning to its end. It is not the result of one force but the result of many. In a Greek play the action is usually dominated by a single protagonist such as Prometheus, Ajax, or Oedipus; but even in a Greek play the over-all movement involves the interaction of several characters. The point is much clearer in the *Iliad,* or in an Elizabethan play like *King Lear,* which has several important characters and a subplot. Action, then, is process and the process involves several forces working together.

Action is represented in literature by plot, which has already been defined as an "arrangement of incidents." The incidents are the raw material whereby the plot is objectified; without incidents there would be nothing. By selecting and arranging the incidents the poet reveals both the steps in the process that takes place between the beginning and the end of the play, and also the principles that cause the process to occur.

The most important requirement of a plot is that it be complete. This means that it must have a beginning, middle, and end. Aristotle defines these terms. A beginning is an incident that does not of necessity follow anything else but leads to something that follows; a middle has antecedents and at least one "following" incident; and an end has antecedents but no "following" incidents.

These definitions are extremely abstract. We may well ask in what sense any incident marks a "beginning" or an "end." In life everything that happens has antecedents and consequences. Consideration of the Christian religious drama of the Middle Ages suggests, in fact, that its writers were baffled by this problem and solved it only by beginning with the beginning of time and ending with the destruction of the world. Christian religious drama, that is, is typically "cosmic." This is apparent not only in dramas that are very close to ritual but also in such elaborate productions as the English *Corpus Christi* plays, which begin with the Creation and end with the Last Judgment.

More self-conscious drama often solves the problem of beginning and ending by the human life span, or by social convention. Birth and death are obvious and natural points for the beginning and ending of a narrative. The trouble with this solution is that it leads the dramatist to the loose "cradle-to-grave" sort of biographical narrative. Aristotle recognized the prevalence of this type of narrative among epic writers, and he complains in Chapter VIII that it produces a false kind of unity. One alternative is to use social conventions for beginnings and endings, as, for example, "They were married and lived happily ever after." This, however, is as arbitrary as birth and death. It relies on something extrinsic to the action—a convention—rather than the action itself.

Another analysis of action, which seems more in accord with Aristotle's approach, is possible. Although life is never stable, societies and individuals tend to seek stability. It often happens that after a period of relative equilibrium something happens to upset the balance, and that later, after the disrupting factor has worked itself out, a new stability, more or less satisfactory than the former one, is achieved. A rightful king is murdered, and society is plunged into turmoil until the usurper is punished and another rightful king restored to the throne. This is the formula for the relatively short action of *Macbeth* as well as for the enormous action of Shakespeare's history cycle extending in eight plays from *Richard II* to *Richard III*. Alternately, a man is shipwrecked on his return from a war and must live as a wanderer and outcast until he finally regains his homeland—the formula for the *Odyssey*. These are actions in Aristotle's sense. A stable situation is disrupted. A disequilibrium sets in that causes change. The change continues until a new equilibrium is established, at which point the action is concluded. Clearly, just as there are many actions in this sense in the life of a society, so there can be many actions in the life of an individual.

It follows that the "beginning" of a plot is the incident that initiates the process of change. In life all incidents have antecedents; but a plot is concerned with only one action. The initiating incident can—from the point of view of art—be said to be without antecedents. It is ". . . not, by necessity, after anything else, but after it something naturally is or develops" (l. 9). If the initiating incident can be said to be without antecedents, the final incident, which depicts the result of the action, can be described with equal justification as without consequences. Again, in life every incident leads on to something else—to a new action. But in a plot the final incident is simply the end. It marks the completion of the action represented. "Beginning" in the *Poetics* thus means the first incident of the play, and "end" the final incident. The "middle" is everything between the first incident and the last.

Aristotle also tells us something about the content of the beginning and end. If we should attempt to describe "actions" in society or in human life in the most general terms, we would say that they tend to change things for the better or for the worse. At the end of Chapter VII, Aristotle says that the proper magnitude for tragedy is one that allows "for change to occur from bad fortune to good or from good fortune to bad" (l. 45). This statement is parallel to the statement in Chapter VI (l. 49) that tragedy is an imitation of "happiness and misery." It characterizes two forms of tragic plot. In the first form, the beginning is "bad fortune" and the end "good fortune." We can call this a "fortunate" plot. The second begins with "good fortune" and ends with "bad fortune." This can be called a "fatal" plot.[1] The fortunate plot is characterized by a rising action; the fatal plot has a falling action. In the first, things change for the better; in the second, for the worse. In a fortunate plot the situation prior to the initial incident is unsatisfactory. When we meet Ulysses in the *Odyssey,* for example, he has been an outcast and a wanderer for ten years. The initiating incident begins the process that will eventually result in his restoration to wife and kingdom. Although the *Odyssey* is leisurely and has many digressions, its action moves more or less constantly toward this goal. In a drama about the return of Ulysses, the upward motion would be much more emphatic because of the greater need for economy. Finally, when Ulysses has achieved "good fortune," the action is complete. The implication is that the "good fortune" of Ulysses will continue indefinitely. Dante's continuation of his saga merely proves that in one life many actions can happen, just as we know that the same marriage may be the end of a comedy and the beginning of a tragedy. Rosalind, for example, may marry Orlando at the end of *As You Like It* only to reappear as Nora at the beginning of *A Doll's House.*

[1] The terms "fatal" and "fortunate" are adopted from Gerald Else.

The two plots that Aristotle has described so far are diagrammed below:

"Fortunate" Plot

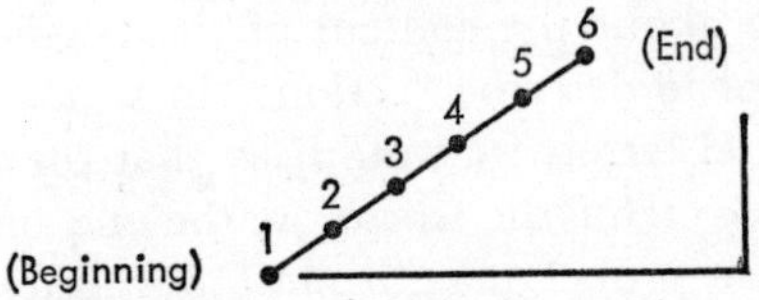

"Fatal" Plot

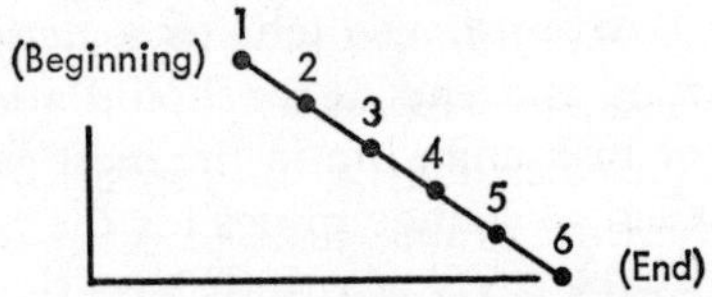

Incidents 1 and 6 in the diagrams are the beginning and end, while incidents 2-5 stand for the "middle." The difference between the beginning and end is symbolized visually by the short legs of the two triangles. They represent the change that occurs as the plot moves toward good or bad fortune, and hence are a measure of the action that the plot imitates. A sequence of incidents that could be represented by a horizontal line would be a sequence without action. The long legs of the two triangles schematically symbolize the dramatic time required for the action to complete itself. This can be a few hours as in *Oedipus,* a few days as in *Othello,* or several years as in *Richard III* or *The Winter's Tale.* Again we are reminded that Aristotle's reference to the normative length of a tragedy in Chapter V is best understood as a reference to duration of performance, not to the dramatic time of the story.

Magnitude (ll. 18-47)

The concept of magnitude is complementary to that of wholeness. Aristotle begins by relating it to the idea of the beautiful (*kalos*). Beauty involves two elements, "proper arrangement" and "magnitude" (l. 22). Both must be present if an object is to be beautiful. Proper arrangement has been dealt with in relation to wholeness. Unless a drama has proper arrangement it will lack wholeness. It will be incoherent, and hence "unbeautiful."

The concept of magnitude places a limit on possible arrangements of incidents. Even if a work has "proper arrangement," it will fail if it is so long and involved that the spectator or reader cannot appreciate the relation of the parts to the whole. This observation holds true for all literature. Many readers, for example, are unable to appreciate Browning's *Ring and the Book* or Joyce's *Finnegans Wake* simply because to appreciate them requires holding so much in the mind at one time. It is especially pertinent, however, to drama, since a spectator cannot turn back to an earlier chapter to recall the name of a minor character or refresh his memory concerning "prior events." This is confirmed by the fact that wherever drama has appeared, it has tended to find a normative length for its performance. Most successful dramas last from two hours (the approximate norm for Greek drama and modern cinema) to four (the outside limit for an Elizabethan drama). A play like Eugene O'Neill's *The Iceman Cometh* stretches the capacity of the audience almost to the limit, and a play like Victor Hugo's *Cromwell* (approximately four hundred pages) is closet drama, for reading rather than performance.

If there is an upper limit to magnitude, there is also a lower one. Dramas that are extremely brief (for example, Yeats' *Plays for Dancers*) may be intriguing because of their poetry, but they cannot produce the effect of a full-scale work. Aristotle illustrates the point by reference to animals. The reference is an analogy and does not imply a quasi-romantic theory of organicism. Its purpose is simply to show that in both nature and art, improper size makes a sense of the whole impossible: "Neither would a very small animal be beautiful (for one's view of the animal is not clear . . .), nor is a very large animal beautiful (for then . . . the unity and wholeness of the animal are lost . . . as would happen, for example, if we should come across an animal a thousand miles in length)" (ll. 23-30).

The emphasis of the analogy is on magnitude in the sense of physical size. The magnitude of a plot, however, is determined by the number of incidents, not the number of words in the text. Aristotle's idea of magnitude cannot, therefore, be separated from the idea of complexity. A two-hour play can contain so many characters and incidents as to be confusing, while a four-hour play can be simple to the point of vacuity.

Aristotle ends with three observations on how proper magnitude should be determined. The first is a pragmatic rule based on the capacity of the audience: "There must be a proper length in regard to plots, and this is one that can be easily taken in by the memory" (ll. 33-34). The second is not a rule but a warning. One way that the length of a Greek drama was determined was by the amount of time allotted by the judges of the dramatic contests. Obviously this is arbitrary and has nothing to do with the art of poetry. If the judges decided to present one hundred tragedies, says Aristotle, the duration of each tragedy would be determined by "water clocks" (l. 39).

The third observation is the most important one, for it relates magnitude to poetic craftsmanship, to "the very nature of the subject itself" (ll. 40-41). The general rule is that the magnitude should be as great as possible, short of becoming unclear. In other words, the dramatist should approach the upper limit but not pass it. But this is *too* general. It is arbitrary in the sense that it does not take into account the fact that different plots have different requirements. The precise rule is that the magnitude should be "whatever . . . is required for a change to occur from bad fortune to good or from good fortune to bad through a series of incidents that are in accordance with probability or necessity" (ll. 43-46). In other words, it is the plot itself, not the audience or the judges, that should determine the magnitude. Each drama is a unique problem in poetic craftsmanship, and what is valid for one may be invalid for another. This is a rule, but it is the very opposite of the "rules" that neoclassic critics ascribed to Aristotle.

Chapter VIII

Unity is closely related to wholeness. Aristotle begins Chapter VIII by rejecting the idea that just because several incidents occur in the life of one man they are part of the same action. As we have seen, an action is a process of change from bad fortune to good, or the reverse. Many such changes may occur in the life of a single man; in fact, two such changes may go on more or less simultaneously. For example, a man's son may die and at the same time he may make important scientific discoveries. One "action" in his life will be the process whereby he adjusts to the loss of his child; another will be the process whereby he gains a Nobel prize. Both actions can, of course, be incidents in a larger action; or they can be entirely separate. In fact, one might become the basis of a "fatal" and the other of a "fortunate" plot.

Aristotle illustrates the point about unity by contrasting two biographical epics with the *Odyssey* and *Iliad.* It is significant that the titles of both biographical epics are derived from the names of their heroes—Hercules and Theseus. Although neither epic has survived, Aristotle evidently has in mind narratives that move chronologically through all or most of the numerous legends associated with lives of their heroes. Homer, on the other hand, is interested in actions, not men. Although the *Odyssey* is named from its protagonist, it is by no means a cradle-to-grave biography. It does not begin *ab ovo* but *in medias res;* and it is concerned not with Ulysses (Odysseus) *per se* but only with "the return of Ulysses." We have already observed in connection with Chapter VII that the return of Ulysses is an action that produces a "fortunate" plot moving from "bad fortune" to good. The *Iliad* is an even more obvious case in point. Its title could be roughly paraphrased as "The Fall of Troy"; and its action is a composite of several forces, of which "the wrath of Achilles" is only one. Aristotle returns to the *Iliad* in Chapter XXIII. There he adds that Homer did not use the whole Trojan war as his action, but merely "one part" (l. 26). The remark confirms—if confirmation is necessary—Aristotle's emphatic differentiation between narrative based on unity of action and biographical narrative.

The comment in Chapter XXIII on the *Iliad* may also clarify Aristotle's reference to Homer's omission of the wounding of Ulysses on Parnassus (l. 14). The reference is puzzling because this episode appears in the *Odyssey* (XIX, 392-466). In Chapter XXIII Aristotle notes that although Homer based his action on one part of the Trojan war, he introduced episodes from several other parts. These episodes are digressions, and in Chapter XXIV Aristotle remarks that epic gains in magnitude and variety by the introduction of such episodes. This ability of epic to admit pleasing digressions is one of its chief differences from tragedy. The digressive episodes remain, however, distinct from the action. Evidently, in "making" the *Odyssey* (that is, in "making" the plot on which the *Odyssey* is based), Homer omitted certain incidents in Ulysses' life that were not part of the action, but later introduced several of them—including the wounding on Parnassus—as digressions. Underlying this line of thought is the notion that biography proceeds chronologically from the beginning to the end of a man's life (*ab ovo*), while poetry, imitating not men but actions, can handle time much more freely. To begin *in medias res* is to begin in the middle of the history of a man's life but at the beginning of an action in that life.

The chapter ends with a summary that combines observations made concerning wholeness in Chapter VII with those concerning unity: "Necessarily, then, just as in other forms of imitation, one imitation is of one thing, so, also, a plot, since it is the imitation of an action, must be the imitation of an action that is one and whole" (ll. 19-22). One corollary is added. It is an important corollary for it provides a simple, decisive criterion for distinguishing between unified and disunified plots: "It is necessary that the parts of the action be put together in such a way that if one part is transposed or removed the whole will be disordered and disunified" (ll. 22-25).

Plot has been defined functionally in Chapter VI as "an arrangement of incidents." We have seen that there are two general types of plot, the "fortunate" and the "fatal." We can symbolize these types in two diagrams:

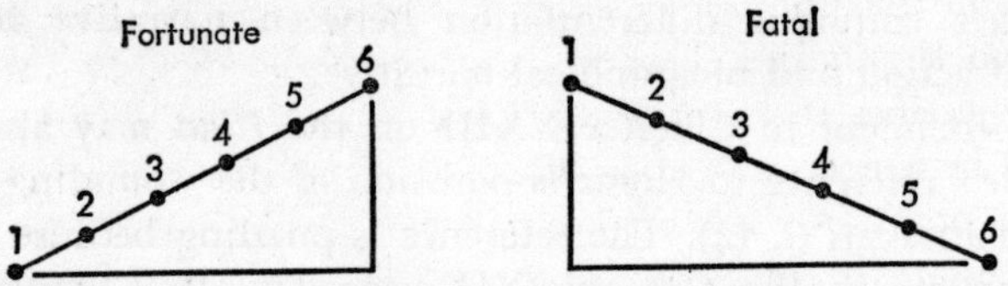

Note that in both diagrams the episodes are arranged so that they objectify the process of change from "misfortune" to good fortune or the reverse. In the fortunate plot, for example, each episode is closer to the end ("good fortune") than the one preceding it. Now consider Aristotle's statement about transposition. If we were to transpose episodes 1 and 6 in the fortunate plot, we would alter the beginning and ending and hence objectify totally new action; whereas to change the order of the episodes in the "middle," although it would not change the action entirely, would certainly obscure it:

(a)

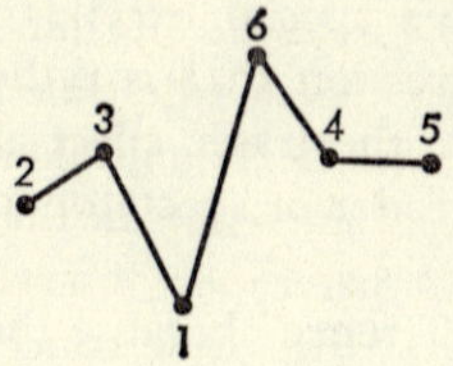

(b)

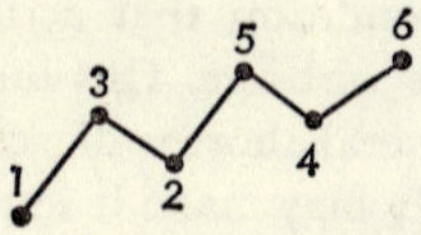

In the first plot, episodes 2 and 5 have been moved from their proper positions so that they seem to be the beginning and ending, respectively; in the second, rearrangement of episodes has made the plot into a series of abrupt and confusing "ups" and "downs." Although the general movement of the plot is "fortunate," the arrangement of episodes implies on two occasions that the movement is "fatal." If this is clear in the abstract, it becomes still clearer when we recall that the episodes are supposed to be related to each other by probability or necessity. If, for example, 3 is the probable or necessary antecedent of 4, the arrangement 1-3-2-5-4 in the second plot will lack probability or necessity. And if probability or necessity are understood as the underlying principles that make the plot coherent, the second plot will simply be "incoherent."

The notion that the omission of an episode will "make a difference" is also significant. The incidents are the elements whereby the plot objectifies the process of change that is the action. Each one should be a necessary or probable result of the one preceding and should point in turn to the episode that follows. If an episode is necessary or probable in this sense, to omit it will leave a gap in the plot. The plot will objectify only a part of the action; and the reader or spectator will be left wondering, for example, how we have suddenly moved from episode 3 to episode 5.

On the other hand, if the omission truly "makes no difference," there are two possibilities. First, the action may be perfectly clear without it. In this case it is a digression. Digressions provide variety and ornament for the epic, but they are inartistic in a drama. In Chapter XXVI, Aristotle observes that compression is the special virtue of tragedy. Tragedy achieves its function with greater economy than epic and for this reason it is superior. The greater economy of the form, we might say, makes for greater intensity of effect. A digression—an episode that "makes no difference"—thus violates the condition that accounts for tragedy's special excellence. It is excess verbiage. Obviously, a single digression that is rather long, or several shorter digressions, will dilute the tragic effect and ultimately may make it impossible for the reader or spectator to gain a sense of the whole.

Second, an episode may "make no difference" because the narrative in which it appears is not an imitation of an action. If there is no difference between the beginning and the end of a drama, there is no action. This kind of narrative can be symbolized by a horizontal line.

Obviously in this case the episodes could be arranged in any order, and episodes could be omitted or added more or less at will. For example, 3-2-1-6-5-4 would be just as satisfactory as the first arrangement. So would 1-1a-1b-2-3-5-6. Nothing really makes any difference because no action occurs, and the selection of incidents is entirely arbitrary. If we must call such an arrangement a plot, it is an extreme form of the "episodic plot" mentioned at the end of Chapter IX; but logically speaking, it is not a plot at all.

It will be helpful to turn briefly from theory to practice. If, for example, we work out the plot line of *Paradise Lost* we are struck by the fact that Milton's sequence violates the chronology of the story. He begins *in medias res* with the debate of the Fallen Angels in Hell rather than with the War in Heaven, which he introduces in Books V-VI through Raphael's narrative to Adam. Why did he choose this sequence, and would a rearrangement of the episodes "make any difference"? The answer to the first question is that beginning in Hell (a) places emphasis on the initiating incident leading to the expulsion of man from Paradise, the plan of the Fallen Angels to attack God by destroying His latest creation; and (b) brings out the heroic stature of Satan, man's antagonist. To have begun *ab ovo* with the War in Heaven would have obscured both points. First, it might have suggested that *Paradise Lost* is a quasi-biographical poem about "the adventures of Satan" rather than a representation of "the fall of Man." Second, since the War in Heaven ends in a disastrous defeat, beginning with this conflict would have emphasized the weakness of Satan, not his strength.

Hamlet provides another example of transposition of incidents "making a difference." In Shakespeare's play, Hamlet is profoundly disturbed by the Ghost's command that he slay Claudius, by his feeling that the kingdom of Denmark is decaying and by his mother's remarriage. His melancholy leads him to consider suicide, and his deliberations are expressed in the famous "To be or not to be" soliloquy. After speaking the soliloquy he meets Ophelia. His conversation with her is brutally harsh, and he leaves her in tears. The necessary or probable relation between the soliloquy and the interview is clear: Hamlet is deeply disturbed, and this disturbance leads him to abuse a woman he loves. When Sir Laurence Olivier prepared a movie version of *Hamlet,* he transposed the two incidents to make the interview with Ophelia precede the soliloquy. The effect of the transposition is striking. Although the text (the speeches; that is, character, thought, and diction) remains Shakespeare's, the rearrangement of episodes changes the playwright's meaning. The new arrangement suggests that Hamlet is tempted to suicide because he finds Ophelia lacking in understanding. The rearrangement of episodes thus threatens to change the play from high tragedy to a melodrama about an adolescent having troubles with his lady friend! Olivier's treatment of the sequence of episodes in *Hamlet* illustrates two points. First, that plot is, as Aristotle insists, more important than character, thought, and diction; and, second, that arrangement of incidents is essentially a device to bring out necessary or probable relations. Moreover, if the relations brought out by the soliloquy-interview sequence are correlated to the over-all action of *Hamlet,* to change the sequence not only changes the relations brought out but also introduces relations that are *not* correlated to the over-all action. Coherence is lost, and the revised version of the play becomes a little more "episodic" than the play that Shakespeare wrote.

Finally, we may consider plots that are nearly episodic, so that episodes can be added, removed, or transposed without making very much difference. Such plots do not need to be considered "bad"; they merely fail to make use of the full potential of plot. The picaresque novel is characteristically episodic; but many picaresque novels are fun to read and a few have become literary classics. The picaresque formula is basically to involve a young, rather roguish man in a series of adventures. The adventures are interesting in themselves. Usually they also reveal a good deal about the social conditions of the time when the story takes place. There is no set number or order for the adventures. The strategy of the picaresque novelist is to create as many adventures as he can, short of risking boring his reader, each adventure being like a separate sketch or short story. The inclusion of several adventures in the same novel is justified simply by the fact that they happened (or are imagined to have happened) to the same person. In fact, they resemble the biographical technique Aristotle evidently had in mind when he criticized epics based on the lives of Hercules and Theseus. Dickens' *Pickwick Papers* is a good modern example of this type of story. Each adventure of Pickwick and company was originally written for magazine publication; and when combined in a book, the adventures are still much more like brief sketches than parts of a larger unity. We read them not for the over-all action (there is none), but for the humorous glimpses of English types and scenes that they offer. An example of a work that is more unified than *Pickwick Papers* but still episodic is Mark Twain's *Huckleberry Finn*. Twain's novel has a beginning (Huck and Jim commence their journey) and an "end" of sorts, when Huck decides not to return Jim to slavery. But the episodes between these points have no very clear design or progression. They all tend to illustrate one point—the depravity of human society—but their order could be changed and episodes could be omitted or new ones added without changing the effect of the whole. In Mark Twain's sequence, for example, the episode of the *Walter Scott* (Chapter 12) is followed by the episode of the *Grangerfords* (Chapters 17 and 18), which is followed by the

Duke and Dauphin (Chapters 19 and 20), and the slaying of Boggs (Chapter 21). There is no reason why these episodes could not be rearranged. Moreover, although we would hate to lose any of them, we would not have missed one if it had never been written—no gap would be left in the action—while, conversely, there is no theoretical reason why Mark Twain could not have added two or three more episodes between Chapters 12 and 21 if he had wished.

Aristotle's criterion for a unified plot is a valuable one. It provides a most effective tool for critical analysis of plot. It also complements Aristotle's emphasis on the primacy of plot.

Chapter IX

Chapter IX is especially rich in fundamental ideas about art. Logically, it moves from the discussion of unity as a general concept to the question of the qualities that relate the incidents in a well-ordered plot. These are probability (*eikos*) and necessity (*ananke*). They are present in poetry, says Aristotle, but not (or not normally) in history. Their presence justifies the statement that poetry is "more philosophical" than history and that its statements are "more concerned with the universal" (ll. 11-14).

The idea that poetry makes universal statements is the prime source, in the *Poetics,* from which renaissance and neoclassic critics derived a didactic theory of literature. In the *Apology for Poetry,* for example, Sir Philip Sidney quotes from Chapter IX to show that poetry combines the particulars of the historian with the universal moral principles of the philosopher to produce "excellent images of the virtues and the vices." The historian, says Sidney, often shows tyrants leading happy and successful lives, while good men are unjustly punished. Moral philosophy, on the other hand, teaches that virtue leads to happiness and vice to unhappiness. Because poetry is more philosophical than history, it can couple the general precept with the particular example so that the tyrant is punished and the virtuous man rewarded. We have already considered this theory in relation to the idea that catharsis is moral purification. It is not Aristotelian, and it represents a misreading of Chapter IX, as well as Chapter VI.

Chapter IX begins with a comment on probability and necessity. This results in a distinction between poetry and history. The distinction leads, in turn, to a discussion of the way that dramatic poets use history. Underlying this discussion is the difference between Aristotle's concept of imitation and the "copy" theory found in Plato's *Republic* and rejected as early as Chapter IV (ll. 15-18). It leads to the well-known observation that the poet is "more a poet of his plots than of his meters." The chapter ends with two corollaries: (1) that plots lacking necessity or probability are "episodic"; and (2) that plots which employ chance rather than necessity or probability should be constructed to seem as though they had these qualities.

Necessity and Probability
(ll. 1-5)

What does Aristotle mean by "necessity or probability"? He gives us a little help when he remarks that plots having these qualities show events "not . . . [as they] have actually happened . . . but . . . as [they] might occur" (ll. 2-3).

The most obvious answer to the question is that necessity and probability are principles of causality. "A" follows "B" in the real world either because it must, or because it is a probable consequence, or because of chance. In the *Nicomachean Ethics* (1139^a), and again in the *Rhetoric* (1356^b-57^a), Aristotle remarks that necessary relations are mostly restricted to nonhuman affairs, whereas social relations are mostly governed by probability. The distinction seems to be between the theoretical sciences (for example, mathematics), which are deductive, and areas like politics and morality, the principles of which are inductive and therefore only statements of what usually happens—of what is probable but not necessary. A triangle must always have 180 degrees; but it is only probable that a tyrant like Macbeth will come to a bad end.

Among other things, this line of thought explains why Aristotle regularly uses not one but both terms when discussing tragic plots. Necessity is not merely a "more rigorous" kind of probability, it is something quite different. An event that is "necessary" is not probable, and vice versa. Accepting the difference between the two, certain commentators have attempted to relate them to specific aspects of drama. Telford, for example, suggests that at episode 2 and in the sequence 1-2-3, the relation between 1 and 2 is necessary because 1 is in the past; but the relation between 2 and 3 is only probable since 3 has not actually happened. He further speculates that pity is related to necessary events, because pity is appropriate only for things that have happened, and fear to probable events, since we only fear what may happen but has not yet happened. An additional speculation concerning necessity and probability is that character is "necessary" since it is a constant throughout the drama, whereas thought is "probable" because it is related to specific events —to contingencies. An agent with the character of an "old man" cannot suddenly grow young in the course of a play; but he will use a variety of different concepts, lines of argument, and maxims when attempting to "reason out" different situations.

These and similar speculations are elegant but extremely abstract. They require a great deal of reference to Aristotelian theory outside the *Poetics,* and they are suspiciously schematic. Their most serious defect, however, is that they assume that the kind of causality operating in nature also operates in art. We have already noted several passages in which Aristotle stresses the difference between nature and art, and in the present passage the distinction is echoed in the emphasis on the difference between history and poetry. Equally important, in Chapter IX we are discussing plots and the relations among incidents, not the actions of living men. In the sequence of episodes 1-2-3, 1 may be presented by the dramatist as the "cause" of 2 and 2 the "cause" of 3 in the simplest, most direct sense of the term. This, however, is by no means always true. The arrival of the messenger in *Oedipus* is the immediate cause for the blinding episode, but what is the cause of the messenger's arrival at just the right moment? Again, in Shakespeare's *Henry IV, Part I,* the scenes alternate between the revels of Hal, Falstaff, and company in the Boar's Head Tavern and scenes in the "rebel camp" featuring Hotspur and his cohorts. In what sense does a scene in the Boar's Head Tavern "cause" a scene at the rebel camp? The answer is plainly, in no sense; yet *Henry IV* is a tightly constructed and effective play. Finally, when we think of causality in drama we usually think of character "causing" action. Yet we have seen that for Aristotle, the action comes first and then the characterization. Therefore the relation between episodes cannot be causal in the sense that the relations between events in real life are often causal.

From Aristotle's point of view, the dramatist begins with the largest possible outline of the plot. This is the "universal form" of the play discussed and illustrated by reference to *Iphigenia in Tauris* near the beginning of Chapter XVII. The form is "universal" because it represents in outline the action being imitated—the change that will occur from bad to good fortune or the reverse. In doing this it also identifies the beginning and end of the play. The next problem is to select incidents for development into the episodes that will comprise the "middle" of the play. In the completed structure the design of the episodes will objectify the movement of the play from beginning to end and thereby will reveal the principles that determine its movement. These will be either necessary, probable, or chance; there can be no others. By definition, a plot based on chance is inartistic. There is no whole because there is nothing to unify the parts; and the result is incoherent. Therefore, in a well-constructed play, the relationships between episodes must be either necessary or probable.

A visual outline of a "fortunate" plot will clarify what Aristotle seems to be getting at:

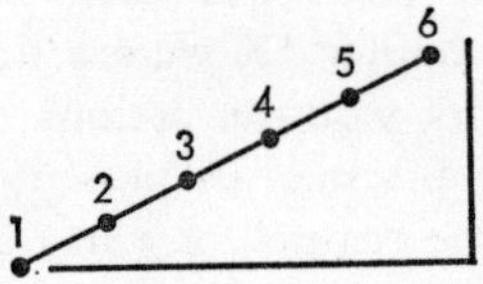

This is a very common—almost instinctive—way to outline plot. As we have seen, the dots represent the incidents; the base line, the time required for performance; and the altitude, the "change" from beginning to end. What does the line connecting the episodes represent? Obviously, it represents what holds the incidents together, the unifying principle. This principle changes from drama to drama. In the *Hippolytus* it may be "scorn of Aphrodite"; in the *Eumenides* it may be "the need for a new moral order"; in *Richard III* it may be "the self-destructiveness of vice"; in *Hamlet* it may be "the ambiguity of truth." There is no need to argue the validity of each of these readings. None is offered as definitive. Rather, they are presented as examples. A critic who denies that "scorn of Aphrodite" is the unifying principle of *Hippolytus* will reject this reading only to offer another, more suitable one in its place.

If the movement of the plot from beginning to end has a unifying principle, the same holds true for the arrangement of incidents in the "middle" of the drama. Episode 2 may or may not be the direct cause of episode 3. If it is not the direct cause, both episodes must be related to larger principles and the relation must be appropriate. The soliloquy and the interview with Ophelia in *Hamlet,* for example, are closely related, but one does not cause the other. Both are ramifications of a larger principle, Hamlet's melancholy, which, in turn, is his response to the situation at the Danish court. They do not "cause" one another, but they are so arranged that to change their order would be to make them objectify a principle (adolescent jealousy) that is both different from the one conveyed by Shakespeare's arrangement and radically inappropriate to the principles objectified by Shakespeare's over-all plot.

If this analysis is acceptable, we can understand probability and necessity simply as those unifying principles brought out by the arrangement of the incidents. "Unifying themes" might be a rough English equivalent. Often they will be directly or indirectly based on the principles of moral philosophy; but they do not have to be. "Men should revere the gods" is a principle of moral philosophy; "Truth is ambiguous and baffling" is not. The most important point, however, is that different principles are conveyed by each successful drama. Hence it is probably wrong to seek an absolute definition of "necessity and probability" in such Aristotelian works as the *Topics* or the *Metaphysics.* If a drama has unity, it has necessity or probability; if it does not, it lacks them—it is episodic. When Olivier rearranged the soliloquy-interview sequence in *Hamlet,* he was treating the play as though it did not have unity. Since it did have unity, the result was negative. The episodes were no longer correlated to the larger design. They became digressions, and as such they were somewhat confusing since the audience naturally assumed that they were "necessary or probable."

One final point. Probability and necessity are presented in the first part of Chapter IX chiefly as they relate to over-all plot. However they are general principles and as such are operative on every level of the poetic art. Later in the chapter (ll. 57-59), Aristotle refers to them as they relate to consecutive incidents. Although not every incident "causes" the one following, this often happens. Linkage by cause-effect is a form of probability or necessity; and when it is possible, it enhances the dramatic effect. We thus have two kinds of causality operating in dramatic plots—the general one in which the unifying principle "causes" all the incidents in the play; and the more specific one in which episode 2 is the direct cause of episode 3.

But the need for necessity and probability does not end with plot. When we say that there is a sense in which plot "causes" character, we are really saying that in an artistic play the dramatist will seek to maintain a necessary or probable relation between what an agent does and the character traits assigned him. A general will normally have traits appropriate to the "military type"; a woman will be "feminine"; a young man bold to the point of rashness, and so forth. By the same token, thought must have a necessary or probable relation to character; and diction, to character and thought. In a perfectly executed play, all these elements will be correlated and hence all will express the play's unity.

Poetry and History
(ll. 5-47)

For Aristotle, the most fundamental job of the historian is to record what has happened. He does not need to understand *why* or *how* events happened; he merely sets them down in chronological order. In fact, precisely because of this requirement the historian often records many events that have no relation to one another. In Chapter XXIII Aristotle makes this clear when he remarks that a history has to deal with "not one action but one period of time" (l. 9), and that two unrelated historical events may occur simultaneously or in succession, as, for example, the Battle of Salamis and the battle with the Carthaginians (l. 13). Notice that this is not a comment on history as written, for example, by Thucydides, but a comment on history in its essential definition. Accordingly, history is said in Chapter IX (l. 14) to be concerned with "the individual"—the event itself—while poetry is concerned with universals—the necessary or probable principles that bind events together.

Aristotle introduces the contrast with another attack on the *ars metrica:* "The historian and the poet do not differ by their writing in prose or verse" (ll. 5-6). To practitioners of the *ars metrica,* a verse chronicle is a poem in spite of the fact that its content has little to do with poetry. From Aristotle's point of view, however, Herodotus in verse would still be history. The true distinction is that the historian writes about "events that have actually happened," while the poet writes about them "as they might possibly occur." This does not mean that the poet must create fictions—things that have not happened but might take place some day. It is, rather, a reference to the way the poet presents events. Obviously, an event that has happened is possible. What the poet does is show *how* it might have happened in terms of probability and necessity. We might say that the poet places the events in a meaningful context so that instead of being "individual" they become pregnant with significance. Probability and necessity are universals. In one way or another they must be embodied in every literary work if it is to succeed. Since the primary concern of philosophy is universals, we can understand why "Poetry . . . is more philosophical and more significant than history, for poetry is more concerned with the universal. . . ." (ll. 11-13).

Aristotle pauses to illustrate the meaning of the term "universal." His illustration is tricky because it appeals to our instinct to see character as the cause of action. This is not his point. To explain the meaning of "universal," he simply chooses the most convenient and clearest example available. We know that in life certain types of people tend to say and do certain things. Moral philosophy and rhetoric provide type descriptions, together with general observations concerning the actions and speech patterns each type is likely to use. These descriptions are universal statements because they are not statements about individual men but about men in general. A universal can thus be defind as the kind of statement that tells ". . . what sort of man turns out to say or do what sort of thing" (ll. 14-15).

Having illustrated the meaning of "universal," Aristotle returns to poetry. We know that poetry seeks to present things in terms of probability and necessity. It shares this objective with moral philosophy. The common goal—probability and necessity—relates the two disciplines and differentiates them from history. The "this" of l. 16 ("this being the goal of poetry") therefore refers to "universal," not to the clause "what sort of man turns out to say or do what sort of thing."

Aristotle now comes to a paradox. Tragedy gives "individual"—that is, historical—names to its characters. History is singular and poetry is universal; but poetry uses proper names. A tragic poet does not write about "King Tyrannus" or "Lady Witch" but about Oedipus or Medea. What is more, although the modern reader makes a very emphatic distinction between legend and history, Aristotle shares the belief of most of his contemporaries that the myths and legends that were the source of most Greek tragedies had historical content. To call a character Agamemnon not only makes him "individual," it reminds us that the poet is drawing on an historical source.

The weight of Greek practice favors a close identification between tragedy and history, but Aristotle has emphasized the difference between the two. This leads him to several observations concerning the use of history by poets.

His first observation is that in comedy, history has been abandoned entirely. The primitive invective poets of Chapter IV lampooned real people and were, in this sense, historical. They are the "iambic poets" who wrote about specific "individuals" (l. 24). Aristophanes and the earlier writers of Old Comedy retained this custom. Such imitation, however, is close to copying. Within Aristotle's historical scheme it is a relic of the primitive age of poetry. Aristotle ignores Old Comedy and turns at once to Middle and New Comedy. The poets of Middle and New Comedy begin properly with the construction of plot. Then they add "any names that happen to occur to them" (ll. 22-23). This does not mean that their naming is haphazard, merely that it is not tied to history. In fact, in New Comedy the names are often chosen to call attention to the types the characters represent. The practice is common in all literatures. English equivalents of the "speaking names" of New Comedy are Shakespeare's Hotspur and Malvolio, and Ben Jonson's Volpone, Mosca, Zeal-of-the-Land Busy, Sir Epicure Mammon, and Truewit.

Whether or not Aristotle has "speaking names" in mind, he clearly approves of the procedure followed by New Comedy. Since tragedy still used "individual names" in his day, he evidently felt that it had not evolved as far as comedy. Note that his concept of comedy is close to what we today would call fiction. Drama with arbitrary names rather than "historical names" is drama "invented" by the author. The fact that this sort of drama exists at all is evidence that poetry need not depend on history. If the relations between "universals," the literary work, and history are parallel to the relations between type, portrait, and model in painting, Aristotle has simply restated the point he made in Chapter IV, namely, that a literary work need not be a "copy" of anything. By nature it tends to seek the universal. Poetry can use history, but can also get along very well without it.

We now move to a series of observations concerning the practice of the tragic poets. Although comedy has abandoned proper names, in tragedy "Our poets cling to the names of the heroes of the past" (ll. 25-26). The first explanation for this practice is verisimilitude. As was noted in connection with probability and necessity, whatever has happened is by definition possible. By using an action and names ratified by history, the poet lulls the audience into suspension of disbelief. The principle clearly includes the pseudo-history preserved in classical myth and legend as well as the more sober chronicles of professional historians.

During the Renaissance this passage became a favorite. It seemed to relate "probability" to "verisimilitude," which was understood to mean "adjusting the drama to the prejudices, limitations, and knowledge of the audience." Castelvetro, for example, defended the historical plot with the argument that a plot about a supposedly great king of whom the audience had never heard would be laughed out of the theater. The audience would not believe that such a king had existed, and the tragedy would fail to have its proper effect. In general, renaissance dramatists thought along similar lines, and almost all renaissance and neoclassic tragedies are based on history or legend.

Verisimilitude, however, is a rhetorical concept. It is foreign to the art of poetry because it relates what the poet does to the psychology of the audience rather than to the requirements of the literary work. Aristotle realizes this, and in the next few sentences he offers proof that the reliance of tragedy on history is fortuitous, not essential. He makes three points:

1. ". . . in some tragedies one or two of the names are well-known and the rest have been invented." In other words, even apparently historical tragedies have an admixture of fiction. The fact that only "one or two" names are known indicates that the fictional element actually predominates.
2. "[In] Agathon's *Antheus* . . . both the incidents and the names have been invented and nonetheless they please us." Agathon's tragedy *Antheus* ("Flower") has not survived, but the point is clear. The *Antheus* is entirely fictional, yet it produces the proper effect. The fact that Aristotle singles out this unique play is further proof that he felt tragedy was evolving (or could evolve) in the direction already taken by Middle and New Comedy. The conclusion to be drawn from the point is stated strongly: "Thus we must not seek to cling exclusively to the stories that have been handed down and about which our tragedies are usually written" (ll. 35-37).
3. "It would be absurd, indeed, to do this since even the well-known plots are known only to a few but nevertheless please everyone" (ll. 37-39). We usually assume that the average Greek theater-goer had an encyclopedic knowledge of the myths and legends on which tragedy was based. According to Aristotle, this is false. Most members of the audience were likely to be unfamiliar with a given legend. For such spectators, the argument that history lends verisimilitude does not hold. If the spectators do not know the historical source, the story might as well be pure fiction. In the sense that it is totally new, it *is* fiction; yet, says Aristotle, it "pleases everyone."

Clearly the renaissance and neoclassic critics who demanded that tragedy be based on history were not merely distorting, they were inverting the *Poetics*. Chapter IX argues against verisimilitude and history, not for them.

Aristotle now pauses to reiterate a favorite point and to strike another blow against the *ars metrica*. The poet, he says, is "more the poet of his plots than of his meters" (l. 41). The emphasis on plot hardly needs comment. It is appropriate here because the fundamental distinction between history and poetry is their treatments of incidents. The historian records particulars, the poet arranges the particulars into plots that objectify unified actions. The discussion of the poet's use of historical names has emphasized the relatively slight part that history plays for the poet. Even when he uses historical names, the poet adds them only after his plot has been constructed. It follows that the essential task of the poet is to construct plots. The implication of this point is clearly stated in Sir Philip Sidney's argument that works in prose are poems just as truly as works in verse; it is also evident in the title of L. J. Potts' translation of the *Poetics,* which is *Aristotle on the Art of Fiction.* The converse of this point is that the *ars metrica,* which makes verse not plots the central element of poetry, is false.

The discussion of poetry and history ends with a qualification. Aristotle has emphasized the difference between tragedy and history. This is appropriate because Greek tragic practice encourages the mistaken notion that the two are intimately related; and this notion, in turn, leads to the "copy" theory of imitation. To say that poetry does not have to use history, however, is not to say that it *must not* use it. Occasionally the poet may find in history a sequence of events that is sufficiently coherent to be used as a tragic plot with little or no modification. As we know, for example, from Shakespeare's use of Holinshed and Plutarch, this seldom happens. Usually the poet must modify—even radically alter—history to make it into a viable plot. But sometimes the poet can use history without change, and when this happens says Aristotle, the poet "is no less the poet for that" (l. 44). Evidently the poet reveals his skill in being able to recognize true actions in the rare cases when they occur in history, just as much as when he constructs his actions independently.

Corollaries (ll. 48-68)

The word "simple" (l. 48) is a technical term referring to a plot that lacks reversal and discovery. The simple plot is defined and contrasted to "complex plot" in Chapter X. The two plot forms that we have examined so far—the fortunate and the fatal—are simple.

Aristotle states the first corollary to the discussion of probability and necessity in terms of the simple plot; but the observation applies equally to complex plots. Plots lacking probability or necessity are called "episodic." We have seen that the theoretical limit of the episodic plot is a plot that has no action at all. Since there is no change between the beginning and the end, the number and arrangement of episodes is arbitrary. This is another way of saying that they have no necessary or probable relation to each other. Aristotle lists two causes of episodic plots. The first is simply the "inadequacy" of poor poets (l. 52). The second is the actors and/or the dramatic competitions. Actors "bring out" spectacle and they demand incidents and speeches that allow their art to achieve maximum effect. But their art is different from the poetic art, and the more the poet is influenced by them, the more "impure" his work will be. By the same token, the contests, as we learned in Chapter VII, are arbitrary. In them, the length of a play is dictated not by its action but by the number of plays to be performed. When the dramatist adds incidents merely to please the actors or to "pad out" his drama to the length required by the contest, he is introducing material that has no necessary or probable relation to the plot. The result is "episodic." It tends to "stretch the plot beyond its capacity" (l. 54).

Having considered what should be avoided in constructing plots, Aristotle now turns the coin over and states what the poet should do to maximize the effect. He begins with a reminder that the tragic plot is composed of incidents that are intrinsically pitiable or fearful. The more pitiable and fearful they can be made, the better. Normally we would say that the way to increase the pathos of an incident is to make it more graphic. A murder, for example, is pitiable and fearful in itself; but its effect can be intensified if it is performed in a brutal manner (strangulation, for example, is more brutal than shooting) or if—say—the victim is a woman or a child. For the present Aristotle ignores the content of the incidents in order to stress ways that their effect can be intensified by the structure of the play. That is, the events are most effective if they occur "unexpectedly yet because of one another" (l. 58).

We have said earlier that probability and necessity manifest themselves in plots in two ways. In a general sense, they can be said to "cause" the movement of the plot from beginning to end; and there can also be a direct cause-effect relation between specific incidents of a drama. Prince Hal's revels in the Boar's Head Tavern do not "cause" the treasonous councils of Hotspur in the rebel camp; but both incidents are consequences of the unquiet conditions in England under Henry IV. If the necessary or probable principle underlying the action of *Henry IV, Part I* is the tendency of an unstable state to move through turmoil back to stability, then all the incidents can be said to be "caused" by this principle. At the same time, a direct cause-effect relation exists between some of the incidents. In the third scene of the play, for example, the demand of Henry IV that Hotspur surrender his prisoners is the cause (or alleged cause) of Hotspur's rage in the latter half of the scene. In the same way, Jason's decision to marry Creon's daughter in *Medea* is the cause of Medea's anger, which, in turn, is the cause of Creon's decree of banishment.

Aristotle does not say that a cause-effect relation will, in itself, intensify the pity and fear evoked by the incidents. A second condition must exist, one that is even more important than the first: the incidents should occur "unexpectedly" (l. 58). This is the heart of Aristotle's argument. An incident such as a murder is pitiable and fearful by itself; it is all the more so if it carries with it the shock of surprise. Finally, the shock will be greater if, after the incident has occurred, we realize that the plot was leading up to it all along. The reference is to a very special set of circumstances that may occur once or twice in a play, and not to the construction of all the incidents. Excessive use of "surprise" produces not tragedy but melodrama.

The special nature of the device that Aristotle has in mind is shown by the fact that he gives it a technical label—*thaumastos*—translated here as "the marvelous" (l. 59). Etymologically, the term suggests "magic" and "miracle." In Chapter XXIV (ll. 57-80) Aristotle observes that the marvelous is usually "irrational" and that it is much more frequently encountered in epic than in tragedy. The term has the general meaning of "events that are wondrous and inexplicable"; and in the *Poetics,* it usually has the connotation of events produced by divine rather than natural agency. The *Iliad* and the *Odyssey* abound with such events, as well as with such nonhuman agents as gods, goddesses, witches, ghosts, and the like. Tragedy uses also "the marvelous," although less often. The most obvious instance is the *deus ex machina.* The gods of *Prometheus Bound,* the Furies of the *Eumenides,* and the dragon-car of *Medea* are additional examples.

Clearly, Aristotle is dubious about the use of "miracles" in drama. His remarks about the statue *Mitys* (ll. 61-65) indicate he felt that they are often attempts to conceal inadequate dramatic skill. It follows that if the dramatist is to achieve "the marvelous," he should make it the result of causes within the plot: "There is more of the marvelous in [the incidents] if they occur in this way than if they occured spontaneously or by chance" (ll. 59-61). Does this mean that Aristotle is opposed to divine agents and events produced by supernatural rather than natural causes? Probably not. The trouble with dramatic miracles is that they are usually extrinsic to plot. The action develops smoothly according to one set of probable and necessary principles and then suddenly changes, as an entirely new set is introduced and the god comes down from the machine. Aristotle only demands that the marvelous be produced by causes within the plot. If the play is about a supernatural figure like Prometheus, or includes a witch like Medea, or a soothsayer like Tiresias, the supernatural is intrinsic to it and to exclude supernatural causality would be just as great a flaw as to introduce it in a naturalistic play. The main point is that the dramatist should accept the conditions of his action and stay within them. In the best sort of tragedy, the marvelous is produced when something unexpected occurs as the necessary or probable result of preceding incidents. The murder of Agamemnon is "marvelous" in this sense although it is the result of natural causes. The "pardon" of Orestes is also a valid instance of "the marvelous" which is brought about with the aid of the goddess Athena.

Consideration of the marvelous reintroduces the notion of "chance" incidents. A play with a large number of such incidents is, as we have seen, episodic. Aristotle ends Chapter IX with a note on how an episodic plot can be given at least the appearance of unity. To illustrate, he recalls the story of the murder of Mitys. This story is also related by Plutarch in an essay titled "Concerning the Eventual Punishment [of Crimes] by God." As the title shows, the story was regarded as an example of the intervention of providence into human affairs. Aristotle is more skeptical. To him the fact that the statue of Mitys fell on Mitys' murderer is "coincidence" (l. 61). If made into a play, the story would be episodic. No reasons exist within the story to make the fall of the statue probable or necessary. On the other hand, the episodic nature of the plot is concealed by the fact that the murderer dies not from, for example, falling into a well, but from being crushed by the statue of his victim. Such a device may not be "artistic," but it will appeal to popular credulity. The story will "appear to have some design" (l. 62) because "such an event, we feel, is not without meaning" (l. 66). Aristotle is unenthusiastic about such "miracles," but he admits that they may be useful in making the best of a bad plot. They make chance plots "superior" (l. 68) to plots without such devices, but not, of course, superior to plots that avoid chance.

Chapter X

The most general distinction among plots is that made in Chapter VII between the fortunate and fatal varieties. Chapter X adds a second distinction. Some plots are simple. The plot line moves uniformly upward toward success or uniformly downward toward failure. Other plots are what Aristotle calls "complex." A complex plot is symbolized schematically by a line that abruptly changes direction. For example, today we normally symbolize the structure of tragedy by using the Freytag pyramid. The hero's fortunes "rise" to a certain point (the climax) and then "fall" rapidly toward the final catastrophe. In a modern comic plot line, the reverse is true. The hero's fortunes decline toward a low point, there is a sudden change, and his fortunes then rise toward the conventional happy ending. Aristotle's definition of tragedy is broader than the modern one, for he includes simple as well as complex plots and fortunate ones as well as fatal. He does, however, prefer the complex to the simple variety.

The basis for calling a plot complex is the fact that it includes a reversal (*peripeteia*) or recognition (*anagnorisis*) or both.[1] Reversals and recognitions are incidents. They are parts of the plot and

[1] *Anagnorisis* is often translated "discovery."

therefore—like the other incidents—"must develop directly from the construction of the plot, itself" (ll. 7-8). This condition can be met only if they are related by necessity or probability to what has gone before. They can be directly caused by the preceding incident —as the blinding of Oedipus is caused by the revelation of the messenger—or they can be consequences of the general principle underlying the action—as the victory at Agincourt in Shakespeare's *Henry V* is caused by the cooperation of providence and English virtue. For complex plots, direct causality is especially important: "It makes quite a difference whether they occur *because* of these events or merely *after* them" (ll. 10-11).

Aristotle has now specified four types of plot. There are no more. Additional variation must be gained (a) by compounding the types or (b) by varying the characters of the agents. Both variations are mentioned in Chapter XIII. The first variation is illustrated by the "double plot," and the second by the different plots produced by different tragic heroes. The four basic types are as follows:

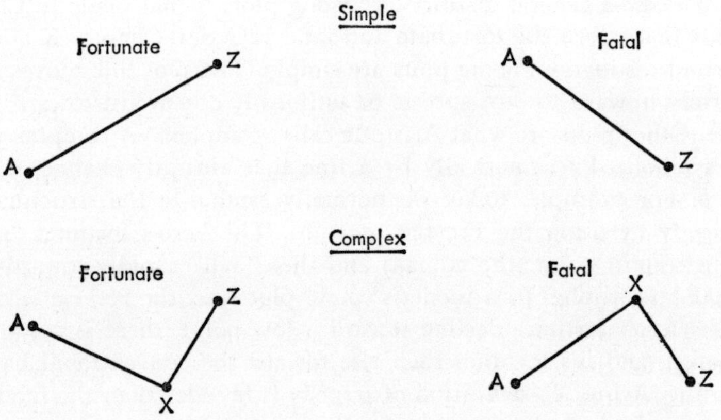

A and *Z* here stand for the first and last episodes of the plot (the beginning and end), and *X* for a reversal and/or recognition.

For Aristotle, reversal and recognition are the two most effective elements of plot (Chapter VI, l. 74). When he discusses them he assumes that the complex play will be built around them. They provide a kind of unity that is not present in simple plots and, of course, they radically alter the nature of the "middle" of the drama. In a simple plot the movement from beginning to end is rather indeterminate. The poet must insert incidents to objectify the movement, and the incidents must be arranged in a definite order; but he has a great deal of latitude in deciding how many incidents are appropriate. In a complex plot the reversal and/or recognition incident is everything. The poet must carefully lead up to it. It should be caused by what has preceded, and what follows should be a natural consequence of it. The definition of what constitutes a probable and necessary series of incidents is thus sharper for the complex plot. The result is a higher degree of unity. The simple plot is organized in terms of beginning and end; but the complex plot is organized, we might say, from the center out.

A dramatist planning a play about *The Sacrifice of Isaac,* for example, would begin with the sacrifice incident. This incident is a reversal since Abraham plans to slay his son until, at the last minute, God sends the ram to be sacrificed instead. Given this incident, the dramatist knows that he must extend the action back to the Lord's command that the sacrifice be performed. He must then include incidents showing Abraham's struggle with and final triumph over his desire to protect Isaac. After the reversal he must extend the action forward far enough to depict the joy of father and son, and their prayer of thanksgiving.

A remarkable description of essentially the same process is given by Henry James in his preface to *The Ambassadors.* The idea or "germ" of the novel, says James, was a bit of dialogue that he overheard one day in Paris between an older man and a young one. The older man was ruefully urging the younger to enjoy life to the full. Using the terms of the *Poetics,* we could call this episode a reversal for the older man, because, in essence, he is admitting that his past values were false. After relating the incident, James describes the process by which he reasoned backward to the "beginning" of the story and selected episodes to show the gradual change in the older man's outlook. The dialogue episode, of course, became the climax of the novel. Although James does not discuss the denouement, a glance at the novel will show that it "follows from" the climax. Interestingly, the criterion that James says he used in designing the plot of *The Ambassadors* is "probability."

Chapter XI

Having introduced the terms reversal and recognition, Aristotle must define them. Reversal is a relatively simple concept. It is "a change of fortune in the action of the play to the opposite state of affairs." An action seems to be proceeding toward success and suddenly veers off in the direction of misfortune. We can call this type of plot "fatal-complex." Aristotle illustrates it with the arrival of the messenger in *Oedipus.* The messenger arrives to help the king but actually destroys him by revealing the key to his true identity. Alternately, an action seems to be proceeding toward misfortune and suddenly veers off in the direction of happiness. This type of plot is "fortunate-complex." It is illustrated by the *Lynceus*—a lost play—in which the principal character is about to be executed, but is suddenly saved. *Iphigenia in Tauris* is also a "fortunate-complex" play, for at the last moment Orestes is recognized by his sister and saved from death.

"Recognition" is a more difficult concept. The introductory definition is fairly broad. It is "a change from ignorance to knowledge" (l. 11); it results in "friendship or . . . hostility" between agents involved in an action; and it is "most effective" when it is closely related to a reversal. The first part of the definition invites misinterpretation. It seems to make recognition a part of character, although in Chapter VI Aristotle has explicitly termed it a part of plot. Moreover, it seems so general that it can be taken to refer to any "knowledge" gained by a character. On this basis it has sometimes been interpreted as including the "self-knowledge" that tragic figures are supposed to achieve through their suffering. "Know thyself" is a Greek aphorism adopted by the Romans and enduringly popular in the Renaissance and beyond. As Francis Fergusson writes of *Oedipus,* "The characters suffer the piteous and terrible sense of the mystery of the human situation. From this suffering or passion, with its shifting visions, a new perception of the situation emerges. . . ." [1] This is an attractive approach to Aristotle's recognition, but it is too broad, no matter how much we would like it to

[1] Francis Fergusson, *The Idea of a Theatre* (New York: Doubleday Anchor Books, n.d.), p. 31.

be true. It might apply to catharsis in the sense of "clarification" (indeed, in Fergusson's treatment it is close to this); but if we are to understand "recognition" as a plot device, we need something much more specific.

The first requirement for a definition of recognition is that it be a change from ignorance to knowledge brought about by the incidents of the plot. By corollary, it must be the "necessary or probable" result of the preceding incidents. The second requirement is that it result in a change in the action—a change from "friendship" to "hostility" (l. 12), or (presumably) the reverse. It is this change rather than the change in knowledge that makes recognition a part of plot; for if "self-knowledge" or "perception" were the only requirement, a recognition scene could form the final incident in a simple plot. But we have seen in Chapter X that the presence of a recognition scene makes a plot, by definition, complex. This is only possible if the recognition occurs in the "middle" section of the play as the result of one sequence of incidents and is followed by at least one other incident defining a new sequence. After the recognition, the plot must "veer off in a new direction"—which is the point of defining the effect of the recognition as a change affecting the "friendship or . . . hostility" of the characters.

Recognition in this sense is closely akin to reversal. A reversal can occur without a recognition if it is caused by something other than discovery of new information. By the same token, a recognition can occur without a reversal if the change in the action happens as the result of new knowledge and for no other reason. The English victory at Agincourt in Shakespeare's *Henry V* is a "simple" reversal; "new knowledge" has nothing to do with it. Although we do not have the play, the reversal in the *Lynceus* was probably also "simple." The typical detective story, conversely, provides examples of "simple" recognitions; as, for example, when the identity of the criminal is revealed by the discovery of his fingerprints at the scene of the crime.

Often, however, it is difficult to separate reversal and recognition. The two are closely allied, and they are easily combined in a single incident. For Aristotle, the combined form is the "most effective." If reversal and recognition are the most important parts of plot taken separately (Chapter VI, l. 74), they will be even more effective when they occur together. Aristotle gives *Oedipus* as his example. The reversal is the arrival of the messenger, which leads to the downfall of the king. The recognition is the discovery by Oedipus of "who he actually is," in consequence of which he blinds himself. In fact, in *Oedipus,* recognition and reversal are so closely interwoven that it is academic to attempt to separate them. The climax of *Oedipus* is not a reversal plus a recognition but something closer to a "reversal-recognition." For convenience we can call this type of episode a "compound recognition."

So much for recognition as a plot element. The content of the recognition incident is also important. As we have seen, the most general definition of its content is "change from ignorance to knowledge." Aristotle recognizes three types: recognition of inanimate things, recognition of events, and recognition of persons. The first two types are commonplace in detective stories and are represented by the investigator's discovering clues or learning of concealed deeds, whether through informers or by the power of deduction. Aristotle has little regard for either type, and this is the last we hear of them in the *Poetics*.

Recognition of persons is a different matter. Aristotle first refers to it indirectly as "the one which has been mentioned" (ll. 20-21). The allusion is to the type of recognition found in Oedipus. Such a recognition involves reversal as well, and Aristotle confirms our suspicion that he is thinking of what we have called "compound recognition" by referring to it in the next sentence as "a recognition and reversal." "Recognition of persons," then, is best understood as compound recognition.

The theoretical reason for the special excellence of recognition of persons is that it is "part of the plot and the action" and is especially evocative of "pity and fear" (l. 22). We were told in Chapter X that pitiable and fearful incidents are made more so by the shock of surprise. Obviously, surprise plays only a small part in a simple plot, in which the incidents all tend in the same direction. In a complex plot, on the other hand, there is a sudden change of direction. The action has been moving toward "happiness" and it suddenly becomes "fatal," or vice versa. If the change is the necessary or probable outcome of the preceding incidents but at the same time unexpected (Chapter IX, l. 58), it will generate surprise; and the inherent pity and fear of the incidents will be enhanced. Both reversal and recognition give a plot this form. When the two are combined as in "recognition of persons," the effect is even greater. Moreover, as Aristotle remarks, "happiness and misery will appear in circumstances of this type" (ll. 23-24). That is, the change in the action caused by personal recognition will lead emphatically to the fatal or fortunate conclusion.

Recognition of persons takes us far from the kind of self-knowledge that figures like Oedipus or Lear are supposed to attain by their suffering. The concept should be understood in its narrow sense. It means just what it says. In *Oedipus,* which is atypical, the hero recognizes himself. He does not gain insight as a result of the information supplied by the messenger; he simply learns who he is. He learns that he is the son of Laius, whom he has slain, and the son of Jocasta, whom he has married. The typical Greek recognition is a recognition of one character by another, and what is more, the characters are usually blood relations. Aristotle lists two types of recognition in this sense. One character can be known and recognize another, or two characters can be known and recognize each other. His example of "mutual recognition of persons" is *Iphigenia in Tauris* where "Iphigenia is recognized by Orestes from her sending of the letter, but it is necessary that there be another recognition of him on her part" (ll. 29-31). This brief passage is supplemented by Chapter XVI, which is an extended discussion of five varieties of personal recognition.

At the very end of Chapter XI, a third plot component is introduced. In addition to reversal and recognition, there is the incident of suffering (*pathos*). The incidents of a tragedy have already been defined as pitiable and fearful as early as Chapter VI. In reversals and recognitions, the pity and fear are enhanced by the structure of the action. Most plays have one—or at the most two—such incidents, for the reason that reversal and recognition tend to occur at, or in relation to, the play's climax. What about the incidents that do not involve reversal and/or recognition? All the incidents of a simple plot and most of those in a complex plot are in this latter class. Clearly, some of them will convey pity and fear through their content rather than through their relation to the structure of the plot. Aristotle's term for such an incident is *pathos* —literally, "a suffering." His examples of incidents of suffering emphasize their pitiable and fearful content: ". . . death on the stage, scenes of very great pain, the infliction of wounds, and the like" (ll. 36-37). Although Aristotle does not state the point explicitly in Chapter XI, most tragedies involve at least one major *pathos* that deeply influences the action. The *pathos* of the *Agamemnon,* for example, is the slaying of the king. As we learn in Chapter XIV, a *pathos* can be "outside the plot" (Oedipus' slaying of Laius); and it can be threatened but fail to happen (Iphigenia's threatened sacrifice of Orestes).

With this, the discussion of reversal, recognition, and *pathos* is concluded. However, many commentators—most recently Gerald Else and Martin Ostwald—have seen an intimate relation between Aristotle's discussion of recognition of persons and his notion of the "tragic error" (*hamartia*) presented in Chapter XIII. The root meaning of *hamartia* is "missing the mark." The term is usually taken to mean a mistake rather than a vice or sin. The mistake, in turn, must be caused by the fact that the hero lacks some essential bit of information; for if he knew all the relevant facts he would presumably not err. According to this view, the tragic hero begins the action of the play in ignorance of precisely the information that he most desperately needs to have. At the climax, a recognition occurs that brings with it a change from ignorance to knowledge. The movement of the plot then changes direction—toward a fatal conclusion as in *Oedipus,* or a fortunate one as in *Iphigenia.* Without anticipating the analysis of *hamartia* in Chapter XIII, we can note that according to at least one line of interpretation, recognition and *hamartia* are complementary concepts. *Hamartia* at the beginning of a complex tragedy requires recognition at its climax.

Chapter XII

Thus far we have been concerned with plot as form. The key terms have been action, plot, incident, probability, necessity, reversal, and recognition. Aristotle now turns to the labels conventionally assigned to the various sections of Greek tragedies: prologue, episode, exode, and "choric song," which is subdivided into parode and stasimon. These labels are matters of Greek theatrical convention, just as it is conventional to divide modern dramas into acts and scenes. Because of this fact, Chapter XII seems rather beside the point. We would expect it in a "handbook of poetry" organized along the lines of the treatises fathered by Greek critics of the Alexandrian period, but it adds little to Aristotle's argument. Scholars have often regarded it as a late classical interpolation. Else, in fact, believes that the last sentence of Chapter XI is completed by the first sentence of Chapter XIII. If so, Chapter XII is not only an interpolation but also badly obscures the flow of Aristotle's thought as it moves from plot components (Chapters VII-XI) to the relative excellence of various arrangements of the components (Chapter XIII).

A conservative approach to the *Poetics* such as the present one must, however, take the Greek text as it stands. Therefore, while admitting the force of arguments against the genuineness of Chapter XII, we will assume that it is loosely correlated to the other chapters and comment on it from this point of view.

In quantitative terms, a dramatic prologue is simply that part of a tragedy that precedes the first choral section. Normally, the prologue makes clear to the audience the situation as it exists at the beginning of the dramatic action. If an action is a process that begins after a period of relative stability as suggested in Chapter VII, the prologue will (a) acquaint the audience with this situation and (b) identify or at least foreshadow the change itself. The prologue, in other words, can be the "beginning" of the plot, or it can prepare for the beginning.

Technically, an episode is simply a passage of monologue or dialogue between a character and the chorus or between two or more characters, preceded and followed by choral sections. The episodes of a drama contain the incidents that define the movement of the plot. In this sense the episodes are the "middle" of the plot. In a simple plot the episodes define a continuous upward or downward movement; in a complex plot they define a movement that changes direction at some point, usually near the end. The episode in which the direction actually changes is one that contains a reversal and/or recognition.

"Episode" (*epeisodion*) is closely related to "incident" (*pragma*) as used in Chapters VII-XI; but "incident" is a more functional critical term because its root relates it to action (*praxis*) rather than to dramatic convention. Presumably, each episode should present one incident; in practice, a single episode can present several incidents. "Episode" is also used in a looser sense in the *Poetics* to refer to an incident that is not related to the probable or necessary movement of the plot. For example, the term for a plot having a great many unrelated incidents is "episodic" (Chapter IX, l. 48); and Homer, after developing a unified action, "introduces many other episodes" from outside the plot to produce the pleasurable variety proper to epic (Chapter XXIII, l. 27). "Episode," therefore, has three different meanings in the *Poetics:* (1) a conventional label for the part of a play between two choral sections; (2) a synonym for "incident"; and (3) "digressive material." In Chapter XII the first meaning is obviously intended, but the reader must be careful to distinguish among the different meanings as they appear in the later chapters.

The exode is the section of the play that is not followed by a chorus. It bears the same relation to the "end" of a tragedy that the prologue bears to the beginning, except that it includes both a final episode and the departure (*exodos*) of the chorus.

Note that if we consider prologue–three episodes–exode a kind of minimum content for tragedy, we can see a dim anticipation of what eventually became the five-act convention of Roman and renaissance drama. The convention that a drama should not have more than five acts is stated by Horace (*Ars Poetica,* l. 189) and in ancient commentaries on Plautus and Terence. It is a byproduct of the fact that as the choral sections of classical drama declined in importance, the episodes came to define the structure of the play.

Little need be said about the choral sections. They divide the episodes. In a Greek drama the chorus reacts to the events, sympathizes with or cautions the characters, and acts as spokesman for the feelings of the audience. The choral passages, says Chapter XII, are divided into parode and stasimon. The parode comes first and contains several meters. The stasimon lacks anapests and trochees. The division seems to be based on the *ars metrica,* and the normal meanings of the terms are not too clear in context. As defined by

Greek dramatic practice, the parode was a song accompanying the entrance of the chorus, whereas the stasima were sung "in one place"—that is, in the orchestra, where the chorus remained after its entrance.

Rather surprisingly, a new term is added almost as an afterthought. The *kommos* is an exception to the general rule that episodes and choral sections are kept separate. During the *kommos* the chorus and actors speak together, and the subject of the *kommos* is "lament" (l. 15). To this rather stereotyped treatment of the chorus can be contrasted the functional approach at the end of Chapter XVIII (ll. 55-64), an additional indication, perhaps, that Chapter XII is a late interpolation.

Chapter XIII

In Chapter XIII the labels offered in Chapter XII are dropped and Aristotle returns to the functional elements of Chapters VI-XI. The reference in the final sentence to "the remarks that have just been made" (l. 4) is clearly to these chapters.

The elements of tragedy can be combined in several different ways, and the purpose of Chapter XIII is to define the combination that best produces the tragic effect or "function." The chapter is divided roughly in half. The first half derives the ideal plot form by a process of elimination. The emphasis is, as we might expect, on structure; but the discussion is complicated by reference to qualities normally associated with character and to the probable response of the audience to various types of plot. In the course of the discussion, Aristotle introduces the idea of the tragic error—the *hamartia*—and this term, itself, creates difficulties of interpretation. The second half of the chapter is devoted to confirmation of two points made in the first half: that the "fatal" is better than the "fortunate" plot, and that the single is better than the double plot.

The Ideal Tragic Plot
(ll. 1-39)

The ranking of types of plot begins with a reminder of two points already established. First, "The best tragedies must be complex, not simple" (l. 5-6), a point asserted in Chapter VI when reversals and recognitions are called the most effective elements in plot, and explained more fully in Chapters X and XI. Second, the tragedy must imitate "pitiable and fearful incidents (for this is the specific nature of the imitation under discussion)" (ll. 6-8). This goes back to the original definition of tragedy in Chapter VI. Since pitiable and fearful incidents are part of the definition of tragedy, they are part of "the specific nature of the imitation under discussion." Further light is cast on such incidents, of course, at the end of Chapter IX and during the discussion of recognition of persons in Chapter XI (ll. 11-32).

We now begin a systematic consideration of possible types of complex plot. There are two basic types—the fatal and the fortunate. These are varied by the type of protagonist—"good," "extremely evil," or "between these extremes"—who is presented in them. Hence, although the discussion is still primarily focused on plot, character begins to become important. How far the discussion involves character is somewhat ambiguous. We have seen in Chapter II that agents are either "noble" (*spoudaioi*) or "base" (*phauloi*) *before* they become "characters" in Aristotle's sense. Their nobility or baseness is thus related to the actions in which they are involved, not to the personality type that is assigned them. Aristotle's most fundamental criteria of character arise from action rather than characterization. On the other hand, in Chapter XIII Aristotle does not use the terms *spoudaios* and *phaulos* to designate the kinds of protagonist discussed. Rather, his terminology tends to be ethical. The Greek term for the "unqualifiedly good" kind of man referred to in relation to the first possible plot (l. 9) is *epieikes*. It means something like "equitable"; and the "equitable man" is defined as the most perfect of all possible types in the *Nicomachean Ethics*, V, 10 (1137^b). He is even superior to the "just man," because he conforms to the spirit rather than the letter of the law at all times. The terms for the "extremely evil" man (l. 11) and the "villainous" man (l. 16) are also definitely ethical, as is much of the later terminology in the chapter. Although we may legitimately detect an echo of the earlier (*spoudaios-phaulos*) distinction in Chapter XIII, a more specific (and less action-oriented) concept of characterization is also present and perhaps predominant. If so, in addition to assuming a necessary and/or probable relation between the incidents of the plot, Chapter XIII introduces a new idea—the need for a necessary and/or probable relation to be established between the incidents and the character traits assigned the agents. It is on this basis that one type of character can be said to be more or less appropriate than another for a complex-fatal plot. When the dramatist follows Aristotle's guidelines, his drama will seem to the audience to reveal natural causality. The illusion will be created that the characters cause the incidents; or—perhaps better—the drama will appear to reveal a relation between character and destiny as defined by the fatal or fortunate conclusion of the plot.

Let us now turn to the plot types.

> First, there is the complex-fatal plot involving the "unqualifiedly good" protagonist.
>
> Second, there is the complex-fortunate plot involving an "extremely evil" protagonist.
>
> Third, there is the complex-fatal plot involving a "villainous" protagonist.
>
> Fourth, there is the complex-fatal plot involving a good man who is "between these extremes" and who makes an error through some "miscalculation" (*hamartia*).

The first two types are related, and both are entirely unsatisfactory. The first is "repellent" and the second is "the most untragic situation of all" since it ". . . violates our human sympathy (*philanthropeia*)." Moreover, both types lack "pity and fear" (ll. 10, 15).

The general sense of Aristotle's thought is clear enough. To see a supremely good man plunged into misfortune, or an evil man gain happiness, is repellent to our moral sense. We are likely to be shocked by the first and disgusted by or indifferent to the second. However, if we carry this line of reasoning very far we risk falling into the didactic interpretations of the renaissance and neoclassic periods, according to which tragedy must show wicked men punished and good men rewarded. This is clearly far from the mark, for plays based on strict poetic justice are usually rather dull and seldom arouse much pity or fear. Aristotle himself will make this point in connection with the third type of plot. In addition, it is still not entirely clear why Aristotle's first type of plot cannot arouse pity and fear. The second type of plot is easy enough. A play in which the villain is successful cannot arouse the proper tragic emotions. We will not pity the protagonist; and because pity and fear are, as we have seen, complementary emotions, neither will our fear be aroused. In Aristotle's terms, such a play will fail to elicit "human sympathy." On the other hand, a plot about a supremely good man coming to a tragic end should, one would think, arouse a great deal of pity and fear. One need only cite the Crucifixion to provide an instance of a fatal action involving an "unqualifiedly good" man that arouses pity and fear.

Actually, the Crucifixion is precisely the example we need in order to understand Aristotle's meaning. The Crucifixion takes place in a profoundly religious context. It is an historical event, but it has cosmic dimensions. Although it happens in a human environment, the agents are only partly responsible. We might say that it takes place simply because it must take place. It is part of a divine plan for man's salvation, a plan that demands a victim who is perfect in every respect. Greek tragedy also evolved in a religious context. It was influenced by Dionysian ritual, and the tragedies of Aeschylus in particular are heavy with fate and the will of the gods. On the other hand, we know that from Aristotle's point of view the tragic plot should proceed in terms of necessary and/or probable principles operating within the action. The worst type of plot is that governed by no principles at all; it is a plot based on "chance." Chance events—like the death of a murderer through the fall of a statue (the story of Mitys in Chapter IX)—are to be avoided. If they cannot be avoided, then they should be given some semblance of meaning through a device that seems to make the death of the murderer a divine punishment. At best, however, this is a way of disguising a weak plot, and in general Aristotle opposes sudden, arbitrary intrusions of the divine into drama. His view is rather more rationalistic than the typical views of twentieth-century criticism, but Aristotle, after all, had read neither Sir James Frazer nor Sigmund Freud. His purpose in the *Poetics* is to analyze those aspects of the subject that lie within the control of "the poetic art." Regarding the art of poetry, the more the incidents are made to develop out of principles innate to the action, and the less the *deus ex machina* needs to be invoked, the better.

Let us return to the first two kinds of plot with these observations in mind. Ethical propositions such as "Virtue brings happiness" may be considered statements of general probabilities. Presumably, the more virtues the individual has, the greater the likelihood of "happiness." The first type of plot in Chapter XIII involves not merely a "fairly good" protagonist, but one who is *epieikes*—"unqualifiedly good." As we have noticed, the "unqualifiedly good" man is superior even to the "just" man. He does not react to situations by "rule," but in terms of equity—in terms of the spirit underlying the rule. Accordingly, "unqualifiedly good" must mean something like "nearly perfect." This interpretation is confirmed when we come to the fourth type of plot, which presents a protagonist who is not "perfect in virtue and justice . . . but . . . who succumbs through some miscalculation" (ll. 27-29). What is the difference between the first and fourth types of tragic hero? The first type *is* and the fourth type *is not* "perfect in virtue and justice"; and the reason for the difference is that the fourth type has a flaw, a tendency toward "miscalculation." If the fourth type has such a flaw, the first type must lack it. In other words, the "unqualifiedly good" man does not miscalculate. Since equity is the avoidance of even the type of miscalculation that comes from unvarying application of a just rule, the contrast of the fourth and first types of protagonist complements the definition of the first type suggested by the term *epieikes*.

A type one plot, then, presents a man who is "unqualifiedly good" and makes no "miscalculation" in a complex-fatal action. Obviously, such a story violates probability. It may faithfully reproduce a sequence of events recorded in history, but if it does, the sequence is based on chance rather than any universal principle. A dramatist who offers such a sequence has violated the requirement of universality and/or probability by failing to relate character to action. From the point of view of the reader or spectator, there is no intelligible relation between the character and his end. Virtue usually brings happiness. The protagonist is outstandingly virtuous and, moreover, does not "miscalculate." Yet instead of succeeding, he fails! The only possible explanation is "chance"; and as we have seen, a plot involving "chance" is the worst possible kind—being episodic, it can hardly be called a plot at all in the technical sense of that term. One further point. Note that the dramatist will not even be able to give the illusion of necessity and/or probability through the use of providential interference, as in the case of the statue of Mitys. In the complex-fatal play involving an "unqualifiedly good" protagonist, to invoke divine agency involves making the gods seem malevolent forces bent on destroying the good man rather than protecting him.

The basic objection, then, to the first type of plot is that it involves a direct violation of the rule of necessity and/or probability. The play will lack unity and appear as a chance sequence of episodes strung together on the hero's name. Because pity and fear are aroused first and foremost by structure—especially by reversal and recognition—the play will lack pity and fear, no matter how harrowing the individual incidents. If this is true of the complex-fatal plot involving an "unqualifiedly good" hero, it is clearly also true for the complex-fortunate plot involving an "extremely evil" one. Note that this reasoning does not imply "poetic justice" or didacticism. Aristotle merely insists that in the best tragedy there must be a relation between character and destiny. If no such relation exists, the tragedy lacks unity—it becomes incoherent and, of course, cannot fulfill its tragic "function." The Crucifixion must be ruled out as a possible subject for tragedy, but the analysis is broad enough to include most drama that is not explicitly ritualistic.

Types one and two are simply poor. Types three and four are more complex. They are both allowable, for in both there is a relation between character and end, but four is much more desirable than three. This fact further emphasizes the difference between Aristotle's theory of drama and the "didactic" theory attributed to him by, for example, Sir Philip Sidney.

Type two has involved consideration of the "extremely evil" protagonist. Type three continues this consideration but in relation to the fatal rather than the fortunate plot. A drama about a villain who eventually destroys himself or is destroyed in consequence of his evil ways is certainly possible. Moral philosophy tells us that "Vice is destructive and brings unhappiness to the sinner," and the third type of drama is solidly based on this notion. From the standpoint of a didactic critic, type three is the best tragedy. It raises no awkward questions about innocent suffering (such as those raised, for example, by The Book of Job), and it is entirely edifying. As Sidney remarks, it "maketh kings fear to be tyrants, and tyrants manifest their tyrannical humors." Aristotle recognizes the validity of the type when he admits that it is in accord with "human sympathy" (l. 18). This quite explicitly contrasts it to type two, which "violates our human sympathy" (l. 14). Yet he considers type three inferior to type four.

The problem for Aristotle is that a type three plot fails to arouse pity and fear. The two emotions are now defined in sentences that closely echo the more extended discussion already cited (p. 118) in the *Rhetoric*: "Pity is aroused by someone who undeservedly falls into misfortune and fear is evoked by our recognizing that it is someone like ourselves who encounters this misfortune" (ll. 19-22). Aristotle's reasoning is cogent. Our reaction to a plot in which the villain is appropriately punished and the hero rewarded is typically not pity and fear but a rather smug, "He got what he deserved." But there is perhaps a deeper point that Aristotle is making. Catharsis, it will be recalled, is a kind of learning. The reason for the failure of a type three plot to arouse pity and fear is that it shows us exactly what we expect to see. Instead of helping us to learn, it confirms our preconceptions. If catharsis involves a clarification of pitiable and fearful incidents, as was suggested in relation to Chapter VI, in a type three plot the incidents are already "clarified." The result—as we all know from exposure to didactic works—may be edifying; but it is also likely to be tedious and sentimental.

Aristotle's type four plot involves an anomaly. If he is simply ringing the changes on possible plot types, the type that most logically follows type three is a complex-fortunate plot involving an "unqualifiedly good" figure. Aristotle does not discuss this type at all. His reason for the omission is not apparent; but we can easily guess what he would have said had he included it. Let us call it type three-a. A type three-a plot is closely related to a type three plot. It too is "moral" and hence will appeal to our "human sympathy." Like a type three plot, however, it is entirely predictable. A supremely good man *ought to succeed*; seeing him do so is doubtless edifying but hardly surprising. No pity and fear are aroused, and the tragic function is not fully achieved. Edification replaces catharsis, and instruction replaces learning.

Like the third type, the fourth type has two forms, only one of which is discussed. If it is possible to have a complex-fatal plot with a flawed hero such as Oedipus, it is also possible to have a complex-fortunate plot with a flawed hero such as Orestes. Aristotle feels that the complex-fatal form is the most artistic, doubtless because it involves a greater excitation of pity and fear than the fortunate variety; but his high regard for the fortunate variety can easily be seen from his many favorable references to *Iphigenia in Tauris,* a play that he evidently found almost as satisfying as *Oedipus Rex.*

The fourth plot type involves a hero "between these extremes" (l. 26). This does not mean that the hero should be a "golden mean" between virtue and vice—such an idea is nonsense. Nor does it mean that the hero should have "average" virtues; we have seen as early as Chapter II that the tragic hero must always be "noble" (*spoudaios*) and be in the "better than" category. The point is emphatically confirmed a little later in Chapter XIII when Aristotle, after referring again to the proper character type, asserts that the hero should be of the type described "or a better rather than a worse one" (ll. 38-39). The good and evil protagonists of the first and second plot types represent extreme poles—the good hero is supremely good, almost infallible; the bad hero is entirely depraved. Anything less than wholly good or wholly bad will fall "between these extremes." Given this fact, the best character type is a figure as close to the good extreme as possible. He is a character who, although just and virtuous, is not "perfect" (l. 27). Why does he fail to excel? Aristotle expressly rules out the idea that he falls through vice or "depravity" (l. 37), a point that further emphasizes his goodness. On the other hand, he is involved in a complex-fatal plot. He must fall for some reason, otherwise the plot will be a type one plot lacking in necessity and/or probability. Aristotle solves this problem by saying that the hero must succumb to some *hamartia,* translated here as "miscalculation."

Logically Aristotle's position is quite clear. We know from Chapter II that the tragic protagonist should be "noble" and in the "better than" category. We also know from Chapters IX-XI that a plot should be as pitiable and fearful as possible. If we carry these requirements to the extreme, the ideal drama is a complex-fatal plot with a supremely "noble" protagonist. This, however, is a definition of a type one plot, and a type one plot is not good but "repellent." As we have seen, the type one plot violates the general requirement of necessity and/or probability. No relation is established between the form of the plot and the traits assigned the hero. A type one plot lacks unity, it fails to arouse pity and fear, and it offends our sense of propriety without showing us wherein that sense is inadequate. On the other hand, if the ideal turns out to be self-contradictory, an approximation of the ideal is still possible. The type three plot preserves the complex-fatal form but ignores the requirement that the protagonist be in the "better than" category. This type is acceptable but rather dull. Type four preserves the complex-fatal form and the goodness of the hero but assigns him a single flaw, which is the crucial element in the dramatic illusion. From the audience's point of view, it explains why the protagonist "fell" and therefore changes an episodic series of incidents into a series creating the illusion of causality.

The flaw is therefore deductively necessary. It is a character trait that is a corollary of the need to preserve necessity and/or probability in a complex-fatal plot. Notice that although the flaw is a character trait, it is so closely related to plot as to be inseparable from it. It is of a different order from the type characteristics dealt with in Chapter XV of the *Poetics,* and discussed more extensively in the *Ethics* and *Rhetoric.*

The nature of the flaw is also determined by the logic of the case. If the general requirement is that the tragic hero be in the "better than" category, and if a complex-fatal plot with a depraved hero is weak, the tragic hero should be as close to the "unqualifiedly good" man as possible. His flaw, therefore, should be slight. In one sense it must be a moral flaw, since it is the factor that makes the protagonist less than "unqualifiedly good." But the moral stigma should not be too great, lest we move toward a type three plot. As Aristotle says a little later, the hero should be "of the type . . . described [that is, "good"] or . . . better" (l. 38). The requirement is met by making the flaw an error of judgment—a mistake or "miscalculation"—rather than a sin. Even the most just men often lack the knowledge needed to make the right decisions. Although ignorance is not, in itself, a moral failing, it often leads to the most terrible consequences, as, for example, when a man is unjustly executed because the jury did not know the facts of the case, or a battle is lost because the commanding general was misinformed about the position of the enemy. "Miscalculation" allows Aristotle to preserve the goodness of the hero while providing the element that explains his downfall and relates his character to his destiny.

Thus far we have considered *hamartia* strictly within the logical context of the first part of Chapter XIII. Although there are still occasional critics of the *Poetics* who interpret the term in the sense of sin (a meaning that it definitely has, for example, in the Greek of the New Testament), the position taken here, that it refers to a "miscalculation," is generally accepted. (Though even "miscalculation" is not entirely satisfactory because it implies an intellectual error, while the root meaning of *hamartia* is simply "missing the mark.")

If "miscalculation," or something like it, is accepted, the term must still be understood in relation to the larger argument of the *Poetics* and in relation to Greek drama, particularly *Oedipus,* which Aristotle cites as an illustration (l. 31). A miscalculation can involve misunderstanding by the protagonist of "things as they are." This interpretation of *hamartia* is rather broad, but it is found in Butcher and in still looser form in A. C. Bradley's *Shakespearean Tragedy,* where the tragic conflict is interpreted as a Hegelian tension leading eventually to synthesis through the victory-defeat of the tragic protagonist. A much narrower—and hence perhaps preferable—meaning is suggested in different ways by Else and Martin Ostwald. Both critics interpret *hamartia* actively, as a tendency to err created by lack of knowledge. Both further suggest that the lack of knowledge characterizes the protagonist from the beginning—(it is a character trait)—and that it is complemented at the crisis of the play by the recognition scene, which involves a sudden change "from ignorance to knowledge." Else supports his argument by reference to *Nicomachean Ethics* III, 1-2 (especially 1110^{b}18-11^{a}14), and V, 10 (1135^{a}15-36^{a}9), adding that in Greek tragedy the ignorance that is the source of the *hamartia* is usually ignorance of blood relatives—a brother fails to recognize a sister, a son a mother, and so forth. Ostwald stresses the point that in *Oedipus* the source of the *hamartia* is the hero's ignorance of who he is, while the recognition scene supplies him with this information at the same time that it insures the "fatal" ending of the play.

To summarize, Aristotle lists four types of plot in Chapter XIII, but these four types clearly imply two additional ones, making three pairs of plot types:

1. Complex-fatal; "unqualifiedly good" hero	"repellent"
2. Complex-fortunate; "extremely evil" hero	"worst of all"
3. Complex-fatal; "villainous" hero	"sympathy, but no pity and fear"
[3a. Complex-fortunate; "unqualifiedly good" hero	? "no pity and fear"]
4. Complex-fatal; good hero with *hamartia: Oedipus*	best type
[4a. Complex-fortunate; good hero with *hamartia: Iphigenia in Tauris*	? next best type]

One and two are simply poor drama. Three and three-a are possible —they can be based on necessity and/or probability—but they lack pity and fear. Actually, the category that is represented by types three and three-a is what we call today didactic literature. It is homiletic, and it is the kind of literature that most renaissance critics wanted Aristotle to advocate. To interpret *hamartia* as "moral flaw" or "sin" is a way of pushing all literature toward the didactic category.

In contrast to his renaissance commentators, Aristotle prefers the kind of tragedy represented by types four and four-a. Note that type four is close to type one. The difference is that in type four the fatal end is caused, while in type one it is not.

Earlier in the discussion of plot types we noticed that a drama about the Crucifixion would probably have to be classified in the first category and would hence be excluded by Aristotle's criteria from the front rank of tragedy. On the other hand, we learn from anthropology as well as from such medieval survivals as the Oberammergau Passion Play that tragedy preserves a ritual element, and that a play on the Crucifixion *can* be absorbing drama. Evidently no defect at all is necessary in a ritual drama; in fact, the sinlessness of the victim is sometimes the central fact of the sacrifice, as is the case in Christian ritual. The need for a defect that makes the fall coherent therefore seems to be an outgrowth of the rationalization of drama. Long after the need for the defect was realized, a further rationalization set in according to which the punishment in a drama should fit the crime, and the reward, the virtue. Historically, the flawless victim is associated with the earliest stages of the development of tragedy, and the theory of poetic justice with the most recent stages. Aristotle's list of types is not based on history but on the relative excellence of the types, moving from least to most satisfactory. If he knew about ritual tragedy at all, it must have seemed nonsense to him; he could not accept it, and it is ruled out in the comment on type one. Neither was he able to accept the thorough rationalization of human experience attempted by didactic writers and represented by types three and three-a. The best type is between ritual and homiletic drama. There is no doubt, however, which of the two it most closely approaches. The hero of the fourth type is as good as possible or "better"; that is, the best plot is as close to type one as it is possible to come without sacrificing necessity and/or probability.

The first half of Chapter XIII ends with a summary sentence. Much of this sentence is already familiar; it asserts that the complex-fatal plot is best, that the change from good fortune to bad should come about through a "miscalculation" rather than "depravity" (l. 37), and that the hero should be of the good variety or "better" than good (ll. 38-39) rather than worse. One apparently new point is introduced—that the single plot is better than the double one. The remainder of the chapter deals with two points: the superiority of the fatal to the fortunate plot, and the superiority of the single to the double plot.

The Superiority of the Fatal Plot
(ll. 40-56)

To confirm the superiority of the fatal plot, Aristotle turns to the Greek theater. All the best tragedies, he observes, are based on a few myths or myth cycles. The families that are the subjects of these cycles were involved in terrible deeds, and the adventures of their offspring furnish ideal materials for fatal plots. The implication is that if fatal plots were *not* best, the dramatists would long ago have turned away from the traditional stories to other, less somber ones.

If "choice of sources" confirms the superiority of the fatal plot, so also does the work of Euripides. Evidently critics of Aristotle's day attacked Euripides for being too pessimistic and over-using the fatal ending. They are mistaken, says Aristotle, "For this is, indeed, the correct procedure" (l. 51). Further confirmation is provided by direct appeal to the theater: The dramas of Euripides are "most tragic" on the stage and in the dramatic contests (l. 54), and this is true in spite of faulty handling of some other aspects of dramatic technique. Aristotle does not say it, but he seems to mean that Euripides was extremely successful both as a playwright and later as a Greek "classic." In spite of his sensationalism, his rhetoric, and his rather frequent use of the *deus ex machina,* he consistently used the fatal plot and therefore "appears to be the most tragic of the poets" (l. 55).

The Inferiority of the Double Plot
(ll. 57-67)

A double plot is one involving two concurrent actions. The term has some relation to the modern term "subplot," except that in a work with a double plot each of the two actions can—at least in theory—be equally important. Aristotle has consistently discussed *one* action and *one* plot, most obviously in Chapter VIII, and his preference for the single plot hardly comes as a surprise. In fact, it is rather surprising to find him permitting the double plot at all, and we are reminded again by his comment that the *Poetics* is an analysis of possible types of drama, not a set of hard-and-fast prescriptions.

Double plots, says Aristotle, are produced to please the audience. His example of a double plot is not a drama but the *Odyssey,* in which we really have two actions—one a fortunate action involving Ulysses, and the second, a fatal action involving the suitors. This produces much pleasing variety and is perhaps consistent with epic freedom from restraint; but it violates dramatic economy. Characteristically, Aristotle adds another, more specific complaint. The double plot ends "in opposite ways for the better and worse characters" (l. 58). The suitors, for example, are destroyed, but Ulysses is reunited with Penelope. Note that this double plot employs two forms that have already been branded inferior when treated separately. The suitor plot is a fatal action involving depraved men (a type three plot), and the Ulysses plot is a fortunate plot involving either an "unqualifiedly good" hero (type three-a) or a good man with a defect (type four-a). Neither type provides the best kind of tragedy.

Finally, the pleasure of such a double plot is not really tragic, says Aristotle, but comic. Here he appears to be using the word "comedy" almost in its modern sense of "having a happy ending." This cannot be entirely right because Aristotle considers *Iphigenia in Tauris* a tragedy and calls its kind of recognition, in which the tragic deed is contemplated and then avoided at the last minute, the best kind of all (Chapter XIV, ll. 63-67). What he must mean in the present context is that comedy involves sudden reversals in which what is seemingly the most implacable hatred suddenly dissolves into joyous reunion—as would be the case, for example, if Orestes and Aegisthus suddenly became fast friends. Such reversals are entirely foreign to tragedy, but they are customary in comedy, especially the Middle and New Comedy that Aristotle evidently admired. Note finally that if tragedy produces a "clarification" of the pitiable and fearful incidents that it presents, there may be some justification on the basis of the present passage for associating comic catharsis with "reconciliation of enemies" and the sudden triumph of love over hate. This is entirely speculative, but it is perhaps as close as we come in the *Poetics* to the concept of comic catharsis.

Chapter XIV

At the end of Chapter XIII, Aristotle explained that the double plot produces inferior tragedy. Chapter XIV begins with a contrast between effects produced by the structure of the plot and those produced by spectacle. The interest of Chapter XIII in ranking possibilities from best to worst persists, but the basis of the scale changes.

As will be seen, the discussion of structure versus spectacle involves the degree to which the content of the incidents contributes to the tragic effect. Its conclusion is that structure is always more important than content. After the structure versus spectacle section, Aristotle turns to content. He does not deny that tragic deeds can in themselves produce pity and fear, and the second half of Chapter XIV discusses various strategies for presenting tragic deeds. Again, there is a ranking of strategies from least to most effective. Since this section treats the most specific element involved in the construction of plot—the content of the incidents—it concludes the treatment that began in Chapter VII. After Chapter XIV, Aristotle turns from plot to character.

Structure vs. Spectacle
(ll. 1-14)

We know from the formal definition of tragedy that the tragic effect depends on the presentation of incidents arousing pity and fear. We have also observed in connection with Chapters IX and XI (pp. 163 and 171) that pity and fear can be aroused (a) by the content of the episodes (*pathos*); and (b) by the structure of the plot, especially by the use of reversal and recognition. Although it is perfectly legitimate—even necessary—to use incidents that are pitiable and fearful in content, the effects gained by proper plot construction are much greater. This is a simple and obvious truth. Two horror movies, for example, may contain the same deserted mansions, secret passages, murders, and narrow escapes; but one may be tedious and the other intensely exciting. The difference is not the content of the incidents but the dramatic craftsmanship with which the incidents are presented. The effects gained by skillful technique are far more important than the effects gained by the mechanical piling of horror on horror.

These ideas are relevant to the comments on spectacle and structure at the beginning of Chapter XIV. In drama—which is based on the third manner of imitation—the spectacle that is provided by "the poetic art" is the way that the text is adjusted to the fact that it may eventually reach the stage. A dramatist who relies on the content of the incidents to arouse pity and fear will write his scenes so that a great many "fearful and pitiable" things will happen on stage when the play is produced. The inclusion of scenes of suffering—*pathos*—will take precedence over considerations of structure. Notice that the effect of such scenes is extremely limited when the play is read. A passage of dialogue implying that Medea is strangling her children may be affecting to a reader; but it will be far less affecting than watching an actress actually performing the deed on stage. Evidently, the enhancement of the effect of the strangulation comes from "the actor's art" or "the producer's art" rather than "the poetic art." It follows that a play relying chiefly on spectacle "does not have much to do with poetic art" (l. 9) and that the search for spectacular scenes will often lead not to pity and fear but to "the monstrous" (l. 11)—to sensationalism.

Again, because reversal and recognition are elements of structure, a play relying on the content of the incidents rather than on structure will often lack precisely those elements most powerfully productive of the tragic effect (Chapter VI, l. 74). On the other hand, a play whose very structure arouses pity and fear will be capable of creating the tragic effect even if its incidents lack the sort of sensationalism exploited by actors and producers. In such a case, the "tragic deed" can be entirely outside the plot, as in *Oedipus* (l. 44).

The first sentence of Chapter XIV simply asserts the conclusion that we have reached by the preceding analysis: "Pity and fear can arise from the spectacle and also from the very structure of the plot, which is the superior way and shows the better poet." Aristotle takes up the idea of creating pity and fear by structure in the next sentence. The plot, he says, should be so constructed that it will create "shudders" of fear and pity even though the drama is not seen on the stage. This point repeats ideas that have appeared earlier. It restates the idea (in Chapter VI) that tragedy can have its proper effect when read. More important, it recalls the advice about how to create pity and fear by the structure of incidents given in Chapters IX-XIII. To do this efficiently requires a unifying principle that is necessary and/or probable (Chapter IX), a sequence of incidents that involves indirect or direct causality (IX), a reversal or recognition (X, XI), and a fatal movement involving a good protagonist with a defect (XIII).

All these elements will be present in a proper outline of the plot of a drama. Such an outline gives what Aristotle will call in Chapter XVII "the universal form" of the drama. Thus Aristotle now observes that even an outline of *Oedipus* can create feelings of pity and fear. He does not mean "the story of Oedipus" in some vague, general sense, but the plot of *Oedipus Rex* just as Sophocles conceived it. The validity of Aristotle's position is evident from experience. Some people are born storytellers. They can turn the poorest experience into a fascinating anecdote; yet others fail to make even the most exciting adventures interesting. The difference, or one major difference, is in the way that the story is told—its structure, its "universal form." Sophocles produced a masterpiece of dramatic construction in *Oedipus,* and an adequate outline of his plot, although no substitute for the whole work, can convey some of its effect.

Having stressed the superiority of structure, Aristotle returns briefly to spectacle. The fact that spectacle is only partly within the poetic art is made explicit in the remark, "The achievement of this [tragic] effect through the spectacle does not have much to do with poetic art and really belongs to the business of producing the play" (ll. 8-10). Finally, some dramatists in their reliance on the content of incident rather than structure move beyond the subject-matter appropriate to tragedy. In order to create the greatest possible sensation, they draw on "the monstrous" rather than "the fearful." It is hard to say what incidents Aristotle had in mind when he referred to "the monstrous" (*teratodes*). He may have been thinking of scenes of unmitigated horror—the sort of scene that classical drama generally avoided—but it is also possible that he was thinking of scenes involving elaborate machines and other striking and apparently magical stage effects. At any rate, "the monstrous" is far removed from pity and fear. It cannot produce the effect proper to tragedy, and "We should not seek every pleasure from tragedy but only the one proper to it" (ll. 12-14).

The idea that there is a pleasure "proper to" tragedy is, of course, an echo of the notion in Chapter IV that all imitation produces pleasure, and of the identification of the tragic pleasure as catharsis in Chapter VI. Having referred to the "proper pleasure" of tragedy, Aristotle defines it once again as one that results from pity and fear in an imitative work. There is nothing new in this definition. It serves primarily as a transition to the consideration of the tragic deed that occupies the remainder of the chapter.

The Tragic Deed (ll. 15-76)

To say that pity and fear should be aroused primarily by the structure of the plot is not to say that the poet should avoid incidents that are pitiable and fearful in themselves. Obviously, the content of the incidents should be consonant with and should reinforce the effect of the tragic structure. The successful tragedy will therefore include incidents that are pitiable and fearful. Aristotle's term for such incidents is "incident of suffering"—*pathos*. One such incident is particularly important. This is what we will call "the tragic deed." The tragic deed involves two factors, the act itself and the knowledge or ignorance of the agent. As an act it is usually a slaying that is intrinsically pitiable and fearful and that deeply influences the mood and action of the tragedy. It can be the climax of the tragedy, but it need not be. Oedipus' slaying of his father Laius, for example, is classified by Aristotle as a tragic deed yet it is, as Aristotle says, "outside the plot" of *Oedipus* (l. 44); the tragic act in *Iphigenia in Tauris* is the sacrifice of Orestes that threatens to occur but does not actually take place. In that the tragic deed involves the knowledge or ignorance of the agent, it also can involve two larger components of tragedy—the *hamartia*, or miscalculation based on ignorance, and the recognition that changes ignorance to knowledge. If so, the tragic deed can extend over several incidents.

The analysis of tragic deeds begins with an appeal from art to life: "Let us try to understand what sort of occurrences appear to be terrifying and pitiable" (ll. 17-18). We then proceed systematically in terms of the various possibilities involved in the performance of a deed involving two parties. Note that a tragic deed involving only one party is never mentioned as a possibility. Oedipus' self-blinding is pitiable and fearful. It is a *pathos* but not a "tragic deed." The Greek tendency to focus tragedy on fearful deeds performed on one another by blood relatives seems to have influenced Aristotle's thinking on this subject.

The first set of possibilities is based on the attitudes toward each other of the two parties involved in the deed. They can be friends, enemies, or strangers who are mutually indifferent. If they are enemies, says Aristotle, the destruction of one by the other is not piteous, although the anguish of the defeated enemy may produce "suffering" (l. 24). Obviously we need have no pity for the victor. He has achieved exactly what he wished. We may, moreover, feel sorry for the vanquished and even pity him in a general sense; but the technical meaning of pity in the *Poetics* involves the idea of undeserved misfortune—misfortune that the individual neither wills nor brings on himself. By the mere fact of being "enemies," the two agents involved in the first kind of tragic deed will each other's destruction and accept the possibility that each himself may be destroyed. The vanquished enemy is therefore not pitiable in the same sense as, for example, Laius, whose death results from the fact that he and Oedipus do not recognize one another.

If the two agents are indifferent, the deed again fails to be "pitiable." Because one indifferent agent would only destroy another accidentally, the tragic deed would depend on chance, and chance produces episodic drama that arouses neither pity nor fear.

On the other hand, when the two parties involved in the deed are friends, the situation is truly conducive to pity and fear in Aristotle's sense. Note that a situation in which one friend slays another almost necessarily involves a mistake. A man does not consciously will the death of his friend; therefore, the performance of the deed implies either ignorance of the identity of the victim or circumstances that make the deed seem something other than what it is. When we mention ignorance, we are touching on *hamartia* and also anticipating the recognition scene, when ignorance is changed to knowledge. There is thus a very close relation in the *Poetics* between the kind of defect assigned the tragic hero, the nature of the tragic deed, the recognition scene that is at the heart of a complex-fatal tragedy, and the pity and fear that lead to the tragic pleasure.

If a tragic deed involving friends is innately pitiable, a tragic deed involving blood relatives will be even more so. The Greeks felt that the bond that united members of the same family was natural and instinctive. This makes tragic deeds perpetrated on blood relatives the most pitiable and fearful of all possible deeds. Aristotle specifies the family relationships that can be involved: brother to brother, son to father, mother to son, son to mother (ll. 28-29). The "traditional stories" of Greek myth and legend tell of several families in which tragic deeds involving relatives occurred frequently, and these stories served as the basis for much Greek tragedy. Aristotle approves the use of these stories (although, we recall, in Chapter IX he also praised Agathon for writing a fictional tragedy). He even advises that they should not be "altered completely" (l. 32) and cites two tragic deeds involving the slaying of a mother by a son—the slaying of Clytemnestra by Orestes and the slaying of Eriphyle by Alcmaeon—to illustrate what the poets should preserve.

Here a qualification is introduced. Having mentioned Clytemnestra and Eriphyle, Aristotle observes that the poets have ample freedom to "adapt" the traditional stories in a way that will maximize their effect. He has in mind the fact that once the poet has selected a tragic deed between blood relatives, he can adjust the circumstances of the deed in several ways.

The basic adjustment has to do with the degree of intent in the perpetration of the deed. That is, the agent can do the deed with full knowledge of the identity of the victim, as Medea when she killed her children; or he can do the deed in ignorance, as Oedipus when he killed his father. Having mentioned Oedipus (l. 44), Aristotle pauses for a moment to observe that in Sophocles' play the deed is "outside the plot." The reference is interesting because it reminds us that a plot in Aristotle's sense is something quite different from a "story," and because it repeats the point that a tragedy does not have to include a tragic deed in its plot to arouse pity and fear. The slaying of Laius would make a most sensational scene on the stage, but the intense, brilliantly developed action in Thebes during the king's quest for the source of contamination is far more gripping than mere sensation and has the advantage of remaining as effective when the play is read as when it is performed. At the same time, *Oedipus* is rather exceptional. The general tendency of

Greek drama is to include the tragic deed. Aristotle mentions a play by Astydamas presumably relating the murder of Eriphyle by her son Alcmaeon (l. 46) and a play by an unknown author about Telegonus, the illegitimate son of Ulysses, who fails to recognize and then fatally wounds his father. The two examples illustrate the two types of tragic deed discussed so far—the deed that is performed knowingly (Alcmaeon's) and the deed that is performed in ignorance (Telegonus'). Aristotle adds immediately that there is a third way: "Someone . . . intends to commit some fatal act through ignorance of his relationship to another person but recognizes this relationship before doing it" (ll. 48-50). The possibilities (but not all the possible combinations) have now been introduced. "Beyond these . . . there is no other way. . . . For it is necessary either to do the deed or not, and either knowingly or in ignorance" (ll. 51-53).

The next section of the chapter simply ranks the possible combinations of action, inaction, knowledge, and ignorance. First, the agent can know all the relevant facts, will the deed, and then desist. This, like the first plot type of Chapter XIII, is "repellent" (l. 55). The reason is identical with that given in Chapter XIII. To will an action with full awareness of the facts and then desist is to act capriciously. A character who does this violates necessity and/or probability, and the illusion of a relation between character and deed is destroyed. In addition, since there is no death, there is no "suffering" (l. 56). As might be expected this type of tragic deed is rare in tragedy. Aristotle cites the example of Haemon in *Antigone.* Evidently he is referring to Haemon's plan to kill Creon in revenge for causing Antigone's death. Haemon thrusts his sword at Creon, misses him, and then commits suicide. Note that the failure to slay Creon is not a reasoned decision based on new knowledge but the result of chance. Since Haemon is a relatively minor character, the incident does not fundamentally damage the play, but it is a blemish—a sensational incident that is not the result of the working of the necessary and/or probable principles underlying the plot. To put the matter another way, *Antigone* would be just as good a play (perhaps better) if Haemon simply committed suicide when he saw Creon approaching. According to Chapter VIII, "That whose presence or absence has no evident effect is no part of the whole" (ll. 25-26).

The second possibility is to know the relevant facts and to do the deed. Little need be said about this possibility. Premeditated murder is common in the life and literature of all ages. From Aristotle's point of view its chief defect seems to be that it precludes recognition, especially the personal recognition that is present in the plots of *Oedipus* and *Iphigenia in Tauris*. We have already had an example of this type of tragic deed in the allusions to Euripides' *Medea* and Astydamas' play about Alcmaeon. Other examples would be the *Agamemnon* of Aeschylus and the *Ajax* of Sophocles, which involves premeditated suicide.

We now come to two types that involve changes from ignorance to knowledge—that is, recognition. They are differentiated according to whether the change occurs before or after the tragic act *per se*. Although plays using deeds of type one or type two can be simple or complex, plays using the last two types must by definition be complex. Notice also that the "tragic deed" is expanded in types three and four to include not only a pitiable and fearful act such as a slaying but also a recognition scene coming before or after the act.

In type three, the recognition follows the act. In this case, "One does the deed in ignorance and after he has done it recognizes his relationship to the other person" (ll. 60-62). As we have seen, this type of tragic deed occurs "outside the plot" in *Oedipus* and within the plot in the story of Telegonus' fatal wounding of his father Ulysses. This type of tragic deed is entirely satisfactory. It is not "repellent" because it does not involve chance; and, as Aristotle says, "the recognition is startling" (l. 63). The effectiveness of this type of tragic deed is evident in Shakespeare's *Othello* as well as in *Oedipus*. In both cases the recognition is profoundly moving and pre-eminently tragic.

Surprisingly, the best type according to Aristotle is the type in which the recognition precedes the act. In this case the act is averted rather than performed. Aristotle gives three examples: the *Cresphontes* of Euripides, the *Iphigenia in Tauris* of Euripides, and the *Helle* of an unknown author. The only one of these plays that survives is the *Iphigenia*. It involves a double recognition (cf. Chapter XI, l. 30); and both recognitions occur before the proposed sacrifice of Orestes by his sister. As a result of the recognition,

Iphigenia decides to help her brother escape, and the plan is successfully executed at the end of the play. Aristotle clearly found this type of "tragic deed" deeply affecting. He calls it the best type (l. 63). It is a type that is familiar in renaissance and later drama, but it usually appears in comedy and romance rather than tragedy. *The Comedy of Errors* and *The Winter's Tale* provide good examples, one rather crude and the other highly sophisticated. Again we are reminded that Aristotle's definition of tragedy is quite different from the modern one, which places major emphasis on the "unhappy ending."

If the fourth type of "tragic deed" is the best one considered by itself, it is not necessarily the best in conjunction with the other requirements of tragedy. Chapter XIII was quite explicit in maintaining that the complex-fatal plot is better than the complex-fortunate. But a type four "tragic deed" produces a complex-fortunate plot, as we see in *Iphigenia.* Given Aristotle's hierarchy of values, we are probably safe in concluding that the best kind of tragic deed may not make the best play. If the best kind of plot is the complex-fatal, the "tragic deed" most suited for it is the third type, involving commission of the act followed sooner or later by recognition, as in *Oedipus, Ulysses Wounded, Hercules Insane,* and *Othello.*

Aristotle's four types of "tragic deed" are derived from the interrelation of two major factors—a tragic deed that is a part of plot and a "lack of knowledge" that is at least in some degree a part of character. If we tentatively assume that "lack of knowledge" is the underlying cause of *hamartia* and that "knowledge" is the result of *anagnorisis,* we can diagram the four types of tragic deed as follows:

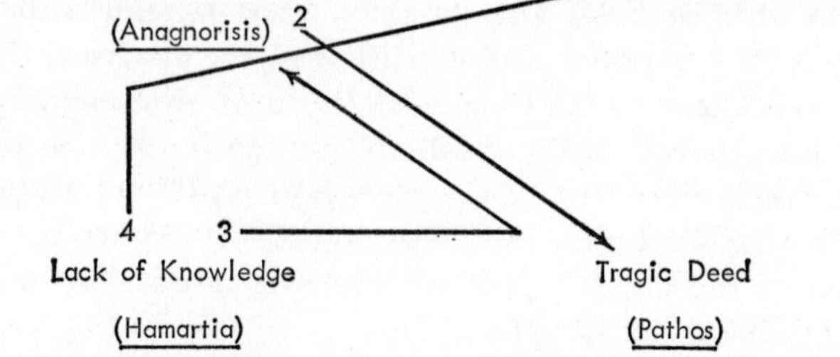

Although the diagram shows the four possible types of tragic deed (the fifth type—from lack of knowledge to no action—is meaningless and never mentioned), it is closely related to the reversal-recognition that makes the complex plot and to the notion of the tragic defect as a miscalculation made on the basis of lack of knowledge. Note especially the close relation in the complex-fatal plot between *hamartia, pathos,* reversal-recognition, and denouement.

Chapter XIV ends with another reference to the "few families" (l. 70) that provide the majority of tragic plots. The distinction between those poets who work by trial-and-error and those who work by art, introduced first in Chapter I (ll. 16-17) and again in Chapter IV (ll. 23-26), is now applied to the selection of plot materials. Early poets lacked knowledge of their art. Proceeding empirically in terms of what "worked" and what did not "work," they discovered that plots based on legendary families with "fatal" histories were the most successful. In fact, says Aristotle, tragic poets still revert to these families. Their practice is evidently the result of custom rather than art. Aristotle's *techne* explains why stories based on the "few families" are appropriate for tragedy. But note that by outlining the general form that tragedy takes, the *Poetics* also liberates poets from exclusive reliance on the "few families," for it points the way to the construction of purely fictional plots, such as the *Antheus* of Agathon.

The last sentence in the chapter is a formal conclusion: "We have now spoken sufficiently about the construction of the incidents and of what type the plot must be." The reference is to the section of the *Poetics* that extends from Chapter VII to Chapter XIV. Appropriately, Chapter XV turns from plot to character. On the other hand, Chapters XVI, XVII, and XVIII return to the subject of plot. They are rather miscellaneous and, although they add significant details to what we know already, they break no really new ground. Chapter XVI is a rather arid extension of the analysis of kinds of recognition. Chapters XVII and XVIII form an extremely miscellaneous list of seven "rules of thumb" for composing tragedies. The evidence, then, suggests that Chapters XVI-XVIII are a kind of appendix to the discussion in Chapters VII-XIV rather than a continuation of the larger argument, which is resumed in the discussion of "thought" in Chapter XIX.

Chapter XV

Although Aristotle does not offer a formal treatment of character (*ethos*) until Chapter XV, several points have already emerged. Chapter II indicated that the agents of a tragedy are "noble" and of "the better sort." Chapter VI confirmed this and made an emphatic separation between character and plot. The corollary would seem to be that the "nobility" of the tragic hero is not part of his character in the technical sense but a byproduct of the action in which he is involved. Chapter VI refined our notion of what character is by emphasizing that it is something added to the agent after the plot has been worked out. In general, what the poet "adds" are traits derived from such sources as the *Nicomachean Ethics* and, especially, the type-formulas found in classical rhetoric. Chapter IX further suggested that there should be a necessary and/or probable relation between the actions an agent performs and the type characteristics assigned him. When such a relation is established, the reader or spectator has the illusion that the character of the protagonist is the "cause" of his actions, as in real life. Pursuing this line of thought further, Chapter XIII suggested that in the best type of plot, the complex-fatal, the goodness of the hero should be qualified by a defect (*hamartia*) that is not (or not necessarily) a vice but that is sufficient to create the illusion of a causal relation between the character and his "fall" from happiness to misery. Finally, Chapter XIV suggested that the tragic hero should have an individual "name" derived from one of the traditional legends, that he should perform or threaten to perform a "tragic deed" against a blood relative, and that he should recognize his victim either after the deed (complex-fatal) or before it (complex-fortunate).

These points are quite specific. They provide, perhaps, Aristotle's basic criteria for the development of an effective drama. How far they are related purely to action and plot and how far they invade the area designated by "character" is hard to say. If they are all corollaries of action and plot, it is very easy to see why Aristotle said in Chapter VI that a tragedy is possible without "character" but not without plot. On the other hand, it is probably safest to assume that the notion of *hamartia* and the strategies related to the tragic deed are part of a kind of middle ground related to plot and character simultaneously, even though these factors appear in the discussion of plot.

Chapter XV is a formal discussion of character *qua* character. It begins with four general principles that serve to guide the dramatist in his selection of character traits. It continues with a reminder that character should be related to action in terms of necessity and/or probability, and it ends with a reminder of the importance of making the characters as good as possible.

One general point should be noted at the beginning. Normally we think of characterization as the art of particularizing. Aristotle does not ignore this matter, but his emphasis is on the generalizing effect of characterization. To "characterize" is to assign type traits to an agent. When Medea is "characterized," for example, she is given traits appropriate to women in general and to a jealous wife in particular. This is necessary because there is no living Medea for the poet to copy; but it is also proper because poetry tends toward the universal in characterization as well as structure. To extend Aristotle's analogy between drama and the visual arts, we can observe that a tragic poet is more like a portrait painter than a photographer. He produces an illusion of particularity, but he stresses those general qualities that seem most appropriate to his action. It is the primitive, not the sophisticated poets who, in Aristotle's history of poetry, imitate real persons.

The Four Principles of Characterization (ll. 1-25)

The four principles of characterization are that the character should be (1) good (*chrestos*), (2) appropriate (*harmotton*), (3) "like" (*homoios*), and (4) consistent (*homalon*). Commentators disagree over the meaning of these terms and perhaps no definitive explanation of them is possible. *Chrestos* has usually been interpreted as roughly synonymous with *spoudaios* in Chapter II and *beltion* ("better") in Chapter XIII (l. 38). It has also been interpreted as "good" in the sense of "dramatically effective" (Telford). "Goodness" has also been seen as a general moral quality evident from the beginning of the drama and more specifically as a moral quality only (or most fully) evident in choices made by the character. *Harmotton* presents few difficulties because Aristotle's examples point quite clearly to rhetorical concepts of character type. *Homoios* again raises problems. Does it mean "realistic" in the sense of "like real life" or "natural"; or does it mean "like" the legendary character whose name is being used; or does it mean "like" in the sense of "like the action that the agent must perform"? *Homalon* is reasonably clear. The requirement that a character be "consistent" is familiar to all readers of drama.

Although we cannot arrive at the final truth concerning Aristotle's terms, we can at least arrive at a probable interpretation by recalling Aristotle's tendency to move from the general to the specific, both in his discussion of literature and in his treatment of plot. We would expect the same pattern in his treatment of character even though the treatment is rather brief. If we take this approach, the most general requirement for character is that it be harmonious with the nature of the agents to whom it is attributed. Since the agents are of the "better sort" by virtue of the action, it follows that their characters should be "good" in the moral sense rather than "bad." Character is manifested in "characteristic speeches," especially those that involve making choices (Chapter VI, l. 96). Although a character may not explain his choice in a speech, if from the audience's point of view the choice seems "good," the character will seem good also. Hence, "If a speech or action has some choice connected with it, it will manifest character . . . and the character will be good if the choice is good" (ll. 3-5). The only problem here is that we have learned to associate action with plot and to draw a sharp line between plot and character. The fact that the line wavers a bit in relation to the first principle of character is actually a good sign. It underscores the relation between *chrestos* of Chapter XV and the "goodness" that is closely related to action in Chapters II, VI, and, especially, XIII. Furthermore, if the two concepts *are* closely related, as seems probable, we do not have to interpret *chrestos* in an exclusively moral sense. The "noble" agents of Chapter II are not paragons of virtue but figures with a special moral grandeur; and the good protagonists of the fatal-complex tragedy have at least one defect, the *hamartia*. Most Greek tragic heroes have high ethical standards, but their standards are quite different from those advocated in textbooks of ethics. *Chrestos* can mean good, brave, or upright, and perhaps some combination of these possible meanings is best. "Righteous" might do for Oedipus, Hippolytus, Orestes, and Antigone; but "fiercely determined" would be better for Clytemnestra and Medea. Aristotle gives twofold confirmation of the idea that there can be no simple meaning for *chrestos*. In the next sentence he says that "goodness" is possible for each class. A woman—and even a slave—can have this quality, although they will have it in different kinds and degrees. And at the end of Chapter XV (l. 49), Aristotle adds that poets have to be able to make men "good" even while making them wrathful or prone to other weaknesses. In other words, the sort of goodness he has in mind can coexist with the stubborn passion so often displayed by tragic figures. The example of Homer's Achilles (l. 50) perfectly illustrates the point.

We can, then, define "goodness" as the quality that provides moral elevation in tragic characters. The specific quality will change from play to play and from character to character, but all tragic protagonists have it in some degree, and the more the better. Unnecessary sacrifice of this quality (as below, l. 21, in the characterization of Menelaus) is a defect. It sacrifices some of the potential effect of tragedy.

We now move from a general quality that is related to both plot and character to a subject that is entirely within the domain of character. "Appropriateness" is close to—if not identical with—what classical rhetoric called "decorum" (*to prepon*). Aristotle cites "manliness" to illustrate an "appropriate" character trait and remarks that the "manly" character is not appropriate to a woman. This is enough to show that he is thinking of the assignment of type characteristics, in rhetoric and rhetoric-related treatises, by sex, age, social class, profession, and nationality. Chapters XII-XVII of Book II of Aristotle's *Rhetoric* contain typical sketches of character types differentiated by age (young, old, middle-aged) and social standing (good birth, wealth, power). Other sources of "appropriate" character traits are ethical treatises, set character sketches such as the "Characters" of Aristotle's pupil Theophrastus, and "scientific" character portraits based on the humours theory or notions of the effect of climate on character. This very rich quarry of material was available to the Greek dramatists, and as Greek tragedy evolved it came to be used more and more. It is least evident in Aeschylus, more so in Euripides; and, of course, it is still more prominent in Seneca's Latin imitations of Greek drama. During the Renaissance it continued to be extremely important. Christopher Marlowe's Tamburlaine has the characteristics of the active warrior-hero; Faustus, those of the contemplative scholar. Shakespeare's Hotspur is the "rash" type, as the name implies; his Iago is an "Italianate" type; his Romeo a "youthful" type; his Antony, in *Antony and Cleopatra* an "effeminate warrior." Hamlet is "melancholic"; and, of course, a great many of Ben Jonson's characters have traits determined by their "humours."

The main point about such character traits is that they should be appropriate to the agent. If "goodness" is the most general character requirement for the tragic character, "appropriate" traits allow his features to be delineated in greater detail and in ways that are necessarily and/or probably related to the action. Again it should be stressed that traits do not "particularize" a character. If anything, they have the opposite effect. They make him a recognizable and well-known "type" and, in this sense, "universalize" him.

The requirment that a character be "like" is perhaps the most perplexing of Aristotle's four criteria. The fact that Aristotle's list of principles moves from most general to most specific is helpful here. "Appropriateness" relates to type traits. After a character has been framed in general terms, what is the dramatist's next task? It is to particularize the character, to give him idiosyncrasies that soften—without obscuring—the general outline. The most probable meaning for "like" is therefore "like an individual." This interpretation is reinforced by the use of *homoios* in reference to painting (l. 45) to mean "likeness to the person being painted." In reference to Greek tragedy, "like" bears two senses. Agathon's *Antheus,* it will be recalled, is entirely fictional, and even in historical tragedies many minor characters are invented. In such cases the dramatist has no model to provide "like" characteristics. He must rely strictly on the relation of action to agent and the more specific relation of agent to "appropriate" characteristics assigned him. If these matters are settled, they will give the dramatist some hint of what "like" characteristics are necessary and/or probable. But Agathon's *Antheus* is exceptional. Most Greek tragedies, as Aristotle notes more than once, are based on legends concerning a few "fatal" families, and the tragic poets, unlike comedy writers, generally preserve "individual names" in their plots. In these cases the poet does have models. Presumably, when depicting Agamemnon, he should use traits that are "like" those traditionally associated with Agamemnon in legend. By the same token, when depicting Zeus, the poet should preserve at least the more presentable myth traditions concerning his character; while Xerxes (Aeschylus' *Persians*) should be given traits that are "like" those assigned him in history. The point is similar to that made by Horace in the *Ars Poetica* (ll. 119-24): "If you introduce . . . 'far-famed Achilles,' let him disown all laws . . . his appeal will be to the sword. In like manner let Medea be high-hearted and unconquerable. Ino tearful, Ixion a traitor, Io a wanderer, Orestes forlorn."

The last principle is that characters should be consistent. Principles one through three relate to the composing of "characteristic speeches." Principle four adds that the traits revealed by the speeches at the end of the play should be the same sort as those revealed by the speeches at the beginning. Note that the criterion of consistency confirms the suggestion made in connection with Chapter VI (p. 125) that character is a relatively constant factor throughout a play. Aristotle adds that if the poet assigns an agent the traits of an erratic man, he should make him "consistently inconsistent" (l. 19)—that is, consistently erratic.

Aristotle next gives examples of abuses of three of the four principles. The lack of an example of abuse of the principle of "likeness" is curious enough to suggest strongly that a line of the Greek has been lost. The first example is a case of gratuitous debasement of a character, a violation of the principle that characters should be good. In the *Orestes* of Euripides, Menelaus is asked to help save Orestes from being condemned to death but refuses through cowardice. Orestes is condemned as expected and the action proceeds. Aristotle's point is clearer in a later reference to the same incident. In Chapter XXV (l. 137), he says that the baseness of Menelaus is an impropriety in the plot because it is superfluous and no use is made of it. In fact, the refusal of Menelaus does not alter the movement of the plot of *Orestes* one iota. It merely retards this movement and, as such, is a digression. Returning to Chapter XV, Aristotle's point is evidently not that Menelaus is base when he should be "good" but that Menelaus is *unnecessarily* base. The baseness is gratuitous. It is not required by the action, and Euripides could have omitted it. By so doing he could have retained at least some "goodness" in his portrait of Menelaus, and the first general principle of characterization is, the more "goodness" retained in the characters of a tragedy, the better. To state the same point in a different way, we recall that in Chapter XIII Aristotle denied that the fall of a "villain" could arouse pity and fear. Tragedies containing unnecessary baseness sacrifice one of the most important sources of pity and fear; hence, they fail to achieve the full tragic effect.

The next examples illustrate violation of the rule of appropriateness. Ulysses is a manly warrior and, by tradition, wily. However in Timotheus' (lost) dithyramb *Scylla,* Ulysses was apparently made to lament in an effeminate way. Clearly Timotheus violated decorum of character. Melanippe's speech—a plea for her life—in the play *Melanippe the Philosopher* survives, although the rest of the play has been lost. It is extremely sophistic, and evidently, from Aristotle's point of view, such cleverness is "inappropriate" to the feminine character type. In Greek psychological theory, the "womanly type" was supposed to be passionate rather than intellectual and to have little capacity for logical argument. Finally, Iphigenia in *Iphigenia in Aulis* changes suddenly from "effeminate" suppliant to heroic figure, clearly a violation of the rule of consistency.

In sum, Aristotle's principles of characterization move from the most general requirement—a requirement that arises from the action imitated as well as from the imaginary psychology of the agents—to the more specific one that the characters be recognizable types, to the still more specific one that they be "like" men in general or the legendary figures whose names they bear, to the final principle that whatever combination of traits is selected, it should remain constant from one scene to the next. Two significant points may be added to this summary. First, throughout the exposition and the examples, the contrast between the manly and the "effeminate" or womanly character tends to recur. The tragic character should be "good" and "such goodness is possible" for a woman or a slave. The character should be appropriate, and the example given is the manly versus the womanly. Menelaus is "base" in the *Orestes* because he acts in a cowardly—that, is effeminate—way; Ulysses utters effeminate lamentations in the *Scylla*; Melanippe shows manly sophistication rather than womanly passion; and Iphigenia vacillates between the womanly and the heroic extremes. The recurrence of the manly-womanly theme in the remarks on character suggests that Aristotle intentionally chose the most clearly distinguishable character types and used them throughout. If so, we have further confirmation for the interpretation of *chrestos* as roughly synonymous with *spoudaios* in Chapter II. "Goodness" is a trait that all humans (including women and slaves) can reveal. It is independent of "type" and hence of what passed in antiquity for deterministic psychology. A woman and a hero—Melanippe and Ulysses—can both be "good." But Ulysses should not be depicted as effeminate; Melanippe should not be given the intellectual traits of a man. And Iphigenia most certainly should not be effeminate and manly in the same play.

The second point is less significant but worthy of notice. The *Orestes* and *Iphigenia in Aulis* are both examples of the abuse of the *deus ex machina,* and insofar as its plot can be reconstructed, *Melanippe the Philosopher* also involved a contrived ending. Is there a trace of the suggestion here that inadequate characterization destroys the illusion of causality in a drama and leads to episodic or contrived plots? This would explain the otherwise somewhat digressive comment on contrived plots in the next section of Chapter XV.

Character and Action (ll. 26-56)

The most basic rule for using the four principles is one that we have already encountered in Chapter IX. "In character, as in the construction of the incidents," says Aristotle, "we must always seek for either the necessary or the probable, so that a given type of person says or does certain kinds of things, and one event follows another according to necessity or probability" (ll. 26-30). The first part of the sentence emphasizes the parallel between the rule in Chapter XV and that laid down in Chapter IX for plot construction. The remainder of the sentence deals with dramatic illusion. For the poet, we recall, the incidents of the plot come first, the characterization later. By selecting a characterization for his agent that is necessarily or probably related to the actions performed, the poet provides for the illusion. The audience knows that the feminine character type, for example, tends to "say or do" certain things and not to say or do others. Thus if the poet assigns Andromache "feminine" traits, her deeds and speeches will seem to the audience to be the consequence of her character; the requirement will be met that the drama seems to reproduce natural causality—". . . a given type of person says or does certain kinds of things, and one event follows from another according to necessity or probability."

Having touched on necessity and probability, Aristotle adds a few more comments concerning plot. The comments appear digressive, but they are perhaps less so than a first glance indicates. The discussion of the four principles of characterization cited plays with contrived endings to illustrate violations of the principles. In addition, the discussion of necessity and probability in characterization suggests that failure to observe these guidelines results in a disruption of the dramatic illusion—the play seems to violate natural causality because the agent's acts do not seem to be caused by his character. If the play is not resolved by factors supplied by characters within the plot, the dramatist must resort to some outside agency, and the most notorious example of such an outside agency is the *deus ex machina.*

Aristotle gives two illustrations. The contrivance in *Medea* is the Sun-chariot in which Medea escapes after murdering her children. Why is it a contrivance? Medea is a sorceress, and a sorceress can certainly command a Sun-chariot. The Sun-chariot must be a "contrivance" because there has been no preparation for it earlier in the play. That is, Euripides' treatment of Medea's character is generally naturalistic. She is primarily a passionate woman, and the "sorceress Medea" of the final scene is insufficiently prepared for by the preceding action. Else has argued more specifically that Medea is (a) cunning, and (b) convinced that the only way to save her children from her enemies is to kill them. Yet if she can summon the Sun-chariot whenever she needs it, their deaths are unnecessary. Her failure to take the Sun-chariot into account makes her seem stupid and contradicts the emphasis on her cunning. The problem arises because Euripides has failed to assign traits to Medea, the agent, that are appropriate to the plot in which she appears. If the final scene is to involve "the marvelous," then much more attention should be given in earlier scenes to Medea's magical powers. Euripides' failure to recognize this fact results in a scene that seems to the spectator like a contrivance—a bit of unmotivated sensationalism.

By the same token, the story of the departure of the Greeks in the *Iliad* (II, 155) involves a sudden, aribtrary manipulation of human affairs by forces "outside the plot." The Greeks, discouraged by nine years of fruitless warfare, decide to raise the siege of Troy and depart. Homer remarks, "Then would the Argives have accomplished their return against the will of Fate, but that Hera spake a word to Athena." The goddess intervenes, and through her the Greeks are persuaded to continue the war. The illustration is clear enough, but it involves an abrupt shift in Aristotle's subject-matter from tragedy to epic. Else therefore suggests that the Greek word *Iliad* should be changed to *Aulid,* making the passage a reference to *Iphigenia in Aulis.* If so, the point of the illustration remains the same. Iphigenia is about to be sacrificed to insure the propitious departure of the Greek fleet for Troy but at the last moment is saved by the intervention of the goddess Artemis. The miraculous salvation of Iphigenia is not found in the modern text of Euripides, but we know that a version of the play existed in antiquity that *did* include the *deus ex machina.* Even more than does *Medea,* this version illustrates inconsistency between a plot involving divine forces and characterization that is generally naturalistic. Up to the appearance of Artemis, the play develops in terms of the conflict between patriotism and piety on the one hand, and love and the instinct of self-preservation on the other. Then suddenly the conflict is abandoned in favor of the miraculous "contrivance." From the spectator's point of view, the play fails to achieve the illusion of natural causality.

Aristotle now turns from specific examples of plays with contrived endings to a general observation: "The *deus ex machina* must be reserved for events that lie outside the plot" (l. 34). We have already been told that the tragic deed of *Oedipus* is "outside the plot" (Chapter XIV, l. 44), and that Homer introduces episodes that are not part of the action of the *Iliad* for the sake of the pleasing variety characteristic of epic. Here the reference is to incidents that influence the action but are far removed from it in time. These incidents may precede or follow the play's action; but they must be described *in the play* if the audience is to appreciate the action and its consequences. Aristotle suggests that the *deus ex machina* is particularly suited to the role of expositor of the past or prognosticator of the future, because the gods have "the power of seeing all things"—past, present, or future (ll. 38-39).

The section ends with a restatement. No incidents should be "improbable"—that is (in the present context) there should be a necessary and/or probable relation between incidents and characterization. If this is impossible, says Aristotle, the improbability should be outside the plot "as, for example, in Sophocles' *Oedipus*" (l. 41). The fact that the tragic deed in *Oedipus* is not part of the plot is recalled. Because the slaying of Laius is the result of chance rather than any necessary and/or probable cause, it is "improbable" —it defies rational explanation. If it were part of the plot, the resulting structure would be episodic.

The references to Iphigenia, Medea, the departure of the Greeks in the *Iliad,* and the *deus ex machina* all involve criticism of plays that are resolved by divine intervention. This problem has been touched on before, most clearly in relation to the statue of Mitys mentioned at the end of Chapter IX. Was Aristotle opposed to the use of divine agents? That is, did he wish drama to be confined wholly to the human sphere? This is not an easy question to answer. Else believes that Aristotle heartily disapproves of divine agents, and he points out that in Chapter II tragedy is defined as an imitation of men in action. On the other hand, Aristotle never overtly criticizes the use of magic, fairies and other mythical beings, or even of gods and goddesses. The emphasis in his discussion is on making the characterization consistent with the ending in order to achieve the illusion that character is causing action, as in real life. The criticism of *Medea* is not that the play ends with a Sun-chariot but that "magical powers" have not been stressed sufficiently in the earlier scenes to provide a convincing and effective "cause" for the final miracle. The best conclusion, then, is that although

Aristotle clearly preferred naturalistic to mythic drama, he did not rule out the latter. Magicians furies, and gods can appear—and, in fact, they must appear—if the illusion of causality is to be sustained in some plays.

We now turn from the relation of action to characterization to the tragic character *per se*. Aristotle advises following the lead of portrait painters who paint men "better than they are" in real life (l. 46). Again we are reminded that for Aristotle characterization is a generalizing technique, not one that particularizes, and the general rule for tragedy is that agents should be "good" or, if possible, "better" than good. The painter draws his portrait so that the quality of "goodness" shines out more clearly than in life. The poet does likewise. This process may be called "universalizing" a character. It should not be interpreted to mean "idealizing." After the poet "universalizes" the most basic quality, "goodness," he adds the type qualities of his characters. Aristotle mentions the type that is disposed to anger, the indifferent type, and those disposed "in other such ways" (l. 48). The fully developed character will thus be a blend of "goodness" and appropriate characteristics, some of which may be vices. Aristotle cites the Achilles of Agathon and Homer as an especially vivid example of a character who is "good" in the sense of having tragic elevation and who at the same time clearly manifests a vice—proneness to wrath.[1]

Chapter XV ends with a curt admonition to pay "close attention" to matters of characterization and an observation, not especially pertinent, that one should also be careful about spectacle—"those [matters] that pertain to the effects upon an audience, that follow necessarily from the art of poetry" (ll. 52-54). The "published work" that he refers to in the last line of the chapter is evidently the treatise *On the Poets* that survives today only in fragments.

[1] The text is corrupt here. Other editors and translators have ". . . characteristics, just as Homer makes Achilles both harsh and good at the same time," in place of the present reading. The point is the same in either case.

Chapter XVI

Chapter XVI is a supplement to Chapters XI and XIV. It lists six "kinds of recognition" from least to most "artistic." By "kinds of recognition" Aristotle means exactly what the phrase suggests—ways that characters recognize each other. Notice that the bases of classification in Chapters XVI and XIV are different. In the earlier chapter, the emphasis was on recognition before or after the commission of the tragic deed. Here, emphasis is on the devices whereby the recognition is brought about. The least artistic is by "signs," that is, arbitrary tags that enable one character to identify another. Aristotle lists birthmarks, scars, and external signs such as necklaces. The scar of Ulysses is the best example of what he has in mind. It is used twice, in a "better" and a "worse" way. In *Odyssey*, XIX, 386ff., the nurse Eurycleia, after remarking on the similarity between the rag-clad stranger and her long-absent lord Ulysses, discovers a familiar scar and recognizes the stranger. The recognition is the outcome of a sequence of incidents, and it occurs despite the fact that Ulysses wishes to keep his identity secret. In *Odyssey*, XXI, 205ff., Ulysses reveals his identity to his swineherd and neatherd by showing them his scar. This recognition is not the result of a series of incidents, and it occurs because Ulysses wishes it. The first use of signs is the more artistic, for it is the result of Penelope's command that the nurse wash Ulysses' feet, a customary way of honoring a stranger. It is also "probable," because the old nurse has already sensed the similarity between the stranger and Ulysses. The scar is not so much the demonstration of Ulysses' identity as the confirmation. The nurse's recognition of the scar derives, Aristotle says, "from the reversal" (l. 18). That is, it grows naturally out of the sequence of incidents leading to the major reversal-recognition scene before the suitors. On the other hand, the swineherd episode is simply an arbitrary act that could have occurred at any time after Ulysses' return to Ithaca. Moreover, the swineherd has not sensed Ulysses' identity. The scar therefore becomes the sole proof of who the stranger is.

The basic trouble with this kind of recognition is that it is too easy. It does not grow out of the plot. At any time he wishes, the author can solve his plot problems by inventing a new "sign" in the same way that a mystery writer can enliven a slow chapter by introducing a new clue. As Aristotle says, recognition by signs is used "mainly . . . through the poverty of . . . inspiration" (ll. 3-4).

The second form of recognition is closely related to the first and, like it, is "inartistic." Some recognitions are manipulated entirely by the poet without regard to necessity and/or probability. Aristotle's example is the recognition of Orestes in *Iphigenia in Tauris.* Just as the sacrifice is about to take place, Orestes exclaims, "My sister, my dear sister, from one sire/ From Agamemnon sprung, turn not away" (l. 800). Such a remark at such a time is improbable to say the least. Orestes makes it because he must make it. It is forced on him by Euripides so that his sister can recognize him and for no other reason. Obviously, as Aristotle remarks, recognition via the contrivance of the poet is closely related to recognition by signs.

The third form of recognition is through memory. In the eighth book of the *Odyssey,* Ulysses appears as a stranger at the palace of King Alcinous. The royal minstrel then sings of the fall of Troy and the words so move Ulysses that he weeps. The king observes the stranger's behavior and recognizes him because of it. Since this incident depends on a chain of prior incidents extending back to the fall of Troy, it is less arbitrary than recognition by signs or by the poet's contrivance.

The fourth type of recognition involves the use of logic. The character must reason his way to the recognition, and the reasoning process must be expressed in the dialogue. The first example is the recognition of Orestes by Electra in the *Choëphoroe,* the second play of Aeschylus' *Oresteia* trilogy. Having found a lock of her brother's hair, Electra reasons in roughly syllogistic fashion, even before she sees him, that the strange visitor must be her brother (ll. 168-234). Aristotle summarizes her logic in a formal syllogism:

> Major Premise: Someone resembling me has come.
> Minor Premise: There is no one like me but Orestes.
> Conclusion: He therefore has come.

The other examples are more brief. Apparently Polyidus the Sophist suggested that as he is about to die, Orestes should exclaim something like, "My sister was sacrificed; therefore it was always likely that I too would be sacrificed." These words, of course, would inform Iphigenia of the identity of her victim and would lead to the mutual recognition. The examples of the *Tydeus* and the *Phinidae* are evidently similar, although the plays (or, perhaps, dithyrambs) do not survive.

Recognition by false reasoning (paralogism) is a notoriously difficult concept, complicated by the fact that the Arabic text of the *Poetics* has a much longer discussion at this point than the Greek text and also by the fact that the play *Ulysses the False Messenger* is lost. A paralogism is defined in Chapter XXIV (ll. 69-73) as a kind of reasoning according to which if A is false but its consequent B is true, then A appears to be true. Exactly how this type of false reasoning applies to Ulysses is unclear; and it is quite possible that Aristotle does not use paralogism here in the technical sense found later in Chapter XXIV. All translations agree that the false reasoning is somehow related to the fact that the ragged stranger says that he will recognize a bow that he has apparently never seen. The false reasoning may simply be the fallacy of having a character claim to recognize something he has never seen. However, the stranger's statement does not in itself bring about the recognition—if the play followed Homer, it was the stringing of the bow that revealed Ulysses' identity. Perhaps the false reasoning is on the part of the suitors. They should have recognized the stranger the minute he admitted being familiar with the bow; instead, they waited until the stringing incident. There is no evidence, however, that the play followed Homer. It might, for example, have contained a recognition resulting from the stranger's admission that he can recognize the bow. The false reasoning might be the fact that his listeners assumed him to be telling the truth. There are other possibilities. The passage exercises the ingenuity of commentators, but fortunately it is not very important to the over-all argument of the *Poetics*.

The best form of recognition, of course, is the kind discussed in Chapters XI and XIV. It arises "from the incidents themselves" (l. 57), which strike us "with astonishment through the very probability of their occurrence." The sentence is a close echo of the general rule at the end of Chapter IX that a plot is most effective if the incidents arise unexpectedly, yet in consequence of one another (l. 58). It is illustrated by Aristotle's two favorite plays, *Oedipus Rex* and *Iphigenia in Tauris*. Both tragedies have already been praised for their recognitions (Chapter XI, l. 15; Chapter XIV, l. 66). Iphigenia is revealed to her brother through a letter that she wishes taken home (l. 582), and as Aristotle observes, it is highly probable that she should wish to send such a letter. The chapter ends with a summary ranking recognitions arising from plot first, recognitions from reasoning second, and recognitions from signs and external aids last.

Chapter XVI adds little to the development of Aristotle's thought. It is focused on precisely those technicalities that separate Greek from renaissance and modern drama, and its discussion adds nothing to the understanding of Greek recognition scenes that we cannot deduce by reading a few plays. The suggestion that the chapter is a "late addition" or an "appendix" is especially attractive and has been widely accepted.

Chapter XVII

Chapters XVII and XVIII provide several corollaries to the discussion of tragedy. In general, Chapter XVII is concerned with the process of constructing plays, and Chapter XVIII, with the formal elements of the plays so produced. Chapter XVII considers tragedy from the point of view of the poet who is "making" it, while Chapter XVIII considers it from the point of view of the spectator or critic analyzing the finished product.

The first sentence of Chapter XVII reveals its dominant interest. "Constructing" and "working out" refer to activity taking place in the present. This active emphasis carries through the whole chapter. When constructing and "working out" plots, the poet should do three things. First, he should "visualize" the action; second, he should work out the incidents "with gestures"; and third, he should begin with the "universal form" of the plot, adding the names and episodes later.

This sequence presents a problem because it is backward. We know from Chapter VI as well as from part three of Chapter XVII that the poet begins with the action, moves to the plot, then develops the character and thought, and then "works out" the diction and spectacle. Yet Chapter XVII begins with a principle—"visualization" —that seems to relate to spectacle. It proceeds with a principle that apparently relates to characterization, and it ends with one that clearly relates to plot construction. The movement is thus from spectacle to character to plot, which is the reverse of what is suggested by the emphasis of the first sentence on "constructing" and "working out" plots. Perhaps the best explanation is that Chapters XVII and XVIII are a somewhat miscellaneous group of practical observations and supplementary notes and lack the vigor of the earlier chapters. Montmollin, as might be expected, regards Chapters XVII and XVIII as "later additions" to the primitive text of the *Poetics.* Although this is pure conjecture, the evidence surely supports the view that these chapters are supplements to—not new developments of—Aristotle's argument. Their primary function is to clarify points that have already been made.

Visualizing the Events
(ll. 1-11)

"In constructing plots and working them out with diction, the poet must keep the action as much as possible before his eyes" (ll. 1-3). The general sense of the sentence is plain enough, but the two processes mentioned need a bit of clarification. Plot construction in the technical sense has been explained in Chapters VII-XIII. It has nothing to do with "visualization." Therefore the present reference must be to construction in the nontechnical sense of "working out the episodes." Plot construction in this sense is closely related to diction, because the episodes are ultimately "worked out" through written speeches. Because the poet uses the third manner of imitation and never comments or describes in his own voice, the text as written will have an element of spectacle. It will be suited for stage presentation, although if it is "artistic" (a) it will be just as effective when read, and (b) the modest quotient of spectacle produced by the poetic art will be greatly supplemented in performance by the actor's and producer's arts.

At any rate, the dramatist's speeches cannot avoid having an element of spectacle; and just as there should be a necessary and probable relation between plot and character, so there should be one between diction and spectacle. The speeches should be written so that they do not require the speakers to behave in ways that are impossible, improbable, or ludicrous. "Visualizing" will help to avoid these defects, and it has the added advantage of making the plays as suitable as possible for performance. To use Aristotle's terms, visualizing insures a text that is "fitting" and free of "incongruities." Note the close parallel between the requirements for character (Chapter XV) and the present ones for spectacle. Character is to be "appropriate" (*harmotton*) and "consistent" (*homalon*). Spectacle is to be "fitting" (*prepon*) and avoid "incongruity" (*hypenantion*).

To illustrate his point Aristotle cites a play by Carcinus. Unfortunately, nothing is known of this play or the character Amphiarus. Therefore, an understanding of the citation involves some conjecture. What is clear is that Carcinus failed to visualize some aspect of the actions of Amphiarus. This failure was of little consequence as far as readers of the play were concerned, a fact that confirms again the idea that the spectacle contributed to a drama by the poetic art is relatively insignificant. However, when Carcinus' drama was performed, the incongruity showed up immediately and the audience was "annoyed." Thus Carcinus' neglect of a minor element (spectacle) led to the "failure" of the play when staged. Exactly what detail was neglected is hard to say in the absence of the drama. Because Amphiarus offended the audience by "coming back" from the temple (l. 8), one reasonable guess is that Carcinus forgot to locate him in the temple in the first place. Perhaps in an earlier speech he indicated that he was leaving the stage; yet his temple speech made it clear that he had just emerged from the temple. Such an oversight would hardly trouble a reader but would create difficulties on stage. By visualizing, the poet places himself in the position of the audience and avoids such oversights. Aristotle's point here may be compared to his observation in Chapter XXIV (l. 58) that epic, which is always read, can use "irrational" incidents more frequently than tragedy. There Aristotle adds that the pursuit of Hector, although perfectly acceptable to the reader, would appear ludicrous on stage.

Incidents and "Gestures" (ll. 12-20)

The second principle of drama-making seems initially like a close cousin of the first. The suggestion that the poet work out the incidents "with gestures" seems to refer to the actor's art and hence to the expression of spectacle. In fact, it does not refer to spectacle but to characterization. Recall that characterization is a matter of assigning type traits to an agent. These type traits involve emotions both indirectly and directly. A young man, for example, is rash, avid for honor, and sexually passionate. An old man is sluggish, phlegmatic, greedy, timid. A woman is less "intellectual" and more emotional than a man. These are the standard rhetorical type concepts. The emotional element is even more important if we turn for type concepts from rhetoric to either ethics or medicine. Ethics provides us with portraits of the irascible man, the courageous man, the cowardly man, and the like; medicine provides characteristics for men of sanguine, melancholic, choleric, and bilious temperaments. If the poet is going to produce more than a mechanical duplicate of his model, he must, when writing speeches, feel empathy for the type being depicted. Aristotle's examples of emotions in Chapter XVII are the man overcome with distress and the wrathful man (ll. 15-16). At least the second example—the wrathful man—recalls the reference in Chapter XV to depicting anger (l. 47). The point is that if the poet feels the distress or anger, he will compose speeches that convey these emotions effectively, thus convincing the audience that the character on the stage truly feels the emotions ascribed to him. Horace has exactly the same point: "If you wish me to weep, you must first feel sorrow yourself; then and only then will your misfortunes move me" (*Ars Poetica,* ll. 103-4).

The comment on gestures is related to the much-disputed passage on the mad poet. Aristotle's suggestion that the poet mimic the characters he is creating recalls a psychological notion that also influenced ancient theories of oratory and acting. This theory is prominent in the *Republic,* where it underlies Plato's feeling that tragedy is especially corrupting to actors (III, 395). As Socrates says:

> Since we are training men, we must not allow them, if we hope they will be good men, to imitate a woman, either young or old, quarreling with her husband or showing anger against the gods . . . nor is she to be imitated when she is in affliction or distress or tears . . . and we must not allow our youths to imitate bad men, cowardly and opposite in character. . . . who revile and defame each other and use foul language. . . . And our pupils must not be allowed to act like madmen in word or deed. They must understand insane and wicked men and women, but must not perform any of their acts or imitate them.

Underlying these prohibitions is the idea that when one imitates another person in the sense of mimicking his expressions and gestures, one is bending one's own soul to the shape of another's. Gestures, that is, are intimately related to the form of the soul. To mimic the gestures of a good man is to train the soul in goodness; to imitate those of a wrathful man is to train the soul in anger, and so forth. Aristotle did not share Plato's fears about the corrupting effects of tragic imitation (recall that his conception of imitation is something quite different from "mimicry" or "copying"), but he did believe that a relation exists between gesture and emotion. The poet needs to create convincing characters. As we have seen, character involves conformity to type, and emotion or "emotional bias" is a key element in the concept of character types. To characterize effectively, the poet therefore mimics the gestures appropriate to the type and mood of the figures he is creating. This mimicking makes the poet's soul conform to some degree with the type and allows him to create his characteristic speeches naturally, from a sense of empathy, rather than mechanically, from the formulas in the rhetoric book.

Aristotle ends the comment on characterization with an offhand observation that has vexed editors and commentators since the Renaissance. According to Bywater's translation, which follows the Greek manuscript tradition, Aristotle says: "Hence it is that poetry demands a man with a special gift for it, or else one with a touch of madness in him—the former can easily assume the required mood, and the latter may be actually beside himself with emotion." This version has always appealed to Platonists and other apostles of the idea of poetic inspiration. In the *Ion,* Socrates quite explicitly (and beautifully) identifies the source of poetry with a kind of poetic madness (*enthusiasmos; furor poeticus*) that results when the poet is inspired by some power higher than himself. Horace ridiculed the notion that genius (*ingenium*) is a substitute for training and experience; but Ovid reiterated it: "There is a god in us; when he moves us we glow with inspiration." In general, the Platonic position remained ascendant through the Middle Ages and on into the Renaissance, culminating with Milton's great invocations of the Muse in *Paradise Lost*. Naturally, the reading of the *Poetics* that makes Aristotle say that the poet should have either a "special gift" or "a touch of madness" was favored during this period. As early as Castelvetro, however, the reading was questioned. Aristotle does not say that art is all that a poet needs—he must have a "special gift" or "talent" as well. However, there is never a suggestion elsewhere in the *Poetics* that the poet can afford to be mad or that such a thing as Platonic inspiration forms an important part of the poetic process. The present chapter, for example, shows that the poetic process is a quite deliberate and methodical one, the opposite of the sort of "enthusiasm" advocated by the Platonists. Indeed, it can be argued that the idea of "enthusiasm," if taken seriously, is fatal to the idea of an "art"—*techne*—of poetry.

Therefore Castelvetro proposed an emendation of the Greek to make it read: "Poetry has its source in men who are gifted rather than ones who are mad." Castelvetro did not have textual evidence for his emendation; he made it merely on the grounds that Aristotle could not possibly have advocated poetic madness. Recent editors, however, have discovered that Castelvetro's reading is supported by the Arabic translation and also by the fifteenth-century Greek manuscript known as Riccardianus 46; and on this basis, the emendation has been incorporated into Gudeman's and Rostagni's texts and several translations. Interestingly, neoclassic critics, including Rapin in France and Dryden in England, followed Castelvetro and repudiated the Platonic reading—a reflection of the general reaction, in the later seventeenth century, against the notion of inspiration.

The present translation reads "well-endowed [rather] than . . .

frenzied." This reading seems intrinsically probable, but there is another, more important reason for accepting it. The notion that a poet who is "either well-endowed or mad" can create effective characters is, to say the least, opaque. As we have seen, Aristotle's suggestion for effective characterization is for the poet to place his soul as far as possible in a condition similar to that imagined for the characters being created. The poet, in other words, must be supremely adaptable—he must be capable of as many moods as there are characters and emotions in his plays. A "well-endowed" poet is obviously fitted for this task. But in what way is a "mad" or "frenzied" poet fitted for it? Aristotle's word for frenzied is *manikos*—related to *mania*. But for Aristotle, as well as for the modern psychologist, the most distinctive feature of a mania is its rigidity. A mania is a fixation; a person suffering from a mania is one whose psyche is locked into a single position from which change is impossible. Thus —far from being better qualified than most people to "characterize" in the Aristotelian sense—the manic poet is the least suited of all! Being frozen into his own emotional configuration, the manic poet cannot make his soul conform to the emotions of an imagined character unless the imagined character happens to be a carbon copy of the poet. Logically then, "either well-endowed or mad" is a contradiction in terms. "Well-endowed rather than frenzied" is what Aristotle must have written, and the sentence is not a bow to Plato but an emphatic rejection of Plato's theory of poetic inspiration. As Aristotle says in the last clause of the sentence, "Poets marked by the former characteristic [that is, "well-endowed"] can easily change character, whereas those of the latter type are possessed" (ll. 18-20).

The Universal Form
(ll. 21-43)

The discussion of the order of procedure for developing plots is fairly clear, but it involves one new concept. As early as Chapter VI, Aristotle began to distinguish between action and plot. Here, he seems to make an additional distinction between "argument" (*logos*) and plot. Used in this sense argument appears to refer to all events that are involved in a significant way in the action of a play or epic poem. Some of these events occur before the play proper begins. They are "outside the plot" but not "outside the argument." Presumably, the slaying of Laius is part of the argument of *Oedipus*, although we know from Chapter XV (l. 40) that it is outside the plot. "Argument" is therefore a larger concept than plot. An incident narrated by, for example, a god who knows both past and future, is part of the argument, but it does not form part of the plot unless it is represented in an episode. Chapter XVII further suggests that an episode can be "outside the argument." In that case, it is either irrelevant and hence digressive, or (under certain conditions) it can be included as a pleasing ornament. Tragedy has little place for digressive episodes, but epic, which is less defined in length, can employ digressions. The point is suggested in Chapter XVII and made explicit in Chapter XXIV (ll. 20-28).

We thus have three possibilities. An episode can be outside the argument and outside the plot; it can be within the argument but outside the plot; or it can be inside the argument and inside the plot. As we have seen in Chapter XII, "episode" is closely related to the term "incident," which is most common in the *Poetics* prior to Chapter XVII. "Episode," as the term is used here, can best be understood as an incident that has been realized in a completed dramatic text *via* the speeches that embody it.

The poet's first task, says Aristotle, is to reduce the argument to its "universal form." This means, essentially, isolating the incidents that directly affect the action of the play and putting them together in a kind of summary. Note that Aristotle again makes the point found earlier in Chapter IX that the poet can either "invent" the argument or use one "already . . . in existence"—that is, one derived from history or legend. The argument embodies the form of the story that is being dramatized. It is "universal" (l. 23) because it involves no accidents. It clearly brings out the principles of necessity and/or probability that determine the sequence of incidents as they move from bad to good fortune or the reverse; and these principles are, as we noted in Chapter IX, in the nature of universals. Once the universal form is established, the poet must "extend [it] by adding the episodes" (l. 23). The incidents chosen from the argument for "episodizing" will constitute the plot. The fully elaborated episodes "extend" the universal form both in the sense of filling it out and in the sense of their being a realization of it in language. As Aristotle makes clear a little later (l. 39), the episodizing process involves more than one step. The first step beyond the construction of the argument is the assignment of names to the agents. This is a crucial step. It determines whether the drama will be fiction or based on legend or history. It also gives the poet important clues for characterization, particularly for the achievement of "appropriateness" and "likeness." Obviously, he must have these matters worked out before he takes the next step, the composition of the dialogue in which the episode is realized.

The first example of the universal form of an argument is *Iphigenia in Tauris,* one of Aristotle's favorite tragedies. Note that the argument outlined by Aristotle is much larger than the plot of Euripides' play. Euripides begins his action in Tauris, but Aristotle begins the argument with the sacrifice and disappearance of Iphigenia in Aulis. The reason is that the sacrifice of Iphigenia has a direct bearing on her presence as a priestess among the Taurians. He then turns to a second aspect of the play, the arrival of Orestes. Curiously, although Iphigenia's past is relevant to his argument, Aristotle adds, "the fact that the god . . . commanded [Orestes] to come is outside the argument; the purpose of his coming is outside the plot" (ll. 31-34). The assertion is all the more puzzling because Orestes mentions the fact that Apollo commanded him to come (ll. 85, 937), and also states his purpose in coming (ll. 85-90; 976-79).

Perhaps the best explanation is that Aristotle considered *Iphigenia* primarily the play of the heroine. Iphigenia's past is definitely relevant. We learn about it through her lengthy and rather bitter complaints. These define the situation at the beginning of the play—the situation from which the complex movement toward "good fortune" starts. If we are to understand the movement, the events alluded to are essential information. They are definitely part of the argument and—through Iphigenia's summary—they are introduced into the plot. On the other hand, the only really important thing about Orestes is that he is Iphigenia's brother, for it is this fact that makes the recognition and the happy resolution possible. That Orestes was sent by Apollo is irrelevant, even though it is mentioned incidentally. He has to arrive, but who sent him is not part of Iphigenia's story. It might therefore be considered outside the argument of Euripides' play, although it would be *within* the argument of a play about Orestes. Orestes' purpose in coming to the land of the Taurians—to return a statue of Artemis to Athens—is a little more ambiguous. Is it or is it not part of the argument of the story of Iphigenia? Aristotle implies that it is (it is "outside the plot" but not "outside the argument"); but he does not say so directly. Fortunately, his main point is quite clear. Since Orestes is seized as soon as he lands, his purpose is totally irrelevant to the action of the play and is quite clearly "outside the plot." The statue is finally reclaimed, not through the cleverness of Orestes, but through Iphigenia's recognition of her brother and the resulting decision to escape with him to Athens. The actual return of the statue is not shown but narrated by the goddess Athena (ll. 1438-41), an excellent example of the proper use of gods to tell of past and future events, as outlined in Chapter XV.

The summary continues with the seizure of Orestes, the preparation for the sacrifice, the recognition, and the "deliverance." In view of the importance of the recognition scene to Aristotle's theory of plot, it is not surprising that even in such a brief summary he pauses to note two possible ways of handling the matter. Euripides' way has good and bad features. The result of the recognition is the best possible tragic change (to be about to do the deed, to recognize the other person, and not to do it—Chapter XIV, l. 60); but Euripides' handling of detail is clumsy. It involves a double recognition. The first is by Iphigenia's letter, which, as Aristotle remarked in Chapter XVI, is a rather inartistic and arbitrary trick. The second is Orestes' speech (ll. 800-30), which does not emerge from the plot but is put into his mouth by the poet as a convenience (Chapter XVI, l. 22). An alternative would have been to use "recognition by reasoning," also mentioned in Chapter XVI (l. 44). We know from Chapter XVI that recognition by reasoning, as suggested by Polyidus, is best. Here Aristotle merely suggests that it is "reasonable" (l. 37). Note that after the recognition, the entire remainder of *Iphigenia* is covered by the single word "deliverance." The "deliverance" constitutes about one third of the play—roughly, from line 1000 on. The reason for such summary treatment is clear. After the recognition, the movement of the action is uniformly upward toward the fortunate ending. The universal form of a play reveals its basic structure and the necessary and/or probable principles underlying it; it is not a detailed scenario. From Aristotle's point of view, "deliverance" is sufficient. Exactly how the deliverance is to be achieved is something to be "worked out" as the dramatist "completes the episodes."

In sum, Aristotle's "argument" for *Iphigenia* falls into three sections. The longest section outlines the conditions at the beginning of the play. Iphigenia, saddened and embittered because of her treatment by the Greeks does not know that Orestes has arrived. The situation at the beginning is thus "bad fortune," and the initial movement is toward worse fortune—a sister's sacrifice of her brother. The second section of the argument describes the recognition whereby the movement abruptly changes from "fatal" to fortunate. The third very briefly looks ahead to the fortunate conclusion. It is noteworthy that Aristotle rules out all reference to divine agency in his argument. The miracle whereby Iphigenia was transported from Aulis to Tauris is not mentioned. The part that Apollo plays in bringing Orestes to Tauris is ruled "outside the argument." Finally, the predictions by Athena at the end of the play that Iphigenia and Orestes will safely reach Athens and return the statue and that Orestes will be "purified" of the blood guilt incurred by his slaying of Clytemnestra are referred to only in the very general term "deliverance." The elimination of divine agency from the universal form is quite understandable. Divine aid is not necessary to the play as it is, say, in the *Eumenides* or *Oedipus at Colonus*. The effect of the elimination is to leave the whole argument within the scope of natural causality. Thus, the necessary and/or probable principles that underlie the plot can be understood within a strictly naturalistic frame of reference. It is probable that a sister and brother coming together will recognize each other and that they will cooperate rather than fight. In terms of character, it is also probable that a woman will be bitter if she has (as she thinks) been mistreated by her people; that she will display love for her brother once she recognizes him; and that, once reunited, the two will attempt to escape from a barbarous land that requires strangers to be sacrificed. Athena, it may be added, does not appear as a *deus ex machina* in *Iphigenia in Tauris,* but in the role of prophet to foretell the future—the role, as Aristotle remarked in Chapter

XV, that is especially appropriate for gods. She does not influence the action; she merely relates the events that are, roughly speaking, the denouement of the play.

After the universal form has been worked out, says Aristotle, the poet assigns names to the agents. The assignment of names determines whether the drama will be fiction, myth, or history and provides guidance in characterization. A "priestess" could have any character suitable to a woman, but when the priestess is assigned the name "Iphigenia," the dramatist has some notion of her age, her general character as established in traditional stories such as the *Cypria* (on which Euripides is supposed to have drawn), and her attitudes toward the Greeks and her brother.

After the names have been assigned, ". . . it is necessary to complete the episodes" (l. 40). Completing the episodes must involve several operations. First, the poet must select which of the incidents comprising the "argument" he will work up in his plot, and which he will omit or bring in through messengers or divine seers. Those worked up in the plot may eventually grow into episodes in the formal sense mentioned in Chapter XII—that is, fully developed scenes between choral sections. "Completing the episodes" means writing them out—realizing them in dialogue. Obviously, when doing this, the poet should follow the advice given earlier in Chapter XVII to "visualize" and imitate through "gestures." In addition, he must be sure that his episodes are "appropriate." The reference is probably to the notion that each episode should be functional in the sense of being related to the plot and chosen to bring out as clearly as possible a step in the necessary and/or probable movement from beginning to end. The narration by a herdsman of Orestes' madness and seizure by the Taurians (ll. 238-339) is an episode in Euripides' drama, as is the narration of his eventual purification by Athena (ll. 1438-55). Another possible interpretation of the two examples of "appropriate" episodes is that "appropriate" refers to episodes that reveal aspects of the agents fitting to their assumed characters. Traditionally, Orestes is represented as crazed by his blood guilt; hence an episode depicting—even at second hand—a fit of madness is "appropriate" and furnishes a fine reason for his capture. Given the madness, it is also appropriate that some reference be made to its cure. The "purification" is this cure. Incidentally, the Greek term for purification is *katharsis.* This is the second and last time that the famous term appears in the *Poetics.*

The chapter ends with a contrast between episode making in drama and in epic. Dramatic episodes are short. If 1500 lines is accepted as a kind of average length for a Greek tragedy, perhaps one third the lines are conventionally spoken by the chorus. This leaves 1000 lines for prologue, episodes, and epilogue. Obviously, the episodes cannot be extended in the leisurely manner characteristic of Homeric epic and modern novels. To make his point still more emphatic, Aristotle gives the argument of the *Odyssey.* The first nineteen years of Ulysses' travels are summed up in two sentences: Ulysses has wandered "for many years"; meanwhile his home is being disrupted and suitors "plot against his son" (ll. 46-50). These two sentences establish the situation at the "beginning" of the epic. It is clearly one involving "bad fortune" for the protagonist. Next we learn of his "storm-driven" arrival, one or more recognitions, and a double ending involving the destruction of his enemies and his own restoration to good fortune. Notice that as in the argument of *Iphigenia,* most of the detail is devoted to the description of the situation at the beginning. Also, as in *Iphigenia,* Aristotle emphasizes the recognition(s) that change the course of the action, concluding with a curt reference to the happy ending: he "is himself saved" (l. 52). The summary is intentionally brief. It is shorter than the argument given for *Iphigenia,* although the *Odyssey* is approximately ten times as long as the drama. In essence, it outlines a complex-fortunate plot in which there is a movement from bad fortune to worse, then a reversal brought about by a series of recognitions (there are three important ones—Ulysses' revelation of himself to the neatherd and swineherd, his recognition by the nurse Eurycleia, and his revelation of himself to Telemachus), and a conclusion manifesting good fortune. In addition, there is at least a hint of the second plot attributed to the *Odyssey* in Chapter XIII—the fall of the suitors from good fortune to bad.

If such a brief summary can comprehend the argument of the *Odyssey,* Aristotle's ideas about epic magnitude hardly need to be debated. The fact is that epic poets can extend their episodes in a much more leisurely way than tragedians can. The story of the adventures of Ulysses, often regarded today as the heart of the poem, is not even mentioned by Aristotle. This section has only a tenuous relation to the universal form of the *Odyssey* for the simple reason that it does not explain Ulysses' condition at the beginning of the change from bad fortune to good. On the other hand, as we know, epic is much more hospitable than tragedy to episodes that are digressive but enjoyable. Ulysses' narration of his adventures to King Alcinous is such an episode. It is delightful, but the events themselves are "outside the plot" and may be "outside the argument" as well. When Aristotle says of his argument for the *Odyssey:* "This is the essence . . . everything else is episode" (l. 53), the word "episode" evidently is close to what we would call today a "pleasing digression."

In Chapter XVII, we find a rather full discussion of the steps in the composition of a drama. The problem is that, in terms of the earlier chapters of the *Poetics,* the order is inverted. If we list the steps in the order suggested by the earlier chapters, Aristotle advises the poet to: (1) establish the universal form of the story; (2) select incidents for episodizing—that is, establish the plot; (3) add names; (4) proceed to "complete the episodes" in the sense of realizing them in dialogue; (5) when writing dialogue, mimic the characters with "gestures" to improve the verisimilitude of their speeches; and (6) visualize the episodes as they are being written, to avoid inconsistencies that will be ludicrous if the work is staged. We move in this sequence from plot to character to spectacle. Thought may be included in the comment on character, and diction is obviously involved in realizing scenes in language. The only part of drama not explicitly or implicitly included in Aristotle's comments on the process of composition is song; and song, being related to the chorus, has little or no connection with dramatic imitation as Aristotle has presented it thus far.

Chapter XVIII

Chapter XVIII deals with four topics: complication-resolution, kinds of tragedy, tragic versus epic magnitude, and the function of the chorus. The theme that appears to hold these subjects together is the concept of dramatic form. The first three subjects proceed in predictable sequence from form within tragedy, to forms of different tragedies, to the tragic genre versus the epic genre. The last subject abruptly jumps from these larger considerations back to what is only a part of tragedy and is a more specific part, one would think, than complication-denouement.

In addition to presenting certain problems of organization, Chapter XVIII has several puzzling features. In the first place, it introduces an entirely new concept—complication-resolution. No hint of such a division of the sections of tragedy has been given either in the technical discussion of plot (Chapters VII-XI) or in the consideration of the quantitative parts of tragedy (XII). In the second place, the four kinds of tragedy listed here are apparently different from the kinds described in Chapters X and XIII. The difficulty of tracing a relation between the "kinds" as described in the two different sections of the *Poetics* is notorious. The difficulty of understanding the four kinds themselves is also great.

These observations make it likely that Chapter XVIII is a late addition of the type described by Montmollin. Moreover, the text may be badly corrupted and in places spurious.

Complication-Resolution (ll. 1-13)

By complication (*desis*) Aristotle means "that part of the play from the beginning up to the first point where the change occurs to good or to bad fortune" (ll. 5-7). The "complication," in other words, is the nexus of circumstances existing before the beginning of the action, if we understand action as a process of change from bad to good fortune or the reverse. "Complication" does not have the common modern meaning of "the sequence of events that leads up to the climax." Normally, Aristotle's type of complication would be presented in the prologue and in expository scenes very early in the play. It may also, evidently, include one or two incidents prior to the beginning of the change that are presented in an episode. Thus complication involves matters "outside the action together with some within it" (ll. 2-3). Using the terminology of Chapter XVII, we would say that the complication is within the "argument" but for the most part outside the plot—a point confirmed by the reference (l. 9) to the *Lynceus*. It occurs before the "beginning" of the plot if "beginning" is understood in the technical sense of "beginning of change" found in Chapter VII. Note that in the two "arguments" in Chapter XVII, Aristotle devoted most of his summary to conditions just prior to the beginning of the action, and, hence, to what he is now calling "complication." By definition then, resolution (*lusis*) must be "the part of the play from the beginning of the change in fortune to the end" (ll. 7-8). "Resolution" in this sense would seem to comprise almost all the play except the introductory exposition and (perhaps) such epilogue-like predictions of the future as those of Athena in *Iphigenia in Tauris*. Clearly, it is quite different from modern "denouement."

Aristotle illustrates by summarizing the lost play *Lynceus* by Theodoctes, a play already cited for its use of reversal in Chapter XI. The summary closely resembles the "arguments" of *Iphigenia* and the *Odyssey* given in Chapter XVII. Like them, it places major emphasis on "complication." Evidently in this play, as a result of family problems, a child is "seized." The problems forming a part of the complication are narrated; the seizings of the child and parents also form a part of the complication—the last incidents, in fact, before the change of fortune begins—and are evidently presented in an episode instead of being narrated. As a result of the these, Lynceus is accused of murder (the beginning of the change), condemned, and about to be executed. Then there occurs the reversal described in Chapter XI (l. 7) when Lynceus is saved and Danaos is killed. The play then moves rapidly toward a "fortunate" resolution similar in general effect to that in *Iphigenia*. The point is that everything that happens from the accusation of murder to the fortunate conclusion is, according to Aristotle, "resolution."

The effect of Aristotle's introduction of the concepts of argument and plot in Chapter XVII and complication-resolution in Chapter XVIII is to refine the general outline of the movement of an action given in Chapter VII, bringing it more closely in line with theatrical practice. Theoretically, the description in Chapter VII remains adequate. An action is a change from bad to good fortune or the reverse. An action must have a beginning, middle, and end; and the beginning is the start of the change while the end is its completion. Even when discussing Chapter VII, however, we noticed that to understand how there could be a beginning in the sense of an event without antecedents and an end in the sense of an event without consequences, it was necessary to posit some "period of stability" before and after the dramatic action. The effect of the concept of argument versus plot in Chapter XVII is to broaden the limits of what can be contained in a drama to include periods before and after the "change" proper. The effect of the term "complication" in Chapter XVIII is to name the material relating to the "period of stability" before the action begins (that is, what is within the argument but for the most part outside the plot) and to differentiate it from the plot proper—the resolution. Neither Greek nor modern drama can get along without some expository material to "set the stage" for the action that follows; Aristotle's terms, therefore, are practical supplements to the theoretical concepts of Chapter VII.

Types of Tragedy (ll. 14-29)

Aristotle says that there are four general kinds of tragedy ". . . for that number of parts has been mentioned" (ll. 14-15). The difficulty of interpreting this last assertion is notorious. The four kinds are (1) complex (with reversals and recognitions), (2) suffering, (3) character, and (4)—assuming a point yet to be established—spectacle. The trouble is that this list crosses two quite different lists given earlier. One would normally interpret "parts" to refer to the six parts derived in Chapter VI. However, only two of the kinds—the tragedy of character and the tragedy of spectacle—are based on this list. We then turn to the three parts of plot defined in Chapters X and XI. These are reversal, recognition, and suffering. They clearly furnish the basis for the first two kinds of tragedy mentioned in Chapter XVIII but not for the last two. Finally, there is some hint, at least, that the first kind is differentiated from the other three in terms of the complex-simple dichotomy of Chapter X.

What do we make of this situation? One solution is to excise as spurious the apparently incorrect allusion to "the number of parts . . . mentioned." Another would be to assume that the allusion is a general one meaning, essentially, "These terms have already been used before in the treatise." Finally, it can be assumed that the whole discussion of types of tragedy is a late addition and only slightly connected to the main argument. Our present solution will be to interpret "parts . . . mentioned" in a general sense and to treat the kinds of tragedy as logical developments from the previous discussion; but the solution is tentative, because there is no really definitive analysis of this section of Chapter XVIII.

The major contrast among the four types of tragedy is that between the first and the remaining three. The first type derives its effect "wholly" from reversal and recognition. It is, of course, the complex form of tragedy illustrated by *Oedipus* (complex-fatal) and *Iphigenia in Tauris* (complex-fortunate). The remaining three types must, by contrast, be simple. Aristotle has not discussed simple plots in detail. His treatment of them here is therefore a kind of coda to Chapters X-XIV. His practice of treating the most highly developed form of plot first and then adding remarks concerning the less developed forms is paralleled in the larger organization of the *Poetics* by the fact that he treats tragedy before treating epic.

A further hint of method is found in the names for the three simple types. The first simple type is the tragedy of suffering. As we know from Chapter XI (l. 33), the incident of suffering is the third component of plot and consists of painful events such as deaths, woundings, and the like. A tragedy of suffering must therefore be a tragedy that derives its effect not from complex structure but from its emphasis on incidents that have a pitiable and fearful content. Aristotle's examples confirm this interpretation. The *Ajax* of Sophocles is a straightforward dramatization of the sufferings of Ajax and his ultimate deliberate suicide. In a sense, all its episodes are episodes of suffering, but probably the suicide episode accounts for its inclusion in the "tragedy of suffering" category. As has been suggested (p. 165), a simple tragedy progresses directly toward its "end." The end is therefore the key episode, just as the episode containing the reversal or discovery is the key episode of a complex tragedy. The simple plot exists to show us how this end is reached.

The *Ajax* may be called a "tragedy of suffering" because its end is the suicide of the hero, which obviously comes within the scope of "deaths, woundings, and the like"; and this end is reached without reversal or recognition. Although no classical *Ixion* play has survived and we do not know which of several possible plays Aristotle had in mind, the reference in the *Poetics* suggests a play depicting Ixion's attempted seduction of Hera, his suffering, and his eventual punishment—being fixed on an eternally revolving wheel. Such a play would parallel the *Ajax*. It would be a continuous movement through suffering to a final, particularly painful episode.

If this line of analysis is valid, the tragedy of suffering has the simple-fatal type of plot outlined in the commentary on Chapter X. Furthermore, the *Ajax,* which features a noble hero, would be a close cousin of the complex-fatal type of Chapter XIII, featuring a noble hero with a defect. On the other hand, because Ixion was a notorious classical villain—a standard symbol of ingratitude—the *Ixion* would be a cousin of the type of play that shows the progress of an evil man from happiness to misery. Aristotle admitted the validity of this type of play in Chapter XIII but asserted that it lacks pity and fear (l. 19).

With the next simple type we move from tragedies depending on elements of plot to those depending on character. Unfortunately, we know nothing of either *The Pithiotian Women* or the *Peleus,* and the reading itself is debatable. Two points, however, are relatively clear. First, the tragedy of character relies primarily on the techniques outlined in Chapter XV, especially the use of moral stereotypes. Second, the tragedy of character will tend to the episodic. Because a drama is impossible without plot according to Chapter VI, a tragedy of character will have some structure—a simple one, as we have seen—but it will tend to invert the normal and proper relation between plot and character. To put the point another way, in a tragedy of character the speeches revealing character will be important for themselves rather than as steps toward the final episode. The sense of forward motion—of an action to which all the elements of the play contribute—will be weak; and the play will tend in the direction of a series of dramatic monologues. Its unity will not come from its action but from the fact that the same "character" appears in all the episodes, a corollary of the requirement of Chapter XV that character be consistent.

Nineteenth- and twentieth-century literature abounds in such works. They reflect modern preoccupation with psychology. Robert Browning's dramatic monologues (*Andrea del Sarto, Fra Lippo Lippi*) and his *The Ring and the Book* are good nineteenth-century examples; and O'Neill's *Strange Encounter* will serve for the twentieth century. The same tendency is reflected in post-romantic criticism. Since the beginning of the nineteenth century, it has been commonplace for critics of Shakespeare to concentrate on characterization—especially Shakespeare's soliloquies—at the expense of his plots; and commentators on the *Poetics* have tended either to reject Aristotle's high estimate of plot or to explain it away by blurring his distinctions between plot and character. For the present, we need only to reassert that Aristotle is quite unambiguous about the primacy of plot. To him the tragedy of character is an inferior kind: As his examples show, tragedy of character is possible and can be treated artistically; but it ignores just those parts of tragedy that are most important to the tragic effect.

A further hint as to the nature of the tragedy of suffering and of character is provided by Chapter XXIV where we learn that the *Iliad* is "simple and exhibits suffering, whereas the *Odyssey* is complex and shows character" (ll. 8-11). The sense in which the *Iliad* is a work based on suffering is plain enough: the poem moves surely and deliberately toward the fatal encounter between Achilles and Hector. It is an epic equivalent of the *Ajax* and the *Ixion*. In what sense, then, does the *Odyssey* concentrate on character? As Aristotle noted in Chapter XVIII, the argument of the *Odyssey* is relatively brief. The work is filled out with digressive episodes, a device possible in epic but not in tragedy. The most important such episode is Ulysses' tale of his wanderings. It does not advance the action (that is, the story of his recovery of his throne), but does include many incidents that reveal his fortitude and ingenuity. These incidents are themselves loosely unified by the fact that Ulysses' "character" appears in them all. On the other hand, the looseness of the unity is clear from the fact that incidents (for example, the Cyclops episode) could be removed, new ones added, and the Homeric order could be changed without much change in the effect of the tale. If this analysis is valid, the *Odyssey* is complex in that it presents an action involving multiple recognitions; and it is a tragedy of character in that it "shows character" in its digressions, especially the tale of Ulysses' wanderings, which is technically "outside the plot." A tragedy of character will have the quality of the narrative of Ulysses' wanderings in the *Odyssey*. It will be simple; its episodes will be loosely strung together; and it will not focus, like the tragedy of suffering, on a single climactic "final scene."

One further point may be added. The final episode of a tragedy of suffering must be some terrible and painful event, and the effect of such a tragedy depends on the suggestion of inevitable progress toward it. We sense from the beginning of the *Ajax* that the hero will commit suicide; our pity and fear are aroused as we see him moving ever closer to the act. Obviously, a tragedy of suffering with a fortunate ending is a contradiction in terms. What about a tragedy of character? In the abstract, a tragedy of character would seem to have no limitations on its ending. The ending could be either fortunate or fatal. Two points, however, can be raised against this position. First, a simple plot with a fatal conclusion would probably be labeled "tragedy of suffering" by Aristotle because its final episode is an "episode of suffering." More important, the existence of the final, fatal episode influences the structure of the play. An artistic treatment of a fatal plot would almost inevitably emphasize the necessary or probable progress of the protagonist toward his destruction; and Aristotle is only considering artistic treatments, that is, treatments that exploit the full potential of the form. The artistic treatment of a simple-fatal plot would thus lead to a tragedy of suffering on the model of the *Ajax*. On the other hand, in a fortunate plot the movement toward the conclusion is not nearly so pronounced. Having no sense of impending disaster, we can enjoy the episodes as they come along without worrying about where they will eventually lead. This is surely true of Ulysses' tale of his wanderings, and it remains true for such fictional forms as the picaresque novel and the *Bildungsroman*. *Humphrey Clinker* and *Huckleberry Finn* are modern cases in point. On this basis, then, we can conjecture very tentatively that the simple-fortunate plot is more suited to the tragedy of character than the simple-fatal one. Second, as several critics—most recently Else—have observed, there is the suggestion of a contrast between Aristotle's "tragedy of suffering" and his "tragedy of character." Because the tragedy of suffering involves a fatal ending, it seems likely that the tragedy of character will tend to have a fortunate one.

The label for the fourth type of tragedy is uncertain. The text is corrupt, and "tragedy of spectacle," which follows Bywater, is merely a conjecture widely accepted by editors of the Greek text. Butcher identifies the fourth type as "the simple" and Else, as "the episodic."

"Spectacle" is the least unsatisfactory conjecture for several reasons. Aristotle's list of types moves from the "most formal" type to the least formal, and spectacle is the tragic part farthest removed from plot. His list moves from plot, to episode (suffering), to character, to—what? Not to "simple," because the second and third types are simple. Not to "episodic," because after plot, episode, and character we expect another "part," not a qualitative adjective. Not to thought, diction, or melody, because thought cannot exist except as a component of characteristic speeches; and "tragedy of diction" or of "melody" would be nonsense. This leaves "spectacle." Spectacle is a formal part of tragedy. It is intimately related to drama, being a product of the dramatic "manner" of imitation. Finally, we learned as early as Chapter XIV (l. 1) that spectacle can produce the tragic effect and arouse the tragic emotions, although they are much better aroused by the structure of the incidents.

Aristotle's examples and comments cast some light on the nature of the fourth type of tragedy. The examples are *The Daughters of Phorcis* and *Prometheus* and those plays that take place in Hades" (ll. 20-21). If this reading of the text is correct—and there are several alternatives—both the plays mentioned are by Aeschylus. The first is lost, but probably dealt with several fantastic adventures of Perseus. The *Prometheus Bound,* however, survives. The main points about it are that (a) it involves a demigod—perhaps represented by a gigantic mannequin—being visited by a series of gods and mortals, and (b) in the play *nothing happens.* The play has neither a fatal nor a fortunate movement. It is simply static. The situation at the end is essentially the same as the situation at the beginning. How does the dramatist compensate for such a total lack of action? The answer is, by writing in such a way as to create maximum opportunities for sensational effects by the actor and costume designer. The fantastic adventures of Perseus and the gigantic figure of Prometheus visited by superhuman beings provide such opportunities. Obviously, so do all plays "that take place in Hades." Note that the artistry of the poet is involved in creating a text with marked opportunities for spectacle. However, in such a play the artistry of the poet is only one element—and a relatively unimportant one, apparently—in the total effect. The arts of the actor and designer are much more important. Inevitably, a tragedy of spectacle will tend to the episodic. A static play like *Prometheus Bound,* in fact, is close to being a pure succession of episodes. The interest of such a play is its appeal, written or performed, to the visual imagination. If it has any unity at all, the unity will be of tone rather than action or even character. Of course, if there is unity of character, the tragedy, by definition, will tend to move from type four to type three.

We can now sum up our observations concerning the four types of tragedy. The four types are given in order from most unified to most episodic, and this order is correlated to their emphasis on elements ranging from reversal and/or recognition to spectacle. The best play is the complex kind discussed in Chapter XIII and reappearing in Chapter XVIII as type one. Such a play gains its major effects from plot, but an artistic treatment will also use the preferred fatal ending of Chapter XIII, as well as characterization, and spectacle. It is the best type not because it *must* have all these elements, but because it has the potential for using them all. A plot that lacks reversal-recognition is simple. It does not have the potential for the most impressive tragic effects, but it can utilize a strong plot line, the fatal ending, characterization, and spectacle. The tragedy of character sacrifices the emphasis on plot and (as we have seen) probably the fatal ending as well. It is loosely unified by the fact that character remains "consistent" throughout, and it can employ spectacle. The play of spectacle *only* utilizes spectacle. If it emphasizes characterization and if the characters are consistent, it will tend to become a tragedy of character. Because it has neither structure nor characterization to hold it together, it is close to "pure episodic." Like *Prometheus Bound,* it gets nowhere, and to be effective it must rely primarily on sensational acting and stage effects.

Note that each type of play can be treated artistically and, if so treated, will produce an acceptable drama. Aristotle's examples demonstrate this. The point is that some types have more potential than others, and the artist will bring out this potential. At all times, says Aristotle, ". . . it is necessary to attempt, as much as possible, to include all elements in the play" (ll. 21-23). The first is best precisely because the artist *can* use all elements; the fourth is least satisfactory because the artist must rely on one element and an inferior one at that. Aristotle adds that different poets seem to have a special facility for different kinds of tragedy (apparently, from Aristotle's examples, Aeschylus, the most primitive tragedian, was especially skilled at tragedies of spectacle); and he implies that the proper critic will take each poet within his limitations rather than following the public, which "unjustly criticizes our poets" (l. 25) by demanding that "one man be superior to the particular virtue of each of his predecessors" (ll. 28-29). The latitude is striking in view of the tendency of Aristotle's commentators to make him a prescriptive critic.

The four types of tragedy are listed below. A few suggestions are included in the last column as to the modern literary forms most closely corresponding to Aristotle's "kinds."

LABEL	TYPE	SOURCE OF UNITY	MODERN FORM
Tragedy of Recognition	Complex (Fatal or Fortunate)	Form of Incidents (Plot)	Tragedy, Comedy
Tragedy of Suffering	Simple-Fatal	Content of Incidents	? Naturalistic Fiction
Tragedy of Character	Simple-?Fortunate	Consistency of Character	Romance, Picaresque, *Bildungsroman*
Tragedy of Spectacle	Episodic	Spectacle (Plus Actors' and Designers' Art)	"Spectacular"; Variety Show

Tragedy vs. Epic (ll. 36-54)

Having discussed the internal form and the types of tragedy—and having recommended that tragedies be composed on the basis of their plots—Aristotle compares tragedy with epic. What he says has already been implied by several earlier comments, beginning with the discussion of the magnitude of tragedy in Chapter VII. Tragedy is innately limited by its manner of imitation, whereas epic is not. Even an epic, however, must be an imitation of a single action. Homer is pre-eminent among epic writers because he recognized this fact (Chapter VIII); and in spite of its length, the *Odyssey* can be reduced to a very brief argument (Chapter XVII). It follows that the tragic poet should avoid epic techniques (l. 37). In this connection, we recall that the early dramatists mentioned in Chapter V (l. 110) followed epic practice—a possible allusion to the connected trilogy—whereas later dramatists wrote more unified plays.

Aristotle now adds illustrations of dramas that failed because they disregarded the need to avoid epic techniques. Certain poets—Aristotle does not say which ones—attempted to dramatize "the entire destruction of Troy" (l. 43) rather than selecting only one phase of it, as did Euripides. Likewise, certain others dramatized the whole life of Niobe and not just a part of it as did Aeschylus. These poets committed the error (defined in Chapter VIII) of thinking that a set of incidents make a unified action simply because they happened at one time or to one person. Agathon is the only "modern" instance of failure to observe proper magnitude, and we do not know which of his plays Aristotle had in mind. Note, in connection with all the examples cited, that the dramatists are not merely imitating epic technique, they are imitating *bad* epic technique. Homer did not attempt to dramatize "the entire destruction of Troy"; in fact, his special genius was that he dramatized only a part of it and then brought in episodes from other parts (Chapter XXIII, ll. 20-29). Likewise, he did not show the whole life of Ulysses but only a single action in it (Chapter VIII, ll. 12-19).

The remainder of this section of Chapter XVIII is obscure. Is the passage an attempt to offset the effect of the previous criticism? That is, having criticized the poets who attempt epic techniques, is Aristotle now complimenting them on their "reversals" and "simple plots"? Perhaps, but this is not a very satisfactory hypothesis. At any rate, having praised the arousal of "human sympathy," the text goes on to say, "This occurs whenever a clever but evil person is deceived as Sisyphus, or a brave but unjust man is defeated" (ll. 50-52). The sentiment echoes Chapter XIII, l. 18, where Aristotle remarked that a fatal plot concerning an evil man elicits "human sympathy" although it lacks pity and fear. The sentence is therefore not a comment on the poets who used epic technique but an illustration of what arouses "human sympathy." The next sentence continues the digression by adding that the fall of a clever (or brave) but evil man is only probable in the sense of Agathon's witty paradox that "It is probable for many things to occur contrary to probability" (ll. 53-54). Aristotle was sufficiently fond of this paradox to use it again in the *Poetics* (Chapter XXV, l. 120) and also in the *Rhetoric* (II, xxiv, 1402^a10); but its significance in the present passage is unclear. Is Aristotle being ironic or cynical? If so, this is the only instance of such an attitude in the *Poetics*. Fortunately, the question is unimportant. The main point of the contrast of epic and tragedy is the greater limitation of tragic magnitude, and this point emerges clearly enough.

The Tragic Chorus (ll. 55-64)

In Chapter IV, Aristotle indicated that as tragedy evolved it became ever less dependent on the chorus; and in later discussion of tragic plot he has said little about the choral sections. His discussion of comedy suggests that he felt the chorus was unnecessary to drama. In Chapter XVIII, he considers two alternative ways of using the chorus. The first way is the proper one. If the chorus is to be used, it should be "one of the actors and . . . an integral part of the drama" (ll. 55-56). The fact is that in later Greek tragedy, the chorus tended to be a mere interlude between the episodes. The tendency emerges in Euripides, whom Aristotle here contrasts unfavorably to Sophocles. The second way is therefore the way of the later poets who follow the tendency already evident in Euripides. In the tragedies of these poets, "the songs . . . are no more a part of that particular plot than they are of any other tragedy" (ll. 58-60).

The practice of using entirely nonfunctional choral pieces, says Aristotle, was introduced by Agathon. The reference to Agathon is interesting because we know from Chapter IX that Agathon experimented with fictional tragic plots similar to those produced by the comedy writers. In composing tragic fictions, Agathon was moving in the right direction. The implication of the present passage is that he erred only in retaining the last remnant of older practice, the chorus, for in his dramas there was no longer a functional role for the chorus to play. Aristotle emphasizes the superfluity of the nonfunctional chorus in the last sentence: "And yet what difference does it make whether one sings an inserted song or adapts a speech or whole episode from one play to another?" The question is rhetorical. It obviously makes no difference. If the chorus cannot be treated as a character, then it should be omitted. Note that the omission of the chorus combined with a fictitious plot such as that of Agathon's *Antheus* would result in a tragic form precisely parallel to the form of New Comedy.

Chapter XIX

With Chapter XIX we return to the main line of Aristotle's argument. He has treated plot and character; now he proceeds to thought, and, in the second half of the chapter, to diction, which occupies his attention until Chapter XXIII. The chapter begins with a general reference to the preceding discussion. "We have already spoken about other matters; it remains for us to discuss diction and thought." The other matters are primarily plot and character; but the allusion may also include spectacle (touched on in Chapters XIV, XVII, and XVIII) and song in its relation to the chorus (Chapter XVIII). At any rate, Aristotle never treats these parts explicitly, and the several references to them in the *Poetics* show clearly that he considered them of secondary importance.

Thought (ll. 1-19)

There are two questions that must be answered in connection with thought (*dianoia*): what is it, and what is its functional significance in relation to tragedy? We will consider these questions separately.

In Chapter VI, Aristotle asserted that thought is revealed whenever characters demonstrate a particular point or enunciate a general truth or maxim (l. 37). Later he added that thought is manifested in speech, that it is derived from the political art and rhetoric, and that it involves saying what is "appropriate" to the occasion (ll. 89-101). The same points are repeated more specifically in Chapter XIX. The relation of thought to speech is clear from the fact that Chapter XIX includes both. The dependence of thought on rhetoric is asserted in the second sentence, which is an explicit reference to Aristotle's own *Rhetoric.* To make the reference clear, Aristotle adds a list of three areas in which thought is manifested: (1) proof and refutation, (2) production of emotional effects, and (3) "indications of the importance or insignificance of anything" (ll. 6-10).

The first area is easy to relate to the *Rhetoric.* Chapters XIX-XV of Book II of the *Rhetoric* are devoted to "lines of argument." The most important subjects considered are maxims (Chapter XXI), enthymemes or rhetorical syllogisms (Chapter XXII), and twenty-eight general "topics of argument" on which demonstrative and refutative enthymemes can be based. These "topics" (also called commonplaces—*loci communi*) are nontechnical in the sense that they can be used on any subject-matter. The argument *a fortiori* (from the stronger reason), for example, can be used for everything from weather forecasting to astronomy to politics, as can be seen in the following enthymemes:

1. If it is hot in New England, it must be stifling in Alabama.
2. If the earth moves around the sun, certainly Mars must move around the sun too.
3. If the Chinese will not attack in Vietnam, they certainly will not attack across the Formosa straits.

Clearly, this and similar "topics" are not part of a specific discipline such as politics or astronomy, but are applicable to any number of subjects. When Aristotle said in Chapter VI of the *Poetics* that the older dramatists made their characters speak like practitioners of the political art, whereas the newer ones make them speak like rhetoricians, he evidently meant that the older dramatists use arguments derived from a specific subject (political art), whereas the newer ones tend to use the "topics" of rhetoric.

There is an obvious relation between thought and the rhetorical "topics." What about the second way thought is manifested—by "production of emotional effects"? This, too, is related to the *Rhetoric*. Today, we tend to separate thought and emotion, but for the classical rhetorician, emotion (*pathos*) was a mode of persuasion and hence could be considered a variety of thought. Aristotle is more emphatic on this subject than many of his successors in the field of rhetoric, among whom the division begins to assume its modern form. Book II of his *Rhetoric* begins with a lengthy list of emotions that the speaker can introduce into his speech for persuasive purposes. Chapters II-XI discuss anger, calm, friendship and enmity, fear and confidence, shame and shamelessness, kindness and unkindness, pity, indignation, envy, and emulation. Each emotion is defined and analyzed so that it can be put to use in speeches; and examples revealing the emotions are included. It is significant that many of the examples are from poetry, especially that of Homer. Thought, then, is present both in speeches that involve reasoning and in speeches intended to reveal the emotions of the speaker.

The third manifestation of thought occurs when a speech includes "indications of the importance or insignificance of anything." The reference is at first a little puzzling for the modern reader, and, in fact, the suggestion has sometimes been offered that it is an interpolation. Perhaps; but good arguments can be offered for its authenticity. At the end of Book II of the *Rhetoric* Aristotle discusses what he calls "amplification and diminution" (Chapter XXVI). These two techniques are standard rhetorical devices, and post-Aristotelian rhetoric books included long lists of figures that have the effect of "amplifying or diminishing" a subject. Amplification and diminution are devices of argument. They can make the subject seem noble, significant, worthy, and the like; or base, trivial, and insignificant. Although Aristotle's vocabulary in Chapter XIX of the *Poetics* is different from that of the *Rhetoric,* he probably has amplification and diminution in mind when he includes "indications of the importance or insignificance of anything" as a part of thought.

So much for the content of the term "thought." In what way does it function in tragedy? We know from Chapter VI that thought is related to character but different from it; that it is closely related to speech; and that it involves things "appropriate" for the occasion. When considering these points in Chapter VI, we observed that character is a constant in drama. It consists of general traits associated with standard character types. In Chapter XV, this concept was refined in terms of four desiderata—characters should be good, appropriate, "like," and consistent. "Appropriateness" is glossed in terms of the concept of character types found in the *Rhetoric,* and "consistency" means that the characteristics chosen for the agents at the beginning should be retained throughout. Note that although character is revealed in speeches, the qualities that determine character are abstract. They are universal propositions, existing independently of the particular series of incidents that the drama presents. The character of a "courageous soldier" or "rash adolescent" can be formulated independently of any "story" in which such a character is involved, as is shown by the *Characters*—generalized character sketches—of Theophrastus, and the numerous renaissance imitations of these pieces.

Let us now follow the dramatist as he proceeds beyond character. Having decided on the type characteristics that he will embody in his agents, he must begin composing characteristic speeches for the various episodes in which they appear. But each episode involves a particular set of circumstances. We no longer have a "brave soldier," but a brave soldier bidding farewell to his wife or exhorting his troops on the eve of battle or debating with himself which of two alternative strategies is best or expressing his thoughts and feelings prior to throwing himself on his sword following a defeat. Clearly the type characteristics assigned him from the beginning will remain constant as required by the principle of consistency; but these characteristics will manifest themselves in special ways appropriate for each occasion. "Bravery," for example, is manifested in one way when the general bids farewell to his wife, in another as he exhorts his troops, and in quite another as he debates the best strategy for the coming engagement.

A new element has entered the picture. The element is thought. But this element cannot exist in the abstract. It appears as the dramatist composes speeches adapted to each of the incidents in his play. Thought is therefore closely related to diction. It can be functionally defined as *the devices used by the dramatist to objectify in language the response of the character to contingent situations.* This response will be manifested in rational reactions, the use of maxims and "topics of argument"; in emotional reactions expressed according to the formulas for the various emotions; and if we accept the third element of thought, in expressions emphasizing or depreciating the significance of the situations that affect the character. Although diction will be discussed later, it may be added here for clarity that thought and diction are separate but closely related. Thought is the objectification in language of reasoning and feeling; diction is the choice of meter, words, and images. One further point. Just as an agent is "universalized" by being assigned general type characteristics, so a character is "universalized" by the fact that his reactions to particular situations are projected in speeches that follow general rules for objectification of logical reasoning and modes of feeling.

We can now return to the text of Chapter XIX. After listing the three ways by which thought is manifested, Aristotle comments on the parallel between the effects produced by the structure of the drama and those produced by artistic use of thought. In fact, they are (or should be) the same. We know from the discussion of plot that the structure of a drama should be probable and should arouse pity and fear; and at the beginning of Chapter XIV, Aristotle said that the plot of *Oedipus* arouses pity and fear in itself, even without the speeches (ll. 3-8). We thus have two quite distinct elements with similar capacities. The first can have its effect even in a brief outline; the second has its effect in speeches. The difference is emphasized by Aristotle: "The effects arise in the case of the incidents without verbal expression, whereas in the speech they are produced by the speaker and arise because of the speech" (ll. 14-16). Because the dramatic plot is much more important than the thought, preceding it in Aristotle's normative outline of the steps in composing a play, we can say that thought is a way of reinforcing the effects intrinsic to plot. That is, the plot of *Oedipus* arouses pity and fear all by itself; but the play as written is far more effective than the bare outline because the implications of the outline are realized and intensified (that is, "universalized") by the speeches. The impossibility of thought in the abstract is pointed out in the next sentence (ll. 16-19) by a *reductio ad absurdum:* "For what would be the function of the speaker if something should appear in the way that is required without being dependent on the speech?"

Diction (ll. 20-34)

Thought has proved inseparable from the speech in which the thought is objectified. This leads immediately to a discussion of diction (*lexis*) that extends from the second half of Chapter XIX through Chapter XXII. The discussion is surprisingly long. Much of it is technical and, to modern tastes, rather picayune. The second half of Chapter XIX is devoted to distinguishing aspects of diction that are not a part of poetic art from those that are.

In brief, Aristotle distinguishes between subjects that are a part of the art of speaking properly and those that are part of the art of writing properly. The former are appropriate for those who will actually utter speeches—students of the art of elocution (including, perhaps, actors), but not for poets. The substance of the discussion comes from the fact that Aristotle evidently considered the forms (*schemata*) of verbal expression a part of the art of elocution. A public speaker needs to know ". . . what a command is and what a prayer is, what a statement is, and threat and question and answer, and any other such matters" (ll. 23-25), if only to enunciate them properly. If Aristotle is referring here merely to the rules for intonation of such forms, his statement is easy to understand. In this case, they would be only a part of delivery, which Aristotle largely ignores in the *Rhetoric* and which at any rate he would have felt to be a concern appropriate to the actor rather than the poet. Likewise, his statement that "In regard to knowledge or ignorance of these matters, no censure worth taking seriously can be made against the art of poetry" (ll. 25-27) is understandable. However, his remarks concerning Protagoras' criticism of Homer suggest that the *schemata* include formulas for writing as well as for speaking. This subject is covered in the third book of the *Rhetoric,* XIV-XIX, and seems to be generally similar to what Hellenistic rhetoric called *schemes* in contrast to *tropes.* If so, Aristotle's position is rather surprising and quite contrary to the later classical feeling that the poet should master the formulas for various kinds of speech along with the other lore of rhetoric.

To support his position, Aristotle quotes the first line of the *Iliad*—"Sing, O goddess, of the wrath of Achilles"—and recalls the criticism of the line by Protagoras, a fifth-century sophist. According to Protagoras, one should pray to a goddess, not command her. Because Homer's line is a command, it is faulty by Protagoras' standards. The criticism, of course, is silly. On the other hand, it is clearly an attack on the *form* of Homer's line, not the tone of voice in which it might have been delivered. Protagoras evidently claimed that Homer did not know (or had violated) the formulas for addressing a deity. Most ancient critics between Aristotle and Longinus would have regarded such a lapse in any poet except Homer as an error of the poetic art.

Whatever the precise content of Aristotle's term *schemata,* it is clear that he opposed the indiscriminate use of rhetorical concepts in the judgment of poetry. If Homer's first line is faulty according to rhetoric, it is splendid according to the art of poetry, a point that he makes quite explicit in the *Rhetoric* (III, XIV; 1415^a15). There is a suggestion here of what would now be called contextualism—judging the parts of a work in relation to the work itself, rather than by abstract prescriptions or conventions.

The chapter ends with the conclusion that we can "disregard" the area represented by the *schemata.* The ground has now been cleared for the treatment of those aspects of diction that fall within the poetic art.

Chapter XX

The analysis of diction begins with the simplest "parts" of speech, letters, and then moves on to complex concepts. After considering the parts, Aristotle proceeds to noun usage in Chapter XXI, concentrating on ways in which words can be used to enhance the literary appeal of a work. He then treats the criteria of effective style in Chapter XXII.

The material in Chapter XX is grammatical and is not specifically within the poetic art. It is evidently included because it is the foundation for the composition of poetry. Another reason for its presence is doubtless that the study of meters was a part of ancient grammar. The types and functions of the meters formed a natural adjunct to the discussion of syllables, because classical prosody was quantitative and syllabic rather than accentual, as modern English. Aristotle does not have a detailed analysis of the meters in the chapters on diction, probably because of his coolness toward the *ars metrica.* Nevertheless, allusion to meter is frequent in the chapters. Syllables are closely related to the "art of metrics" (Chapter XX); writing in meters is said to encourage the lengthening and shortening of words (Chapter XXI); and heroic meter is said to be hospitable to strange, coined, and ornamental words, whereas the iambic meter of tragedy prefers standard words (Chapter XXII). Meter, word choice, and genre are therefore all related to the proper understanding of syllables.

Throughout the discussion of diction, too, rhetorical concepts loom large. Most of the material on noun usage and style (Chapters XXI and XXII) is duplicated in the first half of Book III of Aristotle's *Rhetoric.* This is true of the general criteria of good style, of the use of strange and coined words, of the relation between vocabulary and the form of discourse used, and of the analysis of metaphor.

Chapter XX lists eight "parts" of diction. These are:

1. The letter, which is a sound without meaning.
2. The syllable, which is a sound without meaning made up of a vowel and a consonant.

3. The "connecting word," which is a word showing relation but without content—that is, a conjunction or preposition.
4. The particle, which also shows relation but lacks content.
5. The noun, which has meaning in itself but does not contain a temporal idea.
6. The verb, which has meaning in itself and contains a temporal idea.
7. Inflectional endings, which indicate case and number for nouns, and number, person, voice, tense, and mood for verbs.
8. The "speech," which can be anything from a phrase to a composition such as the *Iliad*. The definition of man—*man: an intelligent animal*—is a "speech" although it lacks a verb.

Characteristically, Aristotle pauses to consider the ways in which a "speech" can have unity. He finds two kinds of unity, simple and compound. Simple unity is achieved when a "speech" is on a single subject—for example, a definition, a treatise on poetry, a biography of Pericles. Compound unity is achieved by combining "speeches" on different subjects into a larger whole. Aristotle cites the *Iliad* as an example. The *Iliad* contains "speech" concerning Agamemnon and additional "speech" concerning Nestor, Hector, Achilles, and so forth. All these "speeches" fit together in the unity of the poem. Evidently, epics, tragedies, and comedies all have compound unity, whereas a dithyramb or a lyric may have simple unity. In view of Aristotle's general tendency to regard the more complex form as higher, we may suspect that compound unity is superior to simple unity, but this point is not made explicit.

Chapter XXI

We now turn from "speech" to a consideration of nouns and the ways that they can contribute to poetic effects. This subject, although shared by rhetoric, is within the poetic art. Chapter XXI lists and defines the different uses of nouns. Chapter XXII will show that certain uses are appropriate for certain types of poetry. Of the "uses" of nouns, metaphor is by far the most important. Aristotle's discussion of metaphor constitutes a highly influential little essay on the nature of figurative language.

Noun Usage (ll. 1-17; 58-66)

Aristotle begins by examining the structure of nouns. Some are simple. These are composed of nonsignificant letters; for example *man* is composed of *m, a,* and *n*. Compound nouns can be composed of a nonsignificant element plus a significant one or of two or more significant elements. The former type is illustrated by the English word *pronoun,* which has a prefix (nonsignificant) plus a noun (significant). The latter type is illustrated by English words such as *mankind* or *daylight* or *watershed.* Aristotle adds that triple and quadruple compounds are quite possible. Greek, like modern German, frequently created new words by forming compounds of old ones. Multiple compounds were therefore common, although jawbreakers like *hermocaicoxanthus* were considered ungainly and even ludicrous. Modern English and French, of course, generally avoid compounds of three or more "significant" words.

The varieties of noun usage are now listed. A noun can be:

1. A "standard" word. That is, the word can be taken from the standard vocabulary; it can be the type of word people use in everyday speaking and writing. The vocabulary of modern newspapers and popular magazines is for the most part "standard" English.

2. A "strange" word. By "strange" Aristotle means a word, standard in one dialect, used in another. The Greeks used several dialects—Attic, Dorian, Ionian, etc.—and writers often used dialect words for ornament or to comply with their meter. More generally, a "strange" word can be understood as a foreign word or phrase, as when we say *sub rosa* for *secretly,* or *adios* for *good-bye.* Nineteenth-century English novelists and poets were fond of using French words and phrases to add elegance to their works.

3. A metaphor. This category includes words used in a figurative rather than a literal sense. If for example we say, "There was a blanket of snow on the ground," the noun *blanket* does not have its standard meaning. Aristotle is particularly interested in metaphor and devotes about one-third of the chapter to it.
4. An "ornamental" word. An ornamental word is a formal or technical word used for effect in place of a standard one. A writer who uses *perambulate* for *walk, endite* for *write, benighted* for *ignorant, ethereal* for *heavenly,* and the like, is using ornamental words. Archaisms might also be included in the ornamental category.
5. A "coined word." The technical term for a coined word is neologism. In English *Coca-Cola, Univac,* and *supercalifragelisticexpialidocious* are "made up" words, having no etymological meaning. Neologisms are, more properly, words with true etymological meaning "made up" to supply a deficiency in the standard vocabulary. The tolerance of Greek for compound words made neologisms fairly common. During the English Renaissance, writers coined many new terms from Latin and French in their eagerness to enlarge the native English vocabulary. Such words were called by linguistic purists "ink-horn terms." Modern examples of neologisms in Aristotle's sense would be words like *semantics, omnibus* (shortened to *bus*), *abreaction, psychoanalysis, cybernetics, supermarket,* and the like.
6. A word "lengthened" for effect or to fit a metrical pattern. The lengthening can come from making a short syllable long or from adding a syllable. Because English is accentual, there is no exact equivalent to the practice of lengthening a short syllable in a Greek word. A rough parallel would be the accenting of normally unaccented syllables. This is common in English poetry, as, for example, *belovéd* for *belov'd.* English can furnish numerous examples of the addition of syllables for effect, for example, *beloved* for *loved, yclad* for *clad,* or *daffodillies* (or even *daffodowndillies*) for *daffodils.* In classical rhetoric, the figures of "lengthening" are prosthesis, epenthesis, and proparalepsis.
7. A word can also be "shortened" by the shortening of a syllable or the omission of one. The English equivalent of the first practice is elision, for example, *heav'n* for *heaven.* The omission of syllables that cannot be elided is less common, but may be illustrated by the use of *even* (as in *evensong*) for *evening.* In classical rhetoric, the figures of "shortening" are apheresis, syncope, and apocope.
8. Finally, a word can be "altered." An "altered" word is one that is partly a standard word and partly a coinage. The coinage can simply lengthen the word, or it can add to the word's meaning. Donne's term *interinanimate* is an altered word. *Inanimate* is standard; adding the prefix *inter* both lengthens it and gives it a new meaning.

Metaphor (ll. 18-57)

After a brief definition of standard and strange words, Aristotle considers metaphor. His analysis is long and detailed, reflecting his interest in the form. This section of the *Poetics* together with the related comments on metaphor and simile in *Rhetoric,* III, IV, X, XI, may seem rather dry to the modern reader. On the other hand, it fascinated critics and poets of the seventeenth century, who elaborated it into an enormous and complex mechanism for inventing poetic imagery. The most prominent writers in this tradition are Baltazar Gracián, author of the influential *Argudeza y Arte de Ingenio* (1642), and Immanuele Tesauro, foremost of the Italian *concettisti,* and author of the *Cannocchiale Aristotelico* (*Aristotelian Telescope,* 1655). In the twentieth century, the section has proved interesting to those "new critics" who treat imagery as the central element in poetry. I. A. Richards' *Philosophy of Rhetoric* (1936) illustrates the "new critical" approach. In this work, Richards asserts that the Aristotelian concept of metaphor is based on resemblance, that is, that the effect of a metaphor depends on its revelation of similarities between the subject of the metaphor and the thing to which the subject is compared. Although he praises Aristotle for recognizing the importance of metaphor, Richards suggests that the difference between the subject and the thing compared is also important and that the best metaphor gains its effect from the interaction of resemblance and diversity. At the opposite extreme, there is the theory of metaphor that maintains that dissimilarity is the basis for the metaphorical effect, a theory worked out in intriguing detail by the French poet André Breton in his *First Manifesto of Surrealism* (1924).

It is true that Aristotle values metaphor; but that he considers it the central element in poetry is clearly false. Plot and character are the most important elements in drama. Diction comes fairly far down on the list, and metaphor is only a part of diction. On the other hand, Richards' suggestion that Aristotle offers a theory of metaphor based on similarity is correct. Aristotle's explanation of metaphor assumes that its function is to reveal similarities. In Chapter XXII (l. 69), he asserts that metaphor is the most important of the artistic uses of language and that the ability to perceive similarities in dissimilarities is a sign of genius.

It is unnecessary to analyze in detail Aristotle's explanation of the way a metaphor works. The explanation is worked out with mathematical precision and is, perhaps, clear enough in the text. He begins by noting that a metaphor ". . . is the transference of a name from the object to which it has a natural application" (ll. 18-19). The transference can operate in two general ways, by a series of species-genus relations or by analogy.

In the first class of metaphors, the transferred noun is (a) appropriate for the species but used for the genus, (b) appropriate for one species within a genus but used for another. Aristotle's own examples are quite adequate to illustrate the types. Metaphors that are today classed as metonymy and synecdoche fall within Aristotle's first general class.

An analogy, if fully stated, begins with the form "A is to B as C is to D." An analogy thus has four terms; and the first tactic in constructing metaphors based on analogy is to substitute A for C or B for D. To use Aristotle's example, if Dionysus (A) is associated with his cup (B) in the same way that Ares (C) is associated with his shield (D), then we can call the cup the "shield of Dionysus" (A and D), and the shield the "cup of Ares" (C and B). The comparisons, in fact, are quoted by Aristotle from Timotheus. Again, if old age is to life what evening is to day, then, as Aristotle observes, we can metaphorically call evening "the old age of day," and old age "the evening of life." Analogical metaphor can be made more complex by converting its terms into metaphors of the first type. Thus, the term *sunset* can be used in place of *evening* by metonymy, and one can speak of old age as "the sunset of life."

Aristotle next points out that at times one of the parts of an analogy will not have a name of its own. He found no Greek word appropriate for the act performed by the sun in projecting its beams over the earth. On the other hand, he felt that this act (B) is related to sunlight (A) in the same way that the act of sowing (D) is related to seed corn (C). It follows that one can speak of the sun as "sowing" its beams (D and A), and the term *beams* can be converted poetically into the expression "god-created rays." The full metaphor then is "sowing the god-created rays." A final note adds that metaphors can be varied by negation, so that, for example, one can call the shield "not the cup of Ares but the wineless cup" (l. 53).

Conclusion (ll. 58-79)

At this point in Chapter XXI the text is imperfect. Probably Aristotle discussed "ornamental words," but the passage has been lost. The discussion of the various ways in which words can be used is concluded with brief examples of "coined," "lengthened," "shortened," and "altered" words. The chapter ends with a paragraph on the genders of nouns and their endings that seems more appropriate for Chapter XX. The explanation may be that in the list of "parts" in Chapter XX nouns and verbs are introduced before case and verbal endings. If so, the body of Chapter XXI can be considered an explanation of the fifth element (nouns) and perhaps the sixth (verbs), and the final paragraph, an explanation of the seventh element (case endings). Chapter XXII, then, can best be understood as an explanation of the eighth and last element, speech.

If we look back over Chapter XXI, one fact is quite apparent. The list of "uses" of nouns is intended as a guide to poetic composition. The Greeks felt that poetic language should be distinguished from the language of ordinary discourse—and even from the consciously artistic language of formal oratory. Hellenistic rhetoricians invented the influential division of style into the "elevated," "middle," and "low" forms; and this division was in due time applied to poetry and poetic genres. There is perhaps a hint of this type of division in *Poetics* XXII (ll. 1-18). In Chapter XXI it is assumed that the poetic language will be different from that of prose, but no simple rule is offered for achieving this objective. Instead, Aristotle lists eight ways in which nouns can be used. These eight ways are also literary strategies. The first ("standard" vocabulary) is the strategy of ordinary speech, of most standard prose, and of a good deal of oratory. By definition, poetry seeks to rise above this level. Therefore, the remaining seven devices may be considered "poetic," although they are used in the more formal and/or emotional kinds of oratory as well as poetry. They are all important. A reading of *The Faerie Queene* or *Paradise Lost* will quickly reveal to the English-speaking reader the powerful effect of "strange" words, coinages, "ornamental" words, and lengthened and shortened words. Metaphor receives most of Aristotle's attention. This accords with Chapter XXII, which asserts that metaphor is the most important of the "usages," and also that it is particularly appropriate for drama.

We may conclude that for Aristotle "diction" is restricted to the use of language to achieve a style distinct from that of ordinary discourse. In a sense everything in a tragedy is language—language is the plastic medium (the "means") whereby plot, character, and thought are objectified. However, from the point of view of the poetic art, these are separate parts of a literary work. If diction is to be distinct from character and thought, its scope must be far less than the scope assigned it by representatives of ancient rhetorical criticism like Longinus or by the "new critics" of the twentieth century. Insofar as language objectifies ethical types and logical and emotional responses appropriate to each incident in the plot, it is character and thought. Insofar as it regularizes and elevates the literary medium by meter and word usage, it is diction. The effect of diction is an harmonious elevation of tone, providing as it were, the key signature in terms of which the melodies of character and thought are played. The point can be practically illustrated by reference to Shakespeare's *As You Like It, Henry V,* and *Hamlet,* and Milton's *Paradise Lost.* Each of these works has a definite tone or "key" that is constant in spite of variations of situation and speaker. It is evidently this tone or key that constitutes Shakespeare's and Milton's diction, in Aristotle's sense.

Chapter XXII

Chapter XXII is in three parts. First Aristotle defines the two objectives of diction. These are "clarity" and "distinction," and they are to some degree contradictory. In the second section of the chapter Aristotle outlines strategies whereby a proper mixture of clarity and distinction may be achieved. Poetic style can thus be understood as a mean between two extremes; and one basic rule for effective diction is moderation. The material in this section appears in slightly different guise in the *Rhetoric,* III, II, III, and VII. In the third section of the present chapter, Aristotle ranks the usages discussed in Chapter XXI according to their importance and adds that they should always be "fitting." This section, although brief, is a consideration of what later criticism called *decorum* of language.

Objectives of Diction
(ll. 1-18)

The definition of what should be sought in diction is given in the first sentence: "Diction achieves its characteristic virtue in being clear but not mean." This is parallel to the requirement for style in Book III of the *Rhetoric*: "Style to be good must be clear, as is proved by the fact that speech which fails to convey a plain meaning will fail to do just what speech has to do. It must also be appropriate, avoiding both meanness and undue elevation" ($1404^{b}1$-5). In the *Rhetoric* Aristotle adds an important qualification: "Poetical language is certainly free from meanness, but it is not appropriate to prose" ($1404^{b}5$-6). The difference between prose and poetic style is that poetic style should have a greater elevation; this elevation is attained by use of strange words, coinages, metaphors, and the other devices listed in Chapter XXI.

Aristotle's term "mean" is the opposite of his term "distinguished." It does not mean "base" or "crude," but "low" in the sense of "close to the usage of ordinary speech." There may be an anticipation here of the doctrine of the low, middle, and elevated styles. The problem is that clarity is best produced by standard words, but standard words, being those used in ordinary speech, produce a "mean" style. Aristotle cites two examples of poets who sought clarity by using standard words and consequently produced "mean" works. Unfortunately, we cannot be sure who Cleophon and Sthenelus were; and in any event their works have not survived. The point, however, is clear enough. A mean style is acceptable in prose, but it is out of place in poetry.

Poetry aims at a "distinguished" style, and to achieve it the poet must use "unusual words," a concept immediately defined as "strange words and metaphor and lengthened words and everything that goes beyond ordinary diction" (ll. 6-7). The reference is clearly to the seven devices that follow "standard words" in Chapter XXI.

We now face a paradox. Poetic diction should be clear and should therefore use standard words. At the same time, it should be distinguished and should therefore use unusual language. Clarity and distinction are in some sense antithetical, for unusual language reduces the clarity of a work. Anything that is strange or figurative or out of the ordinary requires extra effort to understand. Aristotle demonstrate this by *reductio ad absurdum:* "If someone should write exclusively in such forms the result would either be a riddle or a barbarism" (ll. 8-9). "Barbarism" results from excessive use of "strange" words—that is, from a style that is so heavily laden with dialect and foreign words that it is close to being no language at all. "Riddle" is Aristotle's term for a metaphor that tends to puzzle or confuse the reader. In a riddle, he says, "one speaks of a situation that actually exists in an impossible way" (ll. 12-13). Because Aristotle believes that language used properly accurately reflects reality, he feels that one can only treat what exists "in an impossible way" by distorting the normal meanings of the words used, that is, by metaphor. His example is a famous riddle: "I saw a man who welded bronze on another man by fire." The answer to the riddle is that the man was using a bronze bleeding cup that was affixed to a patient's skin, heated to expand the air, and then allowed to cool so that it became attached ("welded") by the resulting vacuum. Two metaphors of the genus-species type are involved. The bronze bleeding cup is called "bronze" (genus for species), and the attaching process is called "welding" (species for species).

The Proper Mixture of Elements
(ll. 19-66)

It follows that diction must seek a compromise between the extremes of clarity and distinction. The poet uses standard words to achieve clarity and is saved from "meanness" by his use of strange words, ornamental words, metaphors, and so forth. This is true of the diction of prose as discussed in *Rhetoric* III, II; and it is far more true for poetry. In exaggerated form, the idea that poetic style should be more distinguished—"elevated" or "heightened"—than prose helped to produce the excessively ornamental style of the late classical period and Middle Ages, together with the long lists of figures, flowers, and colors of rhetoric that were conventionally included in critical treatises of the Renaissance. Aristotle cannot be held responsible for this development, which comes from rhetoric more than from poetic theory; but he is closer to the view that poetic diction should have an ornamental and ceremonial quality than to the view that it should be "colloquial."

Aristotle particularly recommends lengthening and shortening of words as a way to achieve "distinction" (l. 24). This is because words so altered are "unusual," but at the same time they are easily recognizable variations on standard words. They elevate the style while doing the least possible injury to "clarity." He continues by attacking critics who, like the elder Euclid, deny the poet the right to use lengthening and shortening "on the grounds that it is easy to write poetry if you are allowed to lengthen forms as much as you want" (ll. 31-37). One suspects that this statement is another blow against the *ars metrica.* For advocates of the *ars metrica,* the essence of the poet's craft is his skill at prosody. To allow him to lengthen and shorten syllables at will is to remove the difficulty and also to eliminate one of the chief criteria for distinguishing between good and bad poetry. But this position is only valid if writing in verse is an end in itself. If prosody constitutes only part of a larger effect produced by diction, the poet may take liberties with prosody if he achieves the larger effect. Because clarity and distinction are both achieved by lengthened and shortened words, the techniques are desirable even though they take liberties with the rules of prosody.

On the other hand, says Aristotle, it is possible to abuse a device, and "The employment of . . . lengthening in excess is ridiculous" (ll. 38-39). This leads to the first of two general rules for diction: "Moderation is a quality that is commonly needed in all parts of diction" (ll. 39-40). Intemperate use of strange words and metaphors will produce the same absurd effect as overuse of lengthened words.

The discussion thus far has been primarily negative. Now it becomes positive. That one should use restraint in his employment of ornamental devices does not mean that they should be avoided. To prove the value of such devices, Aristotle suggests substituting standard words for the lengthened words, metaphors, and strange words used in well-known lines of poetry. He even adds three examples of his own, the first from a line found in both Aeschylus and Euripides, and the second and third from the *Odyssey*. The reader can try similar experiments on well-known lines from Shakespeare or Milton and will reach conclusions like those in the *Poetics*. The discussion of thc value of "unusual words" ends with a reference to Ariphrades—now unknown, if the text is not corrupt—who ridiculed tragedians "because no one would use their style in conversation" (ll. 59-60). Ariphrades, of course, was merely displaying his ignorance of what poetic diction was all about. Aristotle feels that the special characteristic of poetic diction is its elevation and that it is obviously impossible to produce something more elevated than ordinary speech by using the language and techniques of ordinary speech. The logic of the case makes this evident; but the famous effort of Wordsworth to imitate "the language of ordinary men" is a remarkable and amusing case in point. As Coleridge pointed out in the *Biographia Literaria,* where Wordsworth succeeded in reproducing ordinary speech his poems are failures; his great poems have an elevation that emphatically separates them from ordinary speech, no matter what their author may originally have thought he was accomplishing.

The Fitting (ll. 67-80)

The second general rule for diction is that it be "fitting" (l. 68). Aristotle's word for "the fitting" is *prepon,* the rhetorical term usually translated *decorum*. It is the harmonious integration of language to context. "Fitting language" is language having a proper relation to the other parts of the work. It is the equivalent of the requirements that character and thought be "appropriate" and that the incidents of a plot be related by necessity and/or probability.

Before stating what constitutes "fitting" language for the various genres, Aristotle remarks that metaphor is "the most important matter" and "This skill alone it is not possible to borrow from another, and . . . is, in itself, a sign of genius" (ll. 70-72). The reason is that metaphor involves "the ability to see essential similarities"

(l. 73). It is the ability to see hidden similarities that characterizes both the philosopher and the scientist in Aristotle's system of knowledge, and this ability is largely a matter of "genius" (*euphuia*—Lat. *ingenium,* often translated *wit* or *talent*). It cannot be taught, as, for example, the correct use of the enthymeme can be taught. The passage supports the contention that Aristotle's theory of metaphor is based on similarities revealed rather than the differences of the things compared. It should be noted, however, that the ability to construct metaphors is merely the "most important" part of diction; it does not in itself make a poet.

We now turn to the relation between poetic language and literary genres. The complex meters of dithyramb make the form especially hospitable to compound words that would be difficult to use in simpler meters. The dactylic hexameter of heroic verse is also hospitable to forms that would be difficult to use in iambic verse. In heroic verse, says Aristotle, ". . . all the forms mentioned are serviceable" (ll. 76-77). This is true both in theory and in practice, as can be seen easily in the works of Homer and Virgil. One curious qualification must be noted. Aristotle asserts that strange words are especially fitting for heroic verse. Why is this? Probably he is thinking of Homer, who wrote in the Ionian rather than the Attic dialect. On the other hand, Virgil generally avoided foreign and dialect words in his effort to make the *Aeneid* a model of Latinity. Later epic poets varied in practice. One poet who seems to have followed Aristotle's suggestion is Milton, whose *Paradise Lost* abounds in words derived from Latin and in English words used in the senses suggested by their Latin roots rather than by contemporary English usage. At any rate, Aristotle was thoroughly convinced of the affinity of heroic verse for strange words, for he repeats the point when discussing epic diction in Chapter XXIV (l. 36).

We now come to iambic verse. Iambic trimeter was the Greek meter for tragic and comic dialogue. As early as Chapter IV Aristotle remarked that iambic meter is appropriate for dialogue because it is closely related to the rhythm of everyday speech. Here the point is repeated (l. 78). The natural appropriateness of iambic meter to everyday conversation carries with it the implication that iambic meter will prefer standard words to all other kinds. This will give iambic poetry clarity, but, as we have seen, will prevent it from becoming "distinguished." How can the tragic poet solve the problem? The answer is both simple and logical. Metaphors normally use standard words. They do not demand "strange" words, nor do they require compounds, lengthening, or shortening. On the other hand, they are among the devices that make diction "distinguished." It follows that the tragic dramatist should place special emphasis on metaphor. His language will then be fitting and will have a proper balance of clarity and distinction. Note that the artistic device most fitting for tragic diction is also the "most important" one. Tragedy being the most excellent of the literary forms, this is probably no accident. At the end of the discussion of iambic diction, Aristotle adds that iambic meter can also use "ornamental" words. Ornamental words are native to the poet's language, but are more formal—more elegant—than standard ones. It can safely be assumed that such words elevate the diction of tragedy without doing serious violence to the innate capacities of the iambic meter.

The chapter ends with the remark: "Concerning tragedy and the imitation that is carried out in action, let what has been said suffice." The sentence completes the discussion of diction. It also completes the discussion, begun in Chapter VI, of tragedy and its parts. In the next chapter Aristotle turns from tragedy to epic.

Chapter XXIII

At the end of Chapter V, Aristotle remarked that all the parts of epic are found in tragedy. These parts are plot, character, thought, and diction. Epic lacks melody because it does not have a chorus; it lacks spectacle because it is in the second ("mixed") manner of imitation rather than the third. Because tragedy and epic share the other four parts, much of what might be said about epic has already been said in reference to tragedy.

Chapter XXIII concentrates on the epic action and epic plot. It is thus parallel to Chapters VII and VIII, which discussed the tragic action and tragic plot. These chapters are, in fact, echoed in the first sentence: "It is necessary to construct the epic plot as in a tragedy in a dramatic fashion and concerning a single action that is whole and complete (having a beginning, middle, and end) . . ." (ll. 2-4). The only phrase that is difficult is "in a dramatic fashion." This is not a reference to the dramatic "manner" of imitation of Chapter III but to the fact that epic, being in the "mixed" manner, has a dramatic component that should be stressed. In Chapter IV, for example, Aristotle praised Homer because of all the epic poets he used the dramatic element most fully. The first sentence of the present chapter ends with an added definition of the term "whole": ". . . so that like a single, integrated organism it achieves the pleasure natural to it." This is the most explicit hint in the *Poetics* of what it called "organicism." The term here translated "organism" is *zoön,* meaning either an animal or an image. Elsewhere, Aristotle states that each animal produces a pleasure appropriate to it through its particular integration of its parts.[1] He is not referring to the sort of organicism that sees each part of a literary work as expressive of the whole in the same way that each cell of a plant or animal is a microcosm of the whole. Rather, Aristotle seems to intend what may best be called functional organicism—a requirement that each part contribute to the functioning of the whole, much as each cog in a watch contributes functionally to the whole mechanism. The point is significant because critics who follow Butcher are inclined to regard the hints of organicism in the *Poetics* as anticipations of the biological point of view which became fashionable during the romantic period.

The body of Chapter XXIII is a definition by statement, by contrast, and by example of what constitutes epic unity of action. First, Aristotle asserts, as he had of tragedy in Chapter XI, that

[1] See Butcher, *Aristotle's Theory of Poetry and Fine Art,* p. 188 and note.

epic unity is quite different from the unity aimed at by history. A history achieves unity by treating one period or one person or group of persons, but we already know that this is the reverse of unity of action. After observing that "almost all the poets commit this error" (l. 18), Aristotle points out that Homer avoided it. In the first place, Homer kept his story within proper limits by not attempting to write about the whole Trojan War, "although it had a beginning and end" (ll. 21-22). A composition about the whole war might have had theoretical unity, but we know from Chapter VII that its magnitude would have been too great to keep in the mind and that the work would therefore have lacked (or appeared to lack) unity. As Aristotle says in Chapter XXIII, "that would have been a very large subject and could not have been taken in easily in a single view" (ll. 22-24). Homer's solution was to take only a part of the story (Achilles and Hector) and then to add other episodes, such as the catalogue of ships, for ornament. Such episodes, we recall, are "outside the plot." They are permissible in an epic because, as we will learn in Chapter XXIV, epic has a special capacity for absorbing digressive incidents.

The chapter ends with two "Brand X'" epics that are nominally unified by being concerned with one man and/or one period or one action having an excessive variety of parts. The *Cypria* dealt with the events that led up to the Trojan War, and the *Little Iliad* dealt with the sack of Troy. These epics are lost. Other references to them in antiquity indicate, however, that they were more like chronicles than unified poems. Interestingly, both were much shorter in number of lines than Homer's poems. The *Iliad* has some 15,000 lines and the *Odyssey* about 12,000. The *Cypria,* on the other hand, was about 7,000 lines long; the *Little Iliad* contained only about 2,500 lines. Aristotle is obviously not referring to physical length but to the length of time covered by the plot (or perhaps the "argument"). The measure of epic unity given in Chapter XXIII is the number of tragedies that can be constructed from a single epic. The passage is puzzling since a good many tragedies were constructed from episodes in the *Iliad,* not the "one or two" mentioned by Aristotle (l. 32). Evidently Aristotle means that only one or two tragedies can be constructed by a poet using roughly the same incidents that form the plot of the *Iliad* or *Odyssey*. The truth of this is apparent from Aristotle's summary of the "argument" of the *Odyssey* in Chapter XVII. The "eight" tragedies allegedly constructed from the *Little Iliad* are also something of a problem. Else suggests that the list is a late interpolation and that instead of being a list of tragedies, it is a crude reworking of a summary by Proclus (5th C. A.D.) of the contents of the *Little Iliad*! As usual, the present translation follows the traditional reading.

Chapter XXIV

The second chapter on epic deals with an initially bewildering variety of topics. It begins with a consideration of the types of epic plot that echoes the discussion of the types of tragedy in Chapter XVIII. Telford has argued that this section should be considered part of Chapter XXIII because it continues consideration of the formal aspects of imitation. Actually, it is a list of things that epic and tragedy have in common and thus a prelude to the contrasts that follow. Next come discussions of epic magnitude, of epic meter, of the epic manner of imitation, and finally, of two qualities that are characteristic of epic—the irrational and the marvelous. Since the chapter emphasizes the contrast between tragedy and epic, its numerous parts can be reduced to at least a rudimentary order. Epic has greater magnitude than tragedy, and magnitude is involved in the discussion of epic digressions and epic meter. The epic manner requires an admixture of drama, which Aristotle believes the poet should emphasize; and epic makes greater use of the marvelous and the illogical than does tragedy. The plan of the chapter, therefore, reduces itself to a section of comparison followed by contrasts in regard to magnitude, manner, and use of the marvelous. On the other hand, it would be false to claim any very high degree of organization in this list of topics, and the chapter lacks the clear design of the preceding one.

Comparison of Epic and Tragedy (ll. 1-12)

Epic and tragedy, says Aristotle, have the same forms. The reference is to the forms of tragedy listed in Chapter XVIII. Epic can be complex (epic of recognition), can emphasize character, or can emphasize suffering. Because epic is in the second manner of imitation, it lacks one form found in tragedy—the tragedy of spectacle. Although thought and diction do not produce forms of tragedy or epic, both are as important to epic as they are to tragedy. Again Homer is cited as the prime example of epic artistry. The *Iliad* is simple and exhibits suffering. That the plot of the *Iliad* is simple in Aristotle's sense hardly needs explanation. Its argument is "the wrath of Achilles." Having been aroused by the death of his friend Patroclus, Achilles sets out consciously to destroy Hector, and by the end of the poem he has done so. There is no reversal or recognition in the plot, although some of the episodes added for variety, which are thus "outside the plot," include these elements. The *Iliad* is also an "epic of suffering." From the beginning, the emphasis is on the "tragic deed" that is the "end" of the plot—the slaying of Hector—and this deed is an episode of suffering as defined at the end of Chapter XI. The *Odyssey*, on the other hand, is an epic of recognition and of character. If the analysis offered in the commentary on Chapter XVIII is valid, the *Odyssey* is not both these forms simultaneously. Rather, the plot of the *Odyssey* is complex, involving several recognitions of Ulysses (by Telemachus, the neatherd, the nurse, and, eventually, the suitors). In this sense there is, as Aristotle remarks, "recognition throughout" (l. 10). The parts of the *Odyssey* that emphasize character, however, are "outside the plot." The most important such "part" is Ulysses' tale of his wanderings in Books IX-XII. This story has an episodic plot that is simple in form and "fortunate" in its movement—the type of plot that Aristotle seems to have in mind for the "tragedy of character," as defined in Chapter XVIII.

Having classified Homer's epics, Aristotle adds that "Homer outstrips all others in diction and thought" (ll. 11-12).

Contrasts Between Epic and Tragedy: Plot (ll. 13-30)

The chief difference between epic and tragedy is the greater magnitude of epic. This magnitude is evident in both plot and meter. Aristotle considers plot first. Later (Chapter XXVI), he adds that the greater magnitude of epic is something of a liability. Tragedy produces its "proper pleasure" more economically; and this constitutes one of the most important reasons for its superiority to epic.

The first fact about epic plot is that it must be short enough "to take in the beginning and end in one view" (ll. 15-16—an allusion to the criterion of magnitude established in Chapter VII). Aristotle criticizes "the old epics"—chronicle-like epics such as the *Cypria* and *Little Iliad* mentioned in Chapter XXIII—and sets as a rough limit for length "the number of tragedies that are designated for one performance" (ll. 18-19). This is evidently a reference to the unified trilogy along the lines of Aeschylus' *Oresteia;* it is the only moderately explicit reference to the unified trilogy in the *Poetics.* The passage neatly complements the statement in Chapter V (l. 31) that the earliest writers of tragedy tended to follow epic practice, and it strengthens the suggestion made in the comment on that passage that Aristotle believed the unified trilogy to be more common in the early period of Greek tragedy than in the later.

At this point we should have no trouble in realizing that, when Aristotle refers to the length of the epic plot, he is not referring to the number of lines in a typical epic. Homer's epics contained as many or more lines than other Greek epics, but, as we have seen, his plots were shorter and more unified. We already know from several references that Homer filled out his epic with episodes "outside the plot." Aristotle now explains why epic has the capacity for adding such episodes: "Epic poetry has a very great capacity that is specifically its own, since it is not possible in tragedy to imitate many simultaneous lines of action but only that performed by the actors on the stage" (ll. 20-23). The difference in the magnitude of epic and tragic plot is a byproduct of the fact that they use different manners of imitation. A tragedy must concentrate on the main action. It can introduce brief episodes that are "outside the plot" through messengers and the narrations of gods; but these cannot be so long or so digressive as to divert attention from the plot being represented by the major characters. Epic, on the other hand, is narrative in manner. A narrator can move forward and backward in time, can change locations easily, and can move freely from the actions of human characters to the councils of the gods and back.

This passage is Aristotle's closest approach to enunciating the third of the three neoclassic "rules"—unity of place. Of course, his statement is not a rule at all but a practical observation, as valid for Shakespeare's theater as for the theater of the Greeks. No matter how much freedom is accorded the dramatic poet, the narrative poet has much greater freedom. Shakespeare's liberal shiftings of place notwithstanding, none of his dramas has anything like the fluidity of movement found, for example, in *The Faerie Queene* or *Paradise Lost*. We can pause here to summarize our observations concerning the three unities as follows: (1) Aristotle advocated unity of action without, however, ruling out the theoretical possibility of subplots; and (2) Aristotle does not advocate either unity of time or unity of place as those concepts were understood by neoclassic criticism.

Aristotle concludes his discussion of the magnitude of the epic plot by observing that it accounts for the special quality of epic. This quality is "elegance" (*megaloprepeia,* often translated as "magnificance" in renaissance critical treatises); it is created by the variety of epic episodes. Characteristically, Aristotle adds that, although it enhances an epic, it "makes tragedies fail" (l. 30). "Elegance" is a desirable quality when it is a natural development of the potential inherent in a literary form. When it is not inherent in the form—that is, in drama—it is a blemish. We can add on the basis of Chapter XXVI that in spite of its attractions, epic elegance is inferior to tragic intensity. Not only is epic (even Homeric epic) more primitive than tragedy(Chapter IV), it is also less economical, and hence less artistic.

Contrasts Between Epic and Tragedy: Meter (ll. 31-44)

Heroic meter has a greater magnitude than dramatic meter in the simple and obvious sense of being longer. The dactyl (one long and two short syllables) is longer than the iamb; and dactylic hexameter is much longer than the six feet of iambic trimeter that formed a line of Greek tragic dialogue. The greater length of heroic verse makes it "the stateliest and most dignified meter" (l. 35). It is therefore "appropriate" to epic poetry, and to use another meter would be "inappropriate" (l. 34). Aristotle now repeats the points made in Chapter XXII. Heroic verse is "especially receptive to strange words and metaphors"; and imitation in the narrative manner "is exceptional among the forms of imitation" (ll. 37-38). We can understand easily why heroic verse is more receptive to strange words than iambic verse. It is far removed from everyday speech, and "strange words" emphasize and bring out this quality. They are "fitting" in the sense of being necessary or probable expressions of the form. It is a little surprising to find that heroic verse also uses metaphors frequently, for we learned in Chapter XXII that metaphors are "fitting" for iambic verse. On the other hand, metaphors are the "most important" of the poetic usages, and if they can add elevation to dramatic verse, they can certainly add it to epic verse. The possibility also exists that Aristotle is thinking not of metaphor in the generic sense but of simile, and, in particular, epic simile.

Having noted that poetry using the narrative manner "is exceptional among the forms of imitation" in its use of ornamental diction, Aristotle explains briefly. Iambic and trochaic meters are associated with drama, that is, with forms using the third manner of imitation. As Aristotle noted in Chapter IV (l. 70), trochaic meter was associated with dance; it gave way to iambic meter when the satyr-play gave way to formal tragedy. The chief association of iambic meter is with conversation, but since conversation implies people conversing, it is also associated with action. If trochaic and iambic meters are (a) associated with the third manner of imitation and (b) less hospitable to ornamental diction than the dactylic hexameter of narrative, it follows that narrative poetry is innately more ornamental than dramatic poetry.

The discussion ends with another assertion of the appropriateness of heroic meter for narrative poems. Chairemon (evidently the Chairemon of Chapter I who composed *The Centaur*) attempted to write narrative in mixed meters and produced a "strange" impression (l. 41). Therefore, no serious authors have written long narrative poems "in a meter other than heroic" (l. 43). Not only do we learn from the poetic art that heroic meter is proper for narrative, but "nature herself teaches us to choose the appropriate meter" (ll. 43-44).

The Epic Manner of Imitation (ll. 45-56)

The manner of narrative poetry is "mixed." It involves statements by the poet in his own person and also statements made by the characters. The epic poet can stress either himself or his characters. If he does the latter, he is emphasizing the "dramatic" element in his composition. Since drama is a higher form than epic, the artistic approach is to stress the characters. Aristotle now repeats a point made concerning Homer in Chapter VI. Other poets speak, for the most part, in their own persons, but Homer "alone of the poets" (l. 46) makes maximum use of his characters: "When he has made a brief prelude [he] immediately brings in a man or woman or some other character; and all his figures are expressive of character and none lacks it" (ll. 53-56). Aristotle stresses this point so heavily that he slightly modifies the position taken in Chapter III. There he had said that all three "manners" were forms of imitation; here he suggests that a poet using the first manner (speaking in his own person) "is not fulfilling his function as an imitator" (l. 49). The slight inconsistency is best explained as a byproduct of Aristotle's desire in Chapter XXIV to make the reason for Homer's superiority absolutely clear.

The Marvelous and the Irrational (ll. 57-102)

We have been told in Chapter IX (l. 59) that tragedy should seek "the marvelous." This can be achieved by two strategies. First, the poet can construct a plot in which something occurs unexpectedly but as the result of necessary or probable antecedents. Second, he can rely on chance or fortune or the intervention of divine agency, as in the story of the statue of Mitys. The second strategy is "irrational" (*alogos*) and is often produced by a kind of logical sleight-of-hand known as paralogism.

Aristotle begins by noting that both tragedy and epic use the marvelous. As we know from Chapter IX, tragedy should produce its effects through structure. The marvelous, however, is most readily produced by "the irrational." Because the dramatic manner forces the poet to adapt his effects to stage presentation, an "irrational" incident may appear unconvincing, even ludicrous, in performance. Epic has no such limitation. Therefore it has much greater liberty than tragedy to create the marvelous by "irrational" incidents. The pursuit of Hector (*Odyssey,* XXII, 205) is "irrational" in that the Greeks and Trojans would not have been likely to stand idly by while Achilles pursued and finally destroyed his foe. The irrationality would be patent if the incident were dramatized, but no one is disturbed by it when reading the poem. What Aristotle is pointing out is a qualitative difference between narrative and stage action, one that still exists today. The mere fact of our seeing stories performed by human actors makes us critical of them. Incongruities that we would not notice—or would even enjoy—in a novel become irritating in performance. This does not mean that dramatic fantasies are impossible. It merely means that a dramatic fantasy such as *The Tempest* must be far more carefully constructed, must have greater internal coherence and probability, than a fairy tale or even a romantic adventure story such as *Treasure Island.*[1]

Having demonstrated that epic has a special capacity for producing the marvelous by "the irrational," Aristotle observes that the marvelous is pleasant and that Homer is especially successful in producing it. Homer's technique is to use paralogism, here translated as "false reasoning" (l. 69). A paralogism is a device for "framing lies," that is, for making the false seem true. It is discussed in

[1] Whether or not the point still holds true for cinema is an interesting question. By and large, cinematic effects are so variable and so impressive that they can make a modest success of a work that would fail on the stage, as witness several crude but entertaining cinematic versions of the wanderings of Ulysses.

Aristotle's *Sophistic Refutations,* V, 167^b1-8 and his *Rhetoric,* II, XIX and XXIV. As Aristotle explains the device in the *Poetics,* it consists of creating the illusion that A is true by asserting B, the normal consequence of A. Thus, when an actor utters lines of impassioned anger, we have the illusion the actor himself is angry, although we know logically that he is merely playing a part. As Aristotle says, "whenever one event occurs or comes into existence and is naturally accompanied by a second event, men think that whenever this second event is present the first one must have occurred . . ." (ll. 69-72). To illustrate, Aristotle cites "the Bath Scene in the *Odyssey*" (l. 80). Although there is disagreement concerning what incident Aristotle has in mind, the reference is probably to *Odyssey* XIX, 164-260. Ulysses appears to Penelope disguised as a Cretan. He pretends that he has seen Ulysses, and Penelope accepts his story because his description is accurate. The trouble with this identification of the passage is that Penelope is taken in, whereas Aristotle seems to be referring to an instance in the *Odyssey* involving the deception of the reader. On the other hand, the alternatives that have been suggested are even less satisfactory. If the reference *is* to the deceiving of Penelope, Aristotle is evidently citing the incident simply to illustrate paralogism, not to demonstrate the use of paralogism to achieve the marvelous.

The chapter ends with a discussion of a famous paradox: "The use of impossible probabilities is preferable to that of unpersuasive possibilities" (ll. 81-82). This is Agathon's paradox mentioned in Chapter XVIII (l. 52). "Impossible probabilities" are incidents that do not normally happen (or cannot happen), which, however, are interrelated by necessity or probability. *The Tempest* is an excellent example of a drama consisting of "impossible probabilities"; *The Rime of the Ancient Mariner* is a narrative poem using the same strategy. The *Eumenides* and the *Odyssey* are parallel classical pieces. An "unpersuasive possibility" is, by contrast, an incident that is possible in itself but is not integrated into the plot by necessity or probability.

The next statement is puzzling in view of the fact that Aristotle has just finished praising Homer for using paralogism. Plots, he says, should avoid the "irrational" (l. 83). The most probable explanation is that the reference is to plots in the formal sense, not to ancillary incidents. The *Odyssey* contains many irrational elements, but its plot, as outlined in Chapter XVII, is just the sort recommended for tragedy in Chapter IX. Its incidents are related by necessity or probability, and it achieves the marvelous not by chance, fortune, or the gods, but by its recognitions.

The general rule, then, is to keep the "irrational" outside the plot. To illustrate, Aristotle turns briefly back to tragedy, citing *Oedipus, Electra,* and *The Mysians,* a lost play probably by Aeschylus. Sophocles treated "the irrational" correctly in *Oedipus* by placing the circumstances surrounding Laius' death "outside the plot." On the other hand, he erred in the *Electra* by making the report of the Pythian games "part of the plot." This is another ambiguous reference, but the traditional interpretation, going back to Robortello and Castelvetro, cites the improbability of the Argives' learning of the games from the messenger, because the news would already have been brought back by other spectators. Another explanation is that the games themselves, which did not exist in the days of Orestes and Clytemnestra, are an anachronism. This seems more likely, for it involves a sensational bit of stage action (Orestes in disguise "reporting" his own death), based on a paralogism: the messengers report the games; therefore the theater audience accepts the idea that they existed. Finally, the author of *The Mysians* evidently erred by introducing a character who is alleged to have walked from Tegea to Mysia in perfect silence. Such illogicalities are ridiculous. A plot that requires them is a bad plot; and Aristotle asserts that the solution is "not to construct such plots" (l. 92). They involve "unpersuasive possibilities," and an author who knows his craft will avoid them.

So far Aristotle has indicated (a) that the marvelous should be probable rather than "irrational" and (b) that if it is irrational it should be "outside the plot." He now considers the case of an irrational episode that is in the plot. This is the most unsatisfactory situation of all, but it must be dealt with. As an example of an irrational incident that is part of a plot, Aristotle cites the "casting ashore of Odysseus" (l. 96). This occurs in Book XIII (ll. 1-164) of the *Odyssey*. It involves a magic boat and a miracle performed by Poseidon. Because the plot of the *Odyssey* is based on probabilities, this incident is out of harmony. It occurs, however, in an epic, not a drama; and Homer has the skill to palliate its irrationality. The remaining lines of Chapter XXIV are somewhat obscure. Homer, it would seem, diverted the reader from the irrationality of the incident by his highly artistic diction. Evidently diction can compensate for deficiencies of action, thought, and character. To avoid the suggestion that diction can be an end in itself, Aristotle adds that when the other elements are present—that is, when the incidents have a necessary or probable relation—too much emphasis on diction can obscure character and thought. Used properly, style is the necessary or probable expression of the form employed (Chapter XXII). Occasionally, when the form is defective, it can veil imperfections, but this is at best a lame strategy.

Chapter XXV

Chapters XXV and XXVI conclude the *Poetics* as we have it. They form a unit devoted to "general questions" that can be raised concerning epic and tragedy. Chapter XXV deals with critical problems and their solutions, which essentially means criticisms of poetry and answers to the criticisms. Chapter XXVI is devoted to a single question—whether epic or tragedy is the superior form. The *Poetics* ends with the demonstration that tragedy is the more excellent of the two forms.

Chapter XXV is long and complicated. It does not, however, add substantially to the larger argument of the *Poetics*. A detailed consideration of its problems would be digressive and would involve technicalities of interest only to specialists. Therefore we will treat it summarily. It is divided into three sections. The first is a consideration of the three bases of poetic criticism. The second is a list of criticisms and their answers. On the basis of the final paragraph of the chapter (ll. 138-142) we can be reasonably confident that there are five criticisms and twelve "answers" in this section. Critics have differed widely in their efforts to identify these precisely, and the summary that is offered here is not intended as definitive. The third section of the chapter generalizes about answers to three of the five criticisms.

Notice that throughout the chapter the perspective is a new one. Aristotle is now viewing the work from the reader's (or critic's) point of view, not from the artist's. He is not offering lame excuses for poetic errors but pointing out that a sophisticated critic will take the nature of poetic art into account when approaching a literary work. This is why many of his "answers"—the difference between technical and nontechnical errors, the need to evaluate the moral significance of incidents in context, the need to understand the nature of poetic language, and so forth—are still excellent guides to sensitive criticism.

The Three Bases of Criticism
(ll. 1-22)

The first basis of criticism is related to object of imitation. On the analogy of painting, an analogy used in a somewhat parallel way in Chapters II and IV, Aristotle concludes that the poet may represent his objects as they were or are, as they are said or seem to be, or as they ought to be (ll. 7-9). The critic can draw upon these alternatives to account for "impossible" situations. They form the third, fourth, and fifth "answers" in the list of twelve that forms the body of the chapter. They recur in modified form as general lines of critical argument in the last section of the chapter (ll. 127-129).

The second basis of poetic criticism is the fact that the poet uses language as his medium. As we know from Chapter XXI, poetic language is more "distinguished" than that of prose, and the poet is obliged to make use of the ornamental devices of diction. There are therefore "many variations of diction, for we grant this license to poets" (ll. 10-11). This is the doctrine of poetic license. It is invoked to explain obscurities and to justify departures from standard usage. It provides answers seven through eleven in Aristotle's list.

The third basis of criticism is that the poetic art is different from other arts. Aristotle specifically contrasts it to the art of politics

(l. 12). This point has been discussed in the comment on Chapter I in connection with the "placing" of poetry among the other sciences. Its corollary is that there are two types of error in poetry—the technical and the nontechnical. A technical error is one that does violence to the principles of poetic art. The poet can, for example, disregard necessity or probability in his plot, include digressive incidents "in the plot," make his characters more base than necessary, substitute spectacle for action, fail to use diction appropriate to his form, and the like. These are cases in which "the poet chose to imitate but imitated incorrectly," and they are "essential" errors (l. 14). On the other hand, if the poet observes the principles of poetic art but makes an error in some other art, the error is nontechnical. Aristotle gives two examples. If the poet represents a horse "putting forward both right hooves" (ll. 18-19) he has revealed a lack of knowledge of horses, not poetry. By the same token, if he misrepresents the symptoms of a character who is sick, he has merely shown ignorance of the art of medicine.

The position that poetic art is different from the other arts is central to the whole *Poetics,* and Aristotle here states that the critic as well as the poet must keep it in mind. It directly conflicts with the position taken by Plato in the *Republic* that a poetic representation—of a bed, for example—must be judged by the same criteria that are used to evaluate the real bed. We have already seen that Plato's position is based on the idea that imitation is a kind of copying, and that Aristotle emphatically rejects the copy theory. Here Aristotle's position emerges with particular clarity. The critic who objects to a poetic horse that simultaneously throws out two right hooves is assuming that the validity of an artistic representation is a function of its fidelity to the original. Aristotle flatly denies this. Such an error is "accidental" (l. 15); what counts is the poet's understanding of his art. The idea that poetry must be judged on the basis of artistic principles is the first "answer" in Aristotle's list, and the idea that some errors are "accidental" is the second.

Answers to Critics
(ll. 23-115)

In the last paragraph of Chapter XXV, Aristotle says that he has given twelve answers to five kinds of censure. The five are: impossibility, irrationality, immorality, contradiction, and lack of correctness. Traces of a five-part division of his list of answers occur in the list itself, but they are not sufficiently clear to permit an outline on which all scholars can agree. Telford believes that the list is divided into two parts, one dealing with problems raised by object of imitation and the other with problems raised by means of imitation (diction). He further believes that all five "censures" are answered in each list. This is an interesting but rather radical analysis. The more common approach, taken by Gudeman and Rostagni, is to divide the list into five major categories, each containing one or more "answer." The problem is that the section supposedly devoted to "irrationality" is hard to isolate; and the section on contradiction appears to follow rather than precede the section on correctness. The following outline adopts the Gudeman-Rostagni analysis with some modifications:

I. Answers to the charge of impossibility

(1) 1. Although one should generally avoid impossibilities, they are sometimes justified when they support "the goal of imitation" (l. 29). As an example, Aristotle cites Homer's depiction of the pursuit of Hector. We know from Chapter XXIV (l. 61) that this is "marvelous" and is justified in Homer because it is not represented on the stage, where it would seem ludicrous. Since "the marvelous" is desirable in poetic art, it is justified.

(2) 2. Some impossibilities are "accidental" rather than essential. Aristotle cites the example of a representation of a hind without horns. This is impossible according to the art of zoology; but it does not violate poetic art. It is comparable to the example cited earlier in Chapter XXV of the poet who depicts a horse simultaneously throwing out both right hoofs.

(3) 3. The impossibility may be caused by the poet's wish to present a character "as he ought to be" rather than "as he is." Sophocles tended in this direction, whereas Euripides was more realistic. This defense, of course, echoes both Chapter II and the requirement of goodness laid down in Chapter XV. It is often considered a defense against the second of Aristotle's five kinds of censure (irrationality); but Aristotle seems quite explicit about its relation to "impossibility" in the third section of the chapter (l. 118). Moreover, "the unreasonable" (*alogos*) is associated with miracles and fallacies in Chapters IX and XXIV.

II. Answers to the charge of irrationality

(This category is not explicit in the text. It seems necessary because the next category is quite definitely devoted to the charge of immorality, the third of the categories mentioned at the end of the chapter. It is justified by the fact that the first "answer" is illustrated by reference to classical myths, which are prime examples of what Aristotle normally means by the irrational.)

(4) 1. The charge of irrationality may be met by reference to received opinion. Men often believe what is false (the Furies who pursue Orestes in the *Eumenides* are examples); and the poet can use such beliefs without making an artistic error. Aristotle illustrates by referring generally to "the myths that are told about the gods" (ll. 46-47). Xenophanes, probably the Eleatic philosopher, had complained that the myths were false, but "in accordance . . . with men's opinions" (ll. 49-50). It is questionable, in view of Chapter XI, whether Aristotle approved of defending poetry on the basis of "opinion"; but he dutifully notes the possibility. Later critics, especially critics of the renaissance and neoclassic periods, equated "opinion" with verisimilitude and sometimes advocated ignoring "truth" in favor of "what men believe."

(5) 2. The charge can also be met by pointing out that many things that seem irrational in one period were common practice in earlier periods. Homer's statement that the Greeks held their spears "upright on their butt spikes" (*Iliad,* X, 152) would have seemed erroneous to a contemporary of Aristotle, but the practice was customary in Homeric times.

III. An answer to the charge of immorality

(6) 1. Only one answer is given to the charge of immorality. The critic, says Aristotle, must consider not only the statement or deed but also its context. In particular, he should decide "whether the object is to achieve a greater good or to avoid a greater evil" (ll. 61-62). Striking a person, for example, is an evil in itself; but to strike an assassin in order to prevent him from killing someone is clearly good.

IV. Answers to the charge of lack of correctness

(This section is devoted to diction, and in particular to poetic uses of language that create obscurity or seem to violate standard usage. A case can be made that the idea of "correctness" is not limited to diction *per se* but includes instances of poetic correctness that violate some other art, such as horsemanship or medicine. If so, Aristotle's answers begin with "correctness" of diction and broaden out to "poetic correctness" in general.)

(7) 1. The first answer is that the poet was using a strange word or metaphor. As we know, poets not only use such devices, they are obligated to use them by the principles of poetic art. Aristotle here devotes major emphasis to explaining strange words.

(8) 2. The poet may have used poetic license, creating a difficulty that can be resolved by changing the accent.

(9) 3. Poetic syntax is sometimes ambiguous, and difficulties may be resolved by changing the punctuation. Actually, "punctuation" is merely an English equivalent for Aristotle's meaning. What he has in mind is the fact that in complex sentences, different

words may be grouped together to give different meanings. Aristotle's example is "Suddenly things become mortal . . . and things unmixed before mixed" (ll. 85-87). Even in English the last phrase can be read either, "things unmixed before [became] mixed"; or, "things unmixed [became, that is, came into existence] before mixed."

(10) 4. Poetic language is sometimes ambiguous.

(11) 5. Poetic language often incorporates common usages that involve misuse of standard words.

V. An answer to the charge of contradiction

(12) 1. Only one answer is given. When a passage seems to involve contradictions, we are to consider all its possible senses and then select the one that seems most probable. If Homer says, "The bronze spear was held there" (*Iliad*, XX, 272), "was held" can refer either to an action performed by a human character, or it can be used in the sense of "became stuck" or "embedded." Aristotle takes the occasion to censure critics who assign an impossible meaning to a passage without considering the alternatives and who then attack the poet for writing absurdities. To illustrate further, he recalls that Icarius was Ulysses' father-in-law and that readers commonly assume on the basis of his name that he was a Spartan. If so, it is ludicrous that Ulysses' son Telemachus, who visited Sparta, did not know Icarius. One solution, says Aristotle, is that *Icarius* is a corruption for *Icadius*, a Cephallenian name. If so, Icarius was never in Sparta, and therefore it is perfectly understandable that Telemachus never met him there.

Summary (ll. 116-142)

The chapter ends with a few generalizations concerning the treatment of the impossible, the irrational, and the contradictory, and a brief qualification to the effect that sometimes censure of the irrational and immoral is justified.

The impossible, says Aristotle, is justified (a) by the requirements of poetry, (b) by the fact that it is better than what is, and (c) by opinion. These are the first, third, and fourth answers given in the preceding list of censures and answers. The idea that poets can make men better than they are is further supported by appeal to the theory outlined in Chapter XXIV that "We must prefer a persuasive impossibility to an unpersuasive possibility" (l. 120). It is illustrated by the practice of the painter Zeuxis, already familiar from Chapter II. According to a popular story repeated by Cicero (*De Inventione*, II, 1), Zeuxis combined traits of the five most beautiful maidens of Croton in his painting of Helen, an obvious case of a "persuasive impossibility."

The irrational is generally to be defended on two grounds. First, "what men say" is often irrational but nevertheless accepted. This is number four in the list of answers to critics. Note that it can be used as a justification for both the impossible and the irrational. A second defense is a variation on Agathon's paradox, first mentioned in Chapter XVIII, that it is probable that sometimes improbabilities will happen.

Contradictions are to be handled like refutations in debating, "with reference to whether the same object is involved and in the same relationship, and in the same sense" (ll. 128-130). This is merely a paraphrase of the last of the twelve answers to critics.

Having listed both specific and general answers to critics, Aristotle adds the qualification that not all apparent errors can be justified. Aegeus appears for no reason in the midst of *Medea* (ll. 663ff) to assure the heroine of her safety. His appearance is "irrational" because it is neither necessary nor probable. It is simply a bit of Euripidean decor, and it dilutes the effect of the play. The villainy of Menelaus in the *Orestes* is an example of unnecessary debasement of character. It was cited in Chapter XV (l. 21) as a violation of the first principle of characterization, "goodness."

The chapter ends with a brief enumeration of the five censures and a reference to the twelve answers that Aristotle has supplied.

Chapter XXVI

Chapter XXVI considers one critical question at length. After Chapter V, the *Poetics* concentrates almost exclusively on tragedy and epic, and it is obviously fitting to conclude with an analysis of the relative merits of the two forms. Whether this consideration is the end of the *Poetics* as Aristotle wrote it is another question.

The likelihood is that he composed a second book on comedy that has been lost. The fact that one manuscript ends with a group of words usually translated "Now as to iambic poetry and comedy . . ." strengthens this possibility, although the manuscript (Riccarcianus 46) is an inferior one and the fragmentary sentence may be an interpolation.

The chapter has four distinct parts. First Aristotle summarizes the argument for the inferiority of tragedy. He then points out that the argument applies more to the art of performance than to tragedy itself. Next, he gives the arguments in favor of the inferiority of epic and concludes that these arguments are decisive. Finally, a brief paragraph summarizing the *Poetics* as a whole ends the work.

The argument for the inferiority of tragedy is based on the strong Greek sense of social class. The better literary form is one that appeals to the best class of people. Epic is read or recited, but tragedy is performed by actors. Tragedy is the more "common" form and therefore, according to its detractors, is inferior. Aristotle adds details to this argument. Not only is tragedy performed, but performers as a class over-act their parts. This is true of flute players and rhapsodists as well as dramatic actors. The tendency to overacting evidently increased as time went by, so that, says Aristotle, Mynescus called Callippides "an ape" (l. 12). What is true of the older and newer actors is also said of epic in contrast to tragedy. Epic is restrained and directed toward "a reasonable audience" (ll. 16-17), whereas tragedy is dependent on actors and intended for the commonality. Interestingly, Castelvetro emphasized the vulgar appeal of tragedy heavily in his renaissance commentary on the *Poetics*. In seventeenth-century France, on the other hand, tragedy was considered an extremely elegant form, best suited for a court audience.

The first answer to this charge against tragedy is that it is directed against the actor's art, not the poet's. Aristotle does not discount the value of motion and gesture, but he rests his case primarily on the fact (mentioned first in Chapter VI) that tragedy "achieves its function . . . through reading" (ll. 29-30). If this is so, the fact that tragedy usually achieves its function in performance is accidental. Aristotle does not deny that public performance may be "common" (he probably felt that it was), but he does deny that this is an essential defect. His argument resembles the first of the critical answers in Chapter XXV.

There are four positive arguments in favor of tragedy. First, tragedy contains all the parts of epic plus two more, spectacle and song. These are not the most important parts of tragedy, but they make it richer than epic and are especially effective in performance. Indeed, they are so closely related to performance that Aristotle repeats the earlier point that tragedy can provide a vivid experience in reading as well as performance (ll. 36-37). Second, tragedy achieves its function "in a shorter length of time" than epic (ll. 38-39). The proper function of tragedy is a kind of pleasure, and, says Aristotle, "A more compact action is more pleasant than one that is much diluted" (ll. 39-40). We begin to sense a criterion of economy in Aristotle's aesthetic. The criterion is a good one, and today, we continue to recognize the relation between economy and intensity of effect. It is supported by a theoretical example. What would happen if *Oedipus* were drawn out to the length of the *Iliad*? Obviously, from Aristotle's point of view, it would be far too long—like the epic tragedies of the early dramatists mentioned in Chapter VII—and its effect would be spoiled.

The third argument moves from magnitude to unity. Tragedy is not only more compact, it is also more unified than epic. This is in part a corollary of its compactness, but more important is the fact that tragedy, by its nature, is restricted to a single action and to the avoidance of episodes "outside the plot." Homer managed to achieve a single action in both the *Iliad* and the *Odyssey*, but he could not resist the innate tendency of epic to include much material "outside the plot." We know from Chapter XXIII that Homer's plots can provide material for only one or two tragedies, in contrast to the *Cypria* and the *Little Iliad*; but his poems—as distinct from his plots—provide source materials for a large number of tragedies. This is, of course, not a defect within the epic form. An epic as severely limited as a tragedy would, as Aristotle says, "lack full development . . . or [have] a watered-down quality" (ll. 46-48). After all, "magnitude" is a virtue in epic and is achieved by Homer through the use of episodes "outside the plot." Given the epic form, Homer's solution is the best one possible, but the form of tragedy makes a still more elegant solution possible: the dramatist can concentrate on a single action and exclude all that is not necessary or probable, that is, all that tends to make the drama episodic. That the *Iliad* and *Odyssey* are here said to "have many . . . elements" (l. 50) does not contradict the statement in Chapter XXIII that only one or two tragedies can be made from their plots, for the "elements" referred to are evidently ornamental digressions such as the tale of Ulysses' wanderings or his wounding on Mount Parnassus. Aristotle ends the consideration of unity with an almost apologetic bow to Homer: "And yet these poems are constructed in the best possible way and are, as much as possible, the imitations of a single action" (ll. 51-53). The point is that the more one fulfills the innate potentials of epic, the farther he moves from the kind of unity found in tragedy.

The fourth argument may not be a new argument at all but a kind of drawing together of the implications of what has already been said. If tragedy is superior to epic in having more parts, in having greater compression, and in having greater unity, and it still accomplishes its proper pleasure, "It is apparent that tragedy, since it is better at attaining its end, is superior to epic" (ll. 57-58). The "proper pleasure" is evidently catharsis. The interesting feature of the passage is that it makes explicit what we could only guess at before; namely, that epic and tragedy both strive for the same effect, but that tragedy produces it more efficiently than epic.

The last sentence of the *Poetics* balances the first. Tragedy and epic, their forms and parts, their differences, the reasons for their effectiveness, and criticisms are all mentioned. The sentence is a retrospective outline of everything that we have read from Chapter I to the end.

Epilogue: On Aristotelian Imitation

Intro

Plato assumed that artistic imitation is a kind of copying, and that the excellence of a particular work is to be judged by its fidelity to its "original." Aristotle meant something quite different by imitation, but his theory was largely ignored by later ages. The Hellenistic fusion of poetics and rhetoric evident in Hermogenes' *Peri Epideiktikon,* Horace's *Ars Poetica,* and Statius' *Sylvae* revived the Platonic view in three ways. In later antiquity, imitation came to be understood as "representation of typical human situations," as "description"—the *ekphrasis, notatio,* and *effictio* of rhetoric—or as "imitating the ancient masterpieces."

According to the first view, literature could be understood as a mirror; and the phrase that Cicero was (falsely) said to have used to describe comedy—*speculum consuetudinis* ("mirror of the times") —became a favorite metaphor for literary imitation during the Middle Ages. According to the second view, literature was understood as a kind of painting—*ut pictura poesis,* as Horace has it. Topographical, descriptive, and landscape poetry partly filled the need for a literature that imitated by producing images of real "things." Ausonius' *Mosella* (a long poetic description of the Moselle river) is a fine classical instance of a poem that paints a picture of nature. But poetry was supposed to contain images of men and events as well as "things." To do this, it followed rhetorically approved formulas. The formulas of *notatio* (character sketch) and *effictio* (physical description) are commonplace in Latin rhetoric from the time of the anonymous *Rhetorica Ad Herennium,* and their influence is constantly evident in the character depiction of Statius, Lucan, Claudian, and their medieval successors. For more elaborate character portraits, there were the formulas of the encomium, which if applied with sufficient skill and diligence, could produce "panegyrical biographies" of the type represented by Tacitus' *Life of Agricola* and endlessly repeated in cruder form in saints' lives and in such secular works as Einhardt's *Life of Charlemagne.* For institutions and events, there were still other formulas —the formulas for epithalamia, for birthday-songs (*genethliaca*), funeral elegies, and the like.

The third rhetorically influenced interpretation of imitation is that it consists of "copying the masterpieces of the ancients." This theory is approved by Cicero and Horace; formulated as school exercise by Quintilian; given a Platonic twist by Longinus; exemplified by poetry of no less stature than the *Aeneid* (which "imitates" the *Iliad* and the *Odyssey*), the tragedies of Seneca, and the comedies of Plautus and Terence; and used as a formal topic of criticism by Plutarch.

All these interpretations of imitation are related in that each assumes that copying of some sort—whether of nature or of another work—is an essential part of the poet's task. Needless to say, these ideas did not die in the late Middle Ages. If anything, they gained in importance with the revival of ancient learning and the cult of antiquity characteristic of the Renaissance. Their survival into the late eighteenth century is attested by M. H. Abrams' recent study of the transition from neoclassic to romantic theories of art, *The Mirror and the Lamp*.

The general tendency of rhetorical criticism was to revive the Platonic notion of imitation as copying and to attribute it to Aristotle whenever the meaning of the *Poetics* was an issue. A different current entered criticism through Plotinus and Proclus, among others. Both writers considered themselves in the train of Plato; but both made important revisions in his outlook, revisions that had an especially marked impact on the history of criticism. The Plotinian *nous* is a creative force seeking to emanate outward, to fill all possible gaps in the scale of being, and to realize itself in material creation. By the same token, the "things" of material creation strive to rise above themselves in order to return eventually to their divine source. This is the "divine cycle" symbolized by the life history of Henry Vaughan's drop of dew and by the iconology of countless renaissance fountains. In this view, "things" remain, as they were for Plato, imperfect copies of divine archetypes; but Platonic dualism, the implacable hostility of body and soul, of worldly and divine, has been softened. With a renewed sense of the divinity of the world, there also arises a view of the artist as a creator in a special sense. As Proclus explains in his "Commentary on the Poetical Questions in the *Republic*," the poet, being divinely inspired, sees farther and higher than most men. If he produces a bed, it is a bed charged with divine *energia* and hence truer than the one produced by the carpenter. In other words, instead of being a fabricator of falsehoods and a purveyor of corruption, the poet has the priestlike function of revealing truth to men's clouded vision. He imitates not by copying the things of the world but by looking to their divine archetypes and producing images of them as they might or ought to be.

The neo-Platonic view was a genuinely new ingredient in criticism. It eventually proved capable of harmonizing efficiently with Christian theories about the influence of the Holy Spirit on the Bible and on the mystics and prophetical writers as well. Most of the notable Christian humanist critics of the sixteenth century, including Minturno, Tasso, Ronsard, and Sir Philip Sidney were sympathetic to this view. Naturally, it was attributed to Aristotle; and the interested reader can admire the ingenuity with which sixteenth-century humanist elicit neo-Platonic meanings from the discussion of the difference between poetry, history, and philosophy in *Poetics,* Chapter IX.

In spite of the fact that they were (and to some degree still are) attributed to Aristotle, the rhetorical and neo-Platonic theories of imitation have little in common with *Poetics.* Aristotle's theory of imitation is both simpler and far more subtle than either, and a brief discussion of Aristotelian imitation will provide a useful coda to the preceding commentary.

topic sentence

First of all, Aristotle's imitation is a process. On the basis of Chapter I, we would have to say that in general, poetic imitation is the representation of some action in language elevated above common speech and in one of three possible "manners." When the poet has decided on what action, what diction, and what manner he will use, he has defined the genre in which he will write. At this point, the process can be defined more specifically, at least in ideal terms. If the writer has chosen a "noble action," "speech plus rhythm and harmony, used separately," and the "dramatic manner," he will produce a tragic imitation. Moreover, a tragic imitation has, by reason of the underlying principles of poetry, six distinct parts. The process of composing a tragedy can be analyzed as the process of "constructing" each of the six parts. If the poet follows the order of Aristotle's analysis, he will begin with action and plot, producing the universal form; he will continue to episodes and characterization; and he will then add thought and diction, saving spectacle and song for the last. This is the order first suggested in Chapter VI and outlined in greater detail in Chapter XVII. Aristotle's program need not, of course, correspond with what actually happens in the composition of a play. What actually happens is far less rational, far less subject to analysis or reconstruction than the ideal order made necessary by the inner logic of poetic art. A poet's method of composition is his own. It has much to do with his psychological makeup and with the critical fashions that he happens to accept. Most poets work from trial and error, not to mention sheer luck, as well as design. All that Aristotle says is that *in the abstract* and in terms of the art of poetry, the six parts of a tragedy are also six more or less consecutive steps necessary for the production of a tragedy that fully capitalizes on the potentialities of the tragic genre.

The ideal order of precedence in the process of imitation is also a powerful tool in critical analysis of completed imitative works. During the 1930's, the "new critics" tended to emphasize diction—poetic imagery—in their discussions of what makes poetry work. Their contribution to criticism has been extremely valuable; but they themselves eventually sought a context larger than the image, something within which they could understand the image as functioning. The transition from concern with diction *per se* to concern with diction as an element of structure can be seen in the movement of William Empson from *Seven Types of Ambiguity,* an analysis of language, to *Some Versions of Pastoral,* an analysis—albeit unorthodox—of genre; and again in the contrast between Cleanth Brooks' *Modern Poetry and the Tradition* and his later *Well-Wrought Urn,* subtitled "Studies in the Structure of Poetry." In retrospect, it is clear that the new critical movement from diction to structure was definitely a movement toward Aristotelian norms; but it was neither rapid enough nor decisive enough for many critics of the 1950's. Hence, this period witnessed the development of the notion of literary archetypes—basic "plots" on which all existing literary plots are variations—by critics such as Joseph Campbell and Northrop Frye; and of an avowed (and at times rather brash) "Aristotelianism" among those writers belonging to the "Chicago School" of criticism. The upshot of the trial-and-error evolution of modern criticism, therefore, seems to be a movement toward recognition of the fundamental value of the *Poetics.* Plot, the newer theories affirm, *is* the decisive element in the literary work; and this is true whether the author likes it or not, for it depends not on personal whim but on the nature of literary art. If so, authors might benefit from realizing the fact (though this cannot be proved, because we never know what an author would have done; we only know what he did do), while critics most certainly would gain by accepting the primacy of plot as the starting point of literary analysis.

Tragic imitation, then, can be understood theoretically as a six-part process that begins with plot. The purpose of the process is to get as much out of the form as possible, no more, no less. Homer, we recall, did amazing things with epic; but even that divine poet could not produce an epic that equaled an artistic tragedy. In fact, the more "artistic" Homer made his treatment—the more he exploited the possibilities of epic—the more he precluded the possibility of tragic effects.

It is adherence to the underlying requirement of necessity or probability that determines whether the poet has made the most of his form. The importance of necessity or probability for the plot is self-evident. What the reader of the *Poetics* sometimes misses is the fact that "necessity or probability" continues to be important throughout every stage of composition. The events summarized in the work's argument or "universal form," as that form is explained in Chapter XVII, must follow one another according to necessity or probability. Indeed, the form is "universal" because it has been reduced to those essentials that bring out the necessary or probable principle on which the plot depends. As we have seen, this can be causality or something resembling the "theme" of the drama.

If the form must be universal, the episodes must (a) be part of the plot—that is, related to the other episodes by necessity or probability—and (b) be chosen to bring out a stage in the movement from good to bad fortune or the reverse. We can add that the combination of elements that most fully realizes the tragic potential is a complex plot moving from happiness to misery and including compound recognition.

We now encounter character, as distinct from agent, for the first time in an important context. The type of character most fitting for such a plot is a "good man with a defect," the defect being a *hamartia*. Notice that basic determinants of the ideal character type are deduced from the nature of the plot. In other words, the "good man with a defect" type has a necessary or probable relation to the sequence of incidents already established. The same situation obtains when we turn from character in relation to plot to character in relation to characterization. After the requirement in Chapter XV that the character be "good" comes the requirement that it be "appropriate." But to say that traits are "appropriate" is merely to say that they are necessarily or probably related to the agents that possess them. The theories as to what traits are necessarily or probably related to what kinds and conditions of men are, in turn, derived from rhetoric, ethics, and medicine, rhetoric being the most obvious, and probably the most important, source.

We then move from character to thought. The most important requirement for thought is that it be "appropriate" for the occasion. The devices for making reasoning or emotion "appropriate" (that is, necessary or probable in a given situation) are primarily the maxims, "topics of argument," and emotions of formal rhetoric, although Aristotle observes that the "political art" was used frequently by the older poets. It may be added that just as "goodness" relates character to plot, so "appropriateness to the occasion" links thought to character and, through character, to incident.

Diction comes next. The normal way of construing the first requirement of diction—that it be appropriate to character—has already been dealt with in relation to thought. This leaves two senses in which diction may have a necessary or probable relation to the work as a whole. First, the meter should be appropriate to the manner of imitation. Dactylic hexameter is proper for heroic poetry because of its weightiness and magnitude; iambic meter is appropriate for tragedy because of its natural affinity to everyday speech. Second, diction should be appropriate to the specific means of imitation used; that is, the words should be harmonious with the meter and the form. All poetic language should be elevated above the level of standard speech, but different devices are appropriate in different situations. Epic uses strange words and metaphors and, in general, has the most ornate diction; tragedy uses standard words and metaphors.

The few specific references in the *Poetics* to spectacle make it reasonably clear that spectacle must not only avoid the ludicrous, it must also be appropriate. Aristotle says almost nothing about song,

—the part of tragedy uttered by the chorus—but we know from Chapter XVIII that (a) the chorus should be treated as a character, and (b) the choral passages should not be treated by the dramatist as mere interludes so unrelated to the tragedy that they can be transferred from one play to another. It follows that song, too, must be "appropriate."

If we summarize the imitative process as Aristotle presents it, we see a clearly defined movement from "universal form" to the elaboration of detail. The first and most important step is discovering in history, nature, or the imagination an action that has a beginning, middle, and end. As Aristotle says in Chapter IX, the poet is a poet primarily by virtue of his ability to create plots; and as he observes, in Chapter VI, plot is the soul of tragedy. But plot has agents, and the agents are realized by character. Character, in turn, always manifests itself in relation to contingencies, and its manifestations emerge as thought. Thought involves the composition of speeches for the individual episodes of a work; and these speeches have qualities related to the nature of language which are made appropriate through diction. Since spectacle and song are not treated specifically by Aristotle, we may omit them from this summary and consider dramatic imitation as essentially a five-stage process with each stage having two or more subordinate parts. In outline, the imitative process is as follows:

1. "Reality," "history," or imagination produces (or discovers) "actions."
2. The poet recognizes these "actions," separates them from the surrounding irrelevancy, and expresses them in plots having agents.
3. The agents are defined by character, which must manifest itself in particular (contingent) situations or episodes.
4. The manifestation of character in episodes is expressed by "thought," which is objectified by language.
5. Language is made fully harmonious with manner and means of imitation through diction.

So far so good, as long as we remember that this represents the process of composition according to the art of poetry, and that the theoretical order is not necessarily the one followed by the creating artist. Artists may (and in fact do) begin at any of the five stages. Yet no matter which stage initiates the creative process, (a) all must ultimately be accounted for, and (b) when they are accounted for in the finished composition, they form a hierarchy of relationships like the one established in the *Poetics,* with plot the most basic element—and therefore, properly, the controlling factor, to which all other parts must be related if the work is to be fully expressive. This is so true that Kenneth Burke uses the term *symbolic action* to define the fundamental characteristic of all literary works. According to Burke, even a lyric must be understood as defined by movement from beginning to end. This movement (or action) is a rudimentary plot, and all other elements of the successful lyric will have a necessary or probable relation to it. But the obvious application of Aristotle is to narrative and dramatic literature; and it is interesting to compare the process of composition outlined in the *Poetics* to the process described by Henry James in his preface to *The Ambassadors.* Although James came to his theories and methods of composition through nineteenth-century aesthetic theory and his own experience as a novelist, the process that he describes is remarkably close to Aristotle's; and it is surely an interesting coincidence that James uses the term "probability" to identify the principle that determined his selection of setting, incidents, and character traits.

But what, in essence, does the imitative process accomplish? Here Aristotle has given us several useful leads. In Chapter IV, we learn that imitative pleasure is related to the pleasure all men take in learning; and in Chapter IX, this point is restated in terms of the idea that poetry is "more universal and more philosophical than history."

To appreciate Aristotle's understanding of art, we must remember that he found two extremes in the world. The first is what might be called "the world of undifferentiated singulars." This world is chaotic. It is unintelligible because the singulars seem to have no relation to one another. At the opposite extreme is the world of universals. A universal is simply a proposition asserting a relation, such as "All men are mortal," or "Temperance usually insures good health." Notice that true propositions are statements of necessity or probability. Philosophy subsumes the world of undifferentiated "singulars" under a system of universal propositions. They make the world intelligible, and to the extent that they are true, they bring out the innate order of nature. In addition, they permit us to deal with the unknown. That is, if I am properly equipped with universal propositions, I am able to "understand" new particulars by relating them to appropriate universals. Even though I have never seen a cuttlefish, if I have studied biology I will be able to identify one when I encounter it; to identify it is to classify and therefore to "understand" it.

Now let us return to the poet. His special task is to discover actions—simple, unified processes—in a world of undifferentiated singulars. For the tragic poet, this world is usually history, which includes myth and legend as well as "records of fact." In Chapter IX of the *Poetics,* history is defined as a collection of "singulars"—a record of facts, we might say, like a medieval chronicle. It is for the poet to find patterns in the record. A poetic plot derived from history is therefore an interpretation, an understanding, of history. The poet makes forays on the unintelligible to discover something that can be understood, a pattern or process, called an action.[1] Does the poet create this intelligible pattern? Not necessarily, for Aristotle says in Chapter IX that the poet can sometimes take actions directly from history without change. On the other hand, Aristotle also says that most tragedies involve a good deal of fiction (that is, invention by the poet) and that it is perfectly legitimate for the poet to follow Agathon and make up his plots entirely. If the poet introduces fiction into a narrative based on an historical source, he is clearly modifying history; if he makes up his plot, he is acting independently of history. The poet thus has three alternatives. He can discover his pattern in history, he can modify history, or he can compose fiction.

Whatever course the poet follows, he can never escape the imperative of intelligibility. In other words, he can modify history only because history is often ambiguous or inadequate or false to the incidents it records. By the same token, an invented action is not the exhalation of a fevered brain but a set of incidents constructed purely on the basis of universal (intelligible) principles and involving

[1] Of course, most historians from Thucydides on have exercised a "poetic" function in that they have tried to discover patterns—"meanings"—in their records of fact. Aristotle must have realized this, but he chooses to ignore it in the *Poetics,* perhaps in the interest of keeping his definitions as clear as possible.

the coordination of undifferentiated singulars. On this basis, a fictitious plot could be called a pure imitation of nature in the same way that a mathematical formula like $s = \frac{1}{2}\, gt^2$ is deductive but also a better image of nature than any amount of empirical data.

No matter which of the three alternatives the poet takes to obtain his action, he has started by confronting the unintelligible, and he has abstracted from it something that is in accordance with universal principles of necessity or probability. To do this is to "universalize." The result of "universalizing" is to make a previously "unknown" segment of history or nature intelligible. Already we have touched on the notion that artistic pleasure is related to the pleasure derived from learning.

Notice that a "universalized action" is the opposite of a copy. The purpose of artistic creation is not to copy history or nature but to make new constructs. History and nature are opaque; the art work is translucent.

A poetic action, then, can be understood as a true creation that "universalizes" history or nature. It can be summarized in an outline that Aristotle calls the "universal form" of an action in Chapter XVII. But there are a great many possible "universal forms," some more suited to tragic imitation than others; and, equally important, the universal form remains abstract until realized in a particular plot. We have seen how Aristotle narrows down the possible forms of the tragic plot to four in Chapter XIII and then concludes that of the four, the complex-fatal plot involving the hero who is good but who has a defect is the most effective. The action is not only universal in outline; now its specific shape reflects its conformity to the necessities and probabilities of the tragic form. In other words, at the same time that the selection of a complex-fatal action is a movement from general to specific, it is also a step toward fuller realization of the "universalizing" impulse. The more precisely defined action has more, not less, of the universal in its makeup; it is therefore more, not less, intelligible.

The plotting stage of poetic art ends with "episodizing," when the plot is objectified in particular incidents. The episodes seem to involve contingencies; but because they are intended to bring out the necessities and probabilities that underlie the original action (and unify the finished drama), they too contribute to the "universalizing" of the drama.

There are thus four steps in the creation and objectification of an action. From undifferentiated particulars the poet moves to pure universals, from the wholly unintelligible to the wholly intelligible. From pure universals he then moves toward intelligible particulars—specific episodes that objectify the universals of his plot and make one complex-fatal play different from another. In sum:

1. Undifferentiated particulars: unintelligible; history, nature.
2. Universal form: wholly intelligible; an action.
3. Tragic form: a complex-fatal plot; a noble hero with a defect.
4. Episodes inserted: particulars objectify universals; a particular plot—for example, *Oedipus Rex*.

As the poet works out his plot he discovers that the agents cannot be made intelligible by plot techniques alone. The nature of the tragic action suggests that the agents should be "noble," but "nobility" is a rather vague notion. How are the agents to be "universalized"? The answer, of course, is given in Chapter XV. The agents should be characterized according to the necessities and probabilities of psychology. The poet must "universalize" the nobility of the agents, and this is done by drawing on the concept of goodness formulated in ethics. But the characters must also be differentiated, and the differentiation is accomplished by drawing on the theory of character types found in rhetoric and in medicine (the humours theory). This produces "appropriateness." The next requirement is that the characters be "like." As we noted when intially considering this requirement, it most probably refers to specific characteristics associated with legendary or historical characters, and with personal idiosyncrasies manifested by invented characters. It is thus bound up with what Aristotle calls the "naming" of the character. If a character is "named" Medea, the poet will turn to tradition for "like" characteristics; for one named Pyrgopolyneices, the poet will turn to experience and observation. If we sum up the process of characterization, we find that it involves the following:

1. "Agents"; unintelligible.
2. "Universal" characteristics: "goodness"; defect (*hamartia*).
3. "Appropriate" characteristics: type traits; differentiation by type—for example, the statesman, the miser, the melancholic, the feminine, etc.

4. "Like" characteristics: particulars objectify universals; "named" characters—for example, Medea, Jason, Clytemnestra, Dives, Pyrgopolyneices.

Episodizing and characterization come together in thought, which also involves the working out of speeches. How is the character to respond to the particular incident at hand? Again, the poet must deal with the inchoate, the undifferentiated. Again, he solves his problem by "universalizing." This time, instead of turning to ethics and the type formulas of rhetoric, he turns to general (hence "universal") prescriptions for emotion and logical thought. Applying these prescriptions insures that the thought will be "fitting to the occasion"—that it will have a necessary or probable relation to the occasion and will, therefore, be intelligible. Again, the poet moves from the inchoate to the universal and then shapes the particular to objectify the universal.

Finally, there is diction. Language presents myriad possibilities to the poet. Which should he select, and what does his choice amount to? Again, the poet turns to the universal to solve his problem. Form should follow function, and iambic meter is fitted by its nature to dialogue. The choice of iambic meter "universalizes" the diction by establishing a necessary or probable relation between the meter and the poet's manner of imitation. It quite literally makes the language more intelligible: we can understand why the poet has chosen this verse form. Exactly the same point can be made about poetic usage, except that usage cannot be determined until after the meter is selected. Iambic verse is not suited for strange and compound words; but it is suited for standard words and metaphors. In a very real sense, then, the poet's choice of language is a "universalization" of his meter. When he chooses particular words, these reflect the universal principles that determined from what class (standard, strange, ornamental, and so forth) they are taken. We thus have:

1. Undifferentiated language.

2. Universalized diction: for tragedy, iambic meter, standard words, and metaphor.

3. Particularized diction: individual words objectify the universal principles that determined their choice.

Although there is ample scope for disagreement concerning the details of dramatic imitation as here outlined, three points are beyond debate. First, imitation is a process moving from plot to diction (and evidently to spectacle and song). Second, at each stage of this process, the poet seeks to universalize the part with which he is concerned and then to objectify the universal results in a particular form of his own. And third, at each stage, as one part is universalized, the next part emerges, still inchoate, demanding to be universalized at the next stage. Not all poems, of course, are completely successful. Aristotle generally gives a list of possibilities ranked from worst to best or vice versa instead of asserting that one way is right and all others wrong. In addition, he recognizes that there are degrees of merit in execution at every stage in the creative process and that a competent performance in a form that is intrinsically mediocre may be preferable to a bad rendition of a superior form. Epic is intrinsically inferior to tragedy, but the *Iliad* and *Odyssey* are worth hundreds of mediocre tragedies.

But the main point is that considered from the point of view of poetic art, imitation is a universalizing process. At every stage, the inchoate is made intelligible. If the universalizing is successful, the finished work will have what can only be called total intelligibility. Not only will all its parts be functional, they will all reflect the operation of necessary or probable principles. Notice that the principles themselves are different on the various levels of the work. For example, the principles of characterization come from psychology; those of diction come from prosody. On the other hand, although the principles are different, the fact that the principles used at one stage have a shaping influence on those employed at the next insures that the principles will be harmonious—that they will be interrelated and mutually reinforcing.

This brings us back to the purpose of imitation. Imitative pleasure, it will be recalled, is a kind of pleasure derived from learning. We have already seen that the catharsis clause in Chapter VI can be translated as a reference to "clarification of the incidents" comprising a tragedy, with "clarification" interpreted as "intellectual clarification." We have also seen that for Aristotle the aim of the imitative process is total intelligibility, total translucence. Why is this? Why should the poet strive so mightily to shape all elements of his work in terms of universal concepts of necessity or probability?

The answer is given time and time again in the *Poetics*. He should strive to do so in order to increase the pleasure proper to his form.

But the tragic function is catharsis. If the poet can only achieve catharsis by making his work wholly intelligible, then the tragic function must have something to do with understanding. Of course, this is precisely the conclusion suggested by the discussion of imitative pleasure in Chapter IV. The ideal end product of the process of universalizing is a work in which every particular is understandable both in itself and in its relations to the other particulars. The poet has attempted to make his work wholly intelligible, and the reader or spectator responds to it in terms of what it is. The response is understanding; the result is the type of pleasure associated with learning. Although the incidents of tragedy may be unpleasant—pitiable and fearful—the pity and fear ultimately become irrelevant as the incidents are "clarified." In the very same way, the pictures of corpses and animals mentioned in Chapter IV strike the viewer as interesting rather than repulsive. He enjoys them and learns from them, although he would be repelled by a real corpse and frightened by a real python or scorpion.

A tragedy should be made totally intelligible; the pleasure derived from it is learning; and the pleasure of learning ultimately absorbs the pity and fear aroused by the action. The doctrine is perhaps related to such contemporary aesthetic theories as James Joyce's (and Jacques Maritain's) idea of art as epiphany—a sudden, luminous perception of a previously hidden set of relations; to Benedetto Croce's concept of aesthetic pleasure as the experience of coherence; and to the Jungian view of the aesthetic experience as a sudden "insight" into the archetypal forms of experience. All these doctrines share with Aristotle the notion of art as learning and the notion of learning as pleasure. Less frequently, modern aestheticians share with Aristotle the belief that the utmost resources of the artist's craft must be used to achieve this end.

In considering the pleasure of learning, we have treated as irrelevant the notion that learning about pitiable and fearful events does anything to explain or justify their occurrence. Does catharsis in any way reconcile us to the terrible events that form the basis of the tragic plot? Butcher seems to think that catharsis *does* in some way justify tragic events by showing that they are in accord with the eternal laws of nature. Perhaps. But there is a residue of both didacticism and the copy theory of imitation in Butcher's view. We would all like to believe that "God's in his heaven; all's right with the world." Consequently, we have a strong motive for reading into Aristotle's catharsis the notion that tragedy explains or justifies suffering. Francis Fergusson's belief that the third and final stage of the tragic rhythm is "perception" may be a case in point, insofar as "perception" refers to wisdom gained through suffering rather than to learning in general. Butcher also assumes that the "laws" embodied in tragedy are identical with the "laws" governing nature and human nature. This is no doubt true in some cases; but many of the necessary or probable principles treated in the *Poetics* are derived from "the poetic art" rather than from nature. Aristotle seems to stress this in Chapter XXV when he insists that the art of poetry is different from the art of medicine or horsemanship or zoology. To portray a hind with horns violates the "laws of nature" but is only a "nontechnical error" in a poem or painting. If this is true, the notion that the laws of tragedy are in accord with the laws of nature is a bit hard to retain, at least in its simple form.

On the other hand, Butcher's view is too persuasive and too widely held by readers of tragedy to be wholly dismissed. In some sense, Aristotle demanded that tragedy show (or seem to show) a relation between tragic character and tragic destiny, for he believed that a fatal tragedy with a wholly "good" protagonist was repellent, whereas a fatal tragedy about a good man with a *hamartia* was not only satisfactory but produced the highest kind of tragic pleasure.

If we, as readers or spectators, learn something from tragedy, part of what we learn must be the relation between the character of the protagonist and his end, be it happiness or misery. But the point is difficult and ambiguous, and a final solution may be neither possible nor desirable. Aristotle's catharsis balances with dazzling virtuosity halfway between the religious view that would make the tragic pleasure a variety of the theophany following a ritual sacrifice and the wholly rationalistic view that makes it a purgation of the impulse to vice. Like the *Poetics* as a whole, catharsis looks in two directions—back to primitive literature and forward to didactic tragedy. And like the *Poetics* as a whole, its ambiguities are a source of its fascination.

Bibliography

1. Bibliographies of Studies on Aristotle's *Poetics.*

Cooper, L., and A. Gudeman, *A Bibliography of the Poetics of Aristotle.* New Haven, Conn.: Yale University Press, 1928.

Else, G. F., "A Survey of Work on Aristotle's *Poetics,* 1940-1952," *The Classical Weekly* (now *Classical World*), XLVIII (1955), 73-82.

Herrick, M. T., "A Supplement to Cooper and Gudeman's Bibliography of the *Poetics* of Aristotle," *American Journal of Philology* LII (1931), 168-74.

2. Texts, Translations, and Commentaries on the *Poetics.*

Butcher, S. H., *Aristotle's Theory of Poetry and Fine Art.* New York: Dover Publications, Inc., 1951. Greek text, translation and commentary on selected topics. A paperback reprint.

Bywater, I., *Aristotle on the Art of Poetry.* London and New York: Oxford University Press, 1909. Greek text, translation, and continuous commentary.

Cooper, L., *Aristotle on the Art of Poetry.* Ithaca, N.Y.: Cornell University Press, 1947. An "amplified" translation designed for students of literature.

———, *An Aristotelian Theory of Comedy.* Ithaca, N.Y.: Cornell University Press, 1922. An attempt to develop a theory of comedy from the *Poetics* and other sources, particularly the "Tractatus Coislinianus."

Else, G. F., *Aristotle: Poetics.* Ann Arbor, Mich.: University of Michigan Press, 1967. Introduction, translation, and explanatory notes.

———, *Aristotle's Poetics: The Argument.* Cambridge, Mass.: Harvard University Press, 1957. Greek text, translation, and continuous commentary.

Epps, P. H., *The Poetics of Aristotle.* Chapel Hill, N.C.: University of North Carolina Press, 1942. Translation with some explanatory notes.

Fergusson, F., ed., *Aristotle's Poetics.* New York: Hill and Wang, 1961. Editor's introduction, together with S. H. Butcher's translation.

Fyfe, W. H., *Aristotle: The Poetics* (Loeb Classical Library). Cambridge, Mass.: Harvard University Press, 1953. Greek text with facing literal translation.

Gilbert, Allen, tr., Aristotle's *Poetics,* in *Literary Criticism: Plato to Dryden.* New York: American Book Co., 1940, pp. 63-124.

Gomperz, T., *Aristoteles' Poetik übersetzt und eingeleitet.* Leipzig, 1895. Introduction, translation, and an essay on the theory of catharsis by Alfred Freiherrn von Berger.

Grube, G. M. A., *Aristotle on Poetry and Style.* New York: Library of Liberal Arts, 1958. Translation and fairly extensive explanatory notes. A translation of relevant sections of Aristotle's *Rhetoric* is included.

Gudeman, A., *Aristoteles' PERI POIETIKES.* Berlin and Leipzig, 1934. Introduction, Greek text, notes, and continuous commentary.

Hardy, J., *Aristote: Poétique* (Collection des Universités de France publiée sous le Patronage de l' Association Guillaume Budé). Paris, 1952. Greek text, facing French translation, and notes.

Kassel, R., *Aristotelis de Arte Poetica Liber* (Oxford Classical Texts). Oxford: Oxford University Press, 1965. Greek text with an informative preface describing the state of our knowledge of the text of the *Poetics* at the present time.

Lobel, E., "The Medieval Latin Poetics," *Proceedings of the British Academy,* XVII (1931), 309-34.

Margoliouth, D. S., *The Poetics of Aristotle.* London, 1911. Introduction, Greek text and translation. A Latin translation of the Arabic version of the *Poetics* is included.

Pitcher, S. M., "Aristotle: On Poetic Art," *Journal of General Education,* VII (1952), 56-76. Translation only.

Potts, L. J., *Aristotle on the Art of Fiction.* Cambridge: Cambridge University Press, 1953. Introduction, translation and notes.

Rostagni, A., *Aristotele Poetica.* Turin, 1945. Introduction, Greek text, and continuous commentary.

Telford, K., *Aristotle's Poetics: Translation and Analysis.* Chicago, Ill.: Henry Regnery Co., 1965. Translation, notes, and continuous commentary.

Tkatsch, J., *Die arabische Übersetzung der Poetik des Aristoteles.* 2 vols. Vienna, Leipzig, 1932. Thorough study of the Arabic tradition of the *Poetics,* including the Arabic text and a facing Latin translation with extensive notes.

Valgimigli, E., ed., *Aristoteles Latinus XXIII: De Arte Poetica Guilelmo de Moerbeke, Interprete.* Revised with preface and indices added by A. Franceschini and L. Minio-Paluello. Bruges, Paris, 1953. Text of the thirteenth-century Latin translation of the *Poetics* by William of Moerbeke.

3. General Studies of Aristotle's Philosophy.

Allan, D. J., *The Philosophy of Aristotle.* London and New York: Oxford University Press, 1952.

Cherniss, H., *Aristotle's Criticism of Plato and the Academy.* Baltimore: Johns Hopkins Press, 1944.

———, *Aristotle's Criticism of Presocratic Philosophy.* Baltimore: Johns Hopkins Press, 1935.

Grene, M., *A Portrait of Aristotle.* Chicago, Ill.: University of Chicago Press, 1963.

Jaeger, W., *Aristotle: Fundamentals of the History of his Development,* trans. R. Robinson. London and New York: Oxford University Press, 1948.

Randall, J. H. Jr., *Aristotle.* New York: Columbia University Press, 1960.

Robin, L., *Aristote.* Paris, 1944.

Ross, W. D., *Aristotle.* London: Methuen and Co., 1945.

4. Interpretive Studies of Major Themes in the *Poetics.*

Braam, P. van, "Aristotle's Use of *Hamartia,*" *Classical Quarterly,* VI (1912), 266-72.

Dale, A. M., "Ethos and Dianoia: Character and Thought in Aristotle's *Poetics,*" *AUMLA: Journal of the Australasian Universities Language and Literature Association,* XI (1959), 3-16.

Else, G. F., "'Imitation' in the Fifth Century," *Classical Philology,* LIII (1958), 73-90.

Golden, L., "Catharsis," *Transactions of the American Philological Association,* XCIII (1962), 51-60.

———, "Is Tragedy the 'Imitation of a *Serious* Action'?" *Greek, Roman and Byzantine Studies,* VI (1965), 283-89.

Goldstein, H. D., "Mimesis and Catharsis Reexamined," *Journal of Aesthetics and Art Criticism,* XXIV (1966), 567-77.

Gomperz, T., *Zu Aristoteles' Poetik, II, III.* Vienna, 1896.

———, "Ein Beitrag zur Kritik und Erklärung der Kapitel 1-6," *Sitzungsberichte der Wiener Akademie,* I-VI (1888), 543-82.

Gresseth, G. K., "The System of Aristotle's *Poetics,*" *Transactions of the American Philological Association,* LXXXIX (1958), 312-35.

Harsh, P. W., "*Hamartia* Again," *Transactions of the American Philological Association,* LXXVI (1945), 47-58.

House, H., *Aristotle's Poetics: A Course of Eight Lectures,* rev. by C. Hardie. London: R. Hart Davis, 1956.

Jones, J., *On Aristotle and Greek Tragedy.* London: Oxford University Press, 1962.

Lucas, D. W., "Pity, Terror, and *Peripeteia,*" *Classical Quarterly,* XII (1962), 52-60.

McKeon, R. "Literary Criticism and the Concept of Imitation in Antiquity," in *Critics and Criticism: Ancient and Modern.* ed. R. S. Crane. Chicago, Ill.: University of Chicago Press, 1952, pp. 147-75.

Montmollin, D. de, *La Poétique d' Aristote: Texte Primitif et Additions Ultérieures.* Neuchâtel, 1951.

———, "Le Sens du terme *philanthropon* dans *La Poétique* d'Aristote," *Phoenix,* XIX (1965), 15-23.

Murray, G., "An Essay in the Theory of Poetry," *Yale Review,* X (1921), 482-99.

Olson, E., ed., *Aristotle's "Poetics" and English Literature: A Collection of Critical Essays.* Chicago, Ill.: University of Chicago Press, 1965.

Ostwald, M., "Aristotle on *Hamartia* and Sophocles' *Oedipus Tyrannus,*" in *Festschrift Ernst Kapp.* Hamburg, 1958, pp. 93-108.

Solmsen, F., "The Origins and Methods of Aristotle's *Poetics,*" *Classical Quarterly,* XXIX (1935), 192-201.

Stanford, W. B., "On a Recent Interpretation of the Tragic Catharsis," *Hermathena,* LXXXV (1955), 52-56.

Vahlen, J., *Beiträge zu Aristoteles' Poetik.* Leipzig, Berlin, 1914.

5. General Studies of Greek Tragedy.

Aylen, L., *Greek Tragedy and the Modern World.* London: Methuen and Co., 1964.

Cornford, F. M., *The Origin of Attic Comedy.* London: E. Arnold, 1914.

Else, G. F., *The Origin and Early Form of Greek Tragedy*. Cambridge, Mass.: Harvard University Press, 1965.

Fergusson, F., *The Idea of a Theatre*. New York: Doubleday and Co., 1953.

Fritz, Kurt von, *Antike und moderne Tragödie*. Berlin, 1962.

Kitto, H. D. F., *Form and Meaning in Drama: A Study of Six Greek Plays and of Hamlet*. London: Methuen and Co., 1956.

———, *Greek Tragedy: A Literary Study*. New York: Barnes and Noble, 1961.

Lattimore, R., *The Poetry of Greek Tragedy*. Baltimore: Johns Hopkins Press, 1958.

———, *Story Patterns in Greek Tragedy*. Ann Arbor, Mich.: University of Michigan Press, 1964.

Lesky, A., *Greek Tragedy,* trans. H. A. Frankfort. New York: Barnes and Noble, 1965.

Lucas, D. W., *The Greek Tragic Poets*. New York: W. W. Norton and Co., 1964.

Lucas, F. L., *Tragedy: Serious Drama in Relation to Aristotle's Poetics*. New York: Collier Books, 1962.

Murray, G., "Excursus on the Ritual Forms Preserved in Greek Tragedy," in *Themis: A Study of the Social Origins of Greek Religion,* ed. J. E. Harrison. Cleveland: Meridian Books, Inc., 1962, pp. 341-63.

Norwood, G., *Greek Tragedy*. London, 1920.

Patzer, H., *Die Anfänge der griechischen Tragödie*. Wiesbaden, 1962.

Pickard-Cambridge, A. W., *Dithyramb, Tragedy and Comedy* (2nd ed.), rev. by T. B. L. Webster. London and New York: Oxford University Press, 1962.

Pohlenz, M., *Die griechischen Tragödie*. Leipzig, 1930.

Romilly, J. de, *L'Évolution du Pathétique d'Eschyle à Euripide*. Paris, 1961.

Rosenmayer, T. G., *The Masks of Tragedy: Essays on Six Greek Dramas*. Austin, Texas: University of Texas Press, 1963.

Index of Key Terms

Included in the index below are important or representative references to a selected group of technical terms and key concepts in the *Poetics*. The original Greek word for each term included in the index is given in the form in which it is found in the Lexicon. In the process of translation it is often necessary to render original Greek forms into different parts of English speech. All references are given by chapter (bold Roman numerals) and line number (Arabic numerals).